THE ART OF CURATING

edited by

GERALD A. MATT

NWV

Vienna 2026

Bibliographic information published by the Deutsche Nationalbibliothek
The Deutsche Nationalbibliothek lists this publication in the Deutsche Nationalbibliografie; detailed bibliographic data are available in the Internet at https://portal.dnb.de/opac.htm.

We would like to thank Mag.ª Kathrin Kneißel, Dean Zahtila, Damir Stojnić, Branka Benčić, Christian Oxenius, Aneta Graham, Gerald Muther and Dieter Auracher.

ISBN 978-3-7083-4306-8

NWV im Verlag Österreich
Bäckerstraße 1
1010 Vienna
Austria
office@verlagoesterreich.at
https://www.verlagoesterreich.at

Editing and Translation: Aneta Graham
Typesetting and Layout: Dieter Auracher
Print: Prime Rate Zrt., 1044 Budapest, Hungary

This book is dedicated

to
my family
Kasia, Ava Apolonia und Amalia Gaia

and

to
my very wonderful colleague
Koyo Kouoh

Foreword

> *"The history of criticism is better known then the history of curating... There aren't many books about this parallel activity of creating exhibitions. Maybe it has to do with the fact that the curator wasn't—and maybe shouldn't be—a well-defined figure."*
> DANIEL BIRNBAUM, the curator of the 53rd Venice Biennale 2009

It was in 2020 when I was invited by the director of the Labin Biennial and artist Dean Zahtila to curate the third edition of the Labin Biennial with my colleagues Branka Benčić und Christian Oxenius.

The Labin Biennial initiated by the artists Dean Zahtila and Damir Stojnić, one of the few major avant-garde artistic events in Istria, and in the whole of Croatia, deals with contemporary art on an international level, independently from official cultural politics. Launched in 2016 in the former mining and industrial town of Labin, located southwest of Rijeka, our Biennial of Industrial Art has spread its wings to include keynote exhibitions in Labin and Rijeka and a host of satellite events in Pula, Vodnjan and Raša. Together, we developed a curatorial concept titled *Ride to the Sun*, based on the history of Labin, once a mining and industrial centre, now seeking to redefine itself through tourism. Centred around the problems and challenges of a post-industrial society, it dealt with themes like the decline of industry, the rise of tourism, problems with the working-class history and regional identity of cities and regions. The fact that the Biennial's MMSU Center building itself is located in a former factory, referencing directly the industrial past, made it an obvious venue for our central exhibition where a host of international artists grappled with the complex problems of today's social, economic and cultural changes.

It was within the framework of the Biennial that the idea emerged: to compile a book on curatorial practice in the form of interviews. The work on the Biennial involved numerous discussions with the director and colleagues about its vision in the broader context of contemporary curating—which kindled my desire to continue and deepen the debates with a wider circle of curators. Thus, the idea of writing a book on this topic matured in me.

The aim of *The Art of Curating* is to explore different curatorial attitudes in relation to current developments in the field of art and exhibitions. To provide a concrete example of curatorial work, I included my own interview, in which I share my thoughts and concept for the selection of artists and artworks for the Labin Biennial.

A questionnaire designed to mirror the current discussions on curating served as the basis of the book and provided a framework for the collection of interviews I conducted with a number of leading and highly interesting curators throughout the world. The questionnaire was not rigorously applied; for most of the interviews it just gave a thematic framework for a wide range of possible answers.

Most of the interviews were conducted very freely and associatively. Some of the conversations important to the book and its themes were based on prior interviews published in the media, due to time or organizational constraints.

Since I conducted most of the interviews myself, and the process involved significant logistical and organizational effort, the project took over four years from conception to publication. For example, my highly esteemed friend Koyo Kouoh, who had been preparing her Venice Biennale presentation, tragically passed away shortly after we had arranged to meet. Therefore, I included previously published conversations with her. Out of deep respect for this outstanding curator, I have dedicated the book to her memory. I also included interviews with the brilliant curator Okwui Enwezor, originally published in *Süddeutsche Zeitung*, because I felt his theoretical and practical contributions were essential to the conversation.

A compelling interview with Simon Njami, a curator I had the pleasure of working with during my time as director of Kunsthalle Wien, in which he discusses African perspectives and challenges, was reprinted with kind permission from *Lettre*.

The selection of curators was intended to represent the broadest possible spectrum of the profession—ranging from freelance or independent curators invited by institutions, festivals and biennials (guest curators) to those holding permanent positions in organizations within their specific hierarchical frameworks (e.g., heads of departments, exhibition curators, education curators), and curators in executive positions at small and large institutions. The ambition was to reflect and do justice to the broad range of roles, responsibilities and challenges facing the curatorial profession.

This resulted in a diverse and colourful range of perspectives—from Max Hollein, director of the Metropolitan Museum, to Kasia Matt-Uszyńska, director of the young Neuer Kunstverein Wien; from artist-curators like Francis Ruyter, to former *Kunstforum* editor and academic Paolo Bianchi; and to independent curators, such as Bernardo de Souza from Brazil. The curators were selected from very different regions and cultures, partly in order to gain a global view of the phenomena and the diversity of exhibition design and organization as well as the theory and practice of curatorial work.

Before anything else, it was essential to determine how curators today understand their profession. The question, *"What is a curator?"*, elicited a wide range of answers, revealing that the role has become more wide-ranging and multifaceted than ever before. There is no doubt, however, that a curator is fundamentally a selector and interpreter of art. They may act as a producer, planner, exhibition architect, commissioner of artworks, manager, educator, and promoter. They choose and interpret works of art. While working closely not only with artists but also art institutions, a curator is a catalyst or conduit of ideas. Their job incorporates a wide range of different tasks, including those of an art expert, author, editor and critic, a producer, teacher, commissioner, exhibition planer as well as exhibition architect. They write catalogue and social media texts, support the marketing of artists and shows, and interact with the media, public and visitors. Oftentimes, they are also involved in fundraising and development activities such as sponsor and donor events. They are highly conscious of political correctness, minority rights and diversity approach to work.

A curator interacts with schools and universities, gives lectures and talks, educates and trains assistants towards a further career as curators. As a director of an institution, the curator is in charge of its programme and the distribution and control of projects they assign to other curators.

The curators' responses also highlighted the differences between independent and institutional curating—between those responsible for long-term programming and budgeting, and those focused on one-off exhibitions or festivals. The tasks of a museum senior curator differ massively from those of a young curator who is not yet tied to an institution while those of a biennial curator differ significantly from those of an art association director. The answers also revealed the advantages and disadvantages of independent and institutional work.

The responses and reflections of the curators show how different the tasks and challenges for curators are depending on their function and position and how these have changed in recent years.

The respondents were also asked about their often-divergent career paths and training, as well as their role models and exhibitions or projects that were important, even formative, for their own path. The great curator Harald Szeemann and his projects and exhibitions, which shaped the image of modern, cosmopolitan, innovative curatorship which transcends boundaries in the truest sense of the word, were repeatedly mentioned, as was the progressive MoMA director Alfred H. Barr Jr. The interviews addressed new curatorial perspectives in relation to political and social debates on appropriation, diversity and identity politics which were presented as new responsibilities and sensitivities, on the one hand, and as artistic restrictions and a source of potential censorship, on the other. This led to reflections on current conflicts between freedom of expression and political correctness, and between artistic freedom and moral imperatives. What is the impact of identity politics on the theory and practice of curating? A discourse that ultimately culminates in the question: "Does art have to be moral?"—a question that ultimately also concerns the financing of projects by public funding bodies and public museums.

The curators were also invited to speak about meaningful projects they had realized and how those exhibitions had come to life. Examples of personal career paths (e.g. from the director of one of the world's most important museums to the head of a contemporary art association who has set up her own institution) are also used to illustrate possible scenarios and opportunities for young curators. The interviewees also discuss the often-challenging friction between artistic curatorial visions and desires versus budgetary, spatial and practical restrictions and constraints, and thus also the question of the independence and freedom of curatorial work. The volatile dynamic between artists, collectors and museum directors was also discussed, leading to the central question about the relationship between the artist and the curator.

Other questions posed to the interviewees included: "Are there two different art worlds: the art world of museums, big collectors, star curators, auction houses, and big fairs—and the other art world based on smaller biennales, and independent art spaces and curators, as Robert Fleck once argued? Is there also a gap between curators serving one or the other world?"

Finally, the curators reflected on the future of their profession and passion.

Vienna, November 2025 *Gerald A. Matt*

Table of Contents

It‘s always a process of negotiation

Branka Benčić
in conversation with Gerald A. Matt

GERALD A. MATT: What is a curator? Can you define your understanding and practice as a curator?

BRANKA BENČIĆ: Situated between the creative and the bureaucratic, the practical and the theoretical, and encompassing artistic, academic and administrative trajectories, contemporary curatorial practice is seen as an agency slipping definitions. Curating operates in the space of the in-between as a cross-platform activity, devised to rethink how we see the world through artistic means, with the potential to shape and inform social imagination. I see it as a set of negotiations undertaken in both the long and the short term, negotiations between different institutional politics, financial constraints, between imagination and reality, the history of art, and the social and economic conditions that frame cultural production. It is about creating support structures, opportunities, opening up spaces and making things visible. Through exhibitions we create a space for action and reflection, communication and discourse, giving voice to what is unseen or unheard or offering new perspectives on what we already know.

GM: How can curating be relevant to the challenges we face today and in what way does it differ from previous approaches to curating?

BB: Curatorial and artistic practice—exhibitions, museums, galleries, artistic interventions—can be seen as open forums or platforms that bring relevant ideas and questions into the public discourse, shaping new connections or new perspectives on existing issues, and opening new spaces which provide opportunities and open new possibilities for artists and artworks. It is sometimes emancipatory, but at the same time, in the fragmented world view, critical voices are instrumentalized, and might remain unheard, neutralized, or absorbed. In order to shift from “show” to “tell”, as well as to sustain the notion of exhibitions being a tool for social change and explore different contexts, curating needs to continuously reinvent itself.

GM: How do you see the changing relations between curators, artists, collectors, galleries, museums and critics? Has there been a shift of power and influence?

BB: I am based in Croatia's cultural landscape where private galleries and collectors are almost non-existent, critical reflection is erased from the media, public institutions are weak, and most power and influence are embedded in political corruption. The public space is marked mostly by a nationalist monoculture and processes of privatization and transition. Within this context—characterized by multiple marginalities and perpetual precarity—curatorial interests are shaped by investigating the relationship between art and society. Central curatorial enquiries are anchored in the specifics of urban locations and the contexts, from which social or cultural and artistic scenes arise. They entail developing and unraveling the intertwined voices, identities and narratives that come from the background. The displaced status and the problem of the de/centralized culture are reflected in the dominant cultural or artistic production.

GM: Was there a personal hero, a curator whom you admired? What were their qualities and achievements? Was there a show which you consider a milestone for curatorial thoughts and practice?

BB: There are artists and artworks I have learned a lot from—and continue to do so—they inspire me every day. From Sanja Iveković to the many artists I have worked with for almost two decades that have shaped and informed my thinking within my immediate environment in Zagreb. Historical conceptual artists and artists of my own generation that I would like to bring along to every project. My influences came from curators, writers, friends, musicians and filmmakers who were my allies and sources of inspiration. I still want to think and feel that I am learning every day from the people I interact with. In my formative years, it was Tihomir Milovac who, by opening the doors of the black Gorgona auditorium at Zagreb MSU Museum of Contemporary Art, gave me the opportunity to take my chances and experiment with film curating and exhibiting moving images in a museum context.

GM: Can you describe a personal curatorial work and project you are really proud of, and also a project which did not really work out?

BB: There are projects that helped me grow professionally, shaped how I think and work, and those that I learned a lot from along the way. Or exhibitions that have connected me personally to artists and those I emotionally invested a great deal in. Some more than others. There is an ongoing project *Think Film* at the Pula film festival, which I established 20 years ago. It is an exhibition, along with a research platform, which questions the relationships between the cinema, moving images and contemporary art, and takes place every summer. It emerged from the desire to present works from the world of contemporary art and film. It has been an active context enabling the presentation of artworks—a place where artists, institutions and audiences meet, new forms of collaboration are formed, and where relationships between film and visual arts are discussed, exploring issues such as architecture and film, exhibition as interface, historical heritage of experimental film, spaces of cinema, found footage, video and television, cinematic apparatus, images and power ...

And, of course, there is the Apoteka—Space For Contemporary Art, an independent art organization, in a remote location on Istria, which my dear friend Matija Debeljuh and I established in an abandoned pharmacy. A space of freeedom to experiment, a space of friedship and care. There, we concived the idea of an ongoing exhibition series *This Is (Not) A Museum*, where artists reflect on the critique of the local institutional landscape and the possibilities of institutional imagination. After about 15 years of work as an independent curator, and working as a museum director today, I struggle against the resistance to bring this imagination to the forefront.

GM: Can you describe the path from the first idea to the exhibition based on one of your curatorial projects? What are the most important steps in developing and executing the project?

BB: Sometimes I start with artworks, or an artwork, that stirs some ideas, and work my way around it. Sometimes I start with a footnote, a note on the margin, as the basis for a text that then expands. I really enjoy this early vague moment when a project begins to take shape, when everything is not clear yet. At this point, I produce some notes, visual notes, images, texts, a sort of mood board, read and look at more art. This is when you start to see the future and things get easier. Or if we're lucky to land a new commission; it is great happiness to join the artist on the unknown journey and the emergence of a new work of art.

Around 2009, I became obsessed with early photocollages by Croatian artist Antun Motika—his unknown and unexplored experimental works—and I curated a solo exhibition of his historical conceptual collages. From then on, collage seemed to follow me, from experimental footage film I found to artists of my own generation such as Vlatka Horvat and Damir

Očko. This was a long journey of research and learning which culminated in a large scale panorama of collage practices in Eastern Europe from the avantgarde until today—the REZ / CUT exhibition I curated with Tihomir Milovac at the Museum of Contemporary Art in Zagreb in 2018, which explored criticality, representation, feminist collage, social and political messages, relations between collage and architecture as well as collage and film, and unfolded questions about the archive and the document, popular culture, image as a found object, the fragmented image—the image of dis/continuity. Collage is a medium which by definition incorporates fragments and deals with opposing tensions, broken images, hidden desires, and collective myths, trauma and discontinuity.

GM: Is curating always a struggle between vision and practical constraints? Can you give an example?

BB: It is always a process of negotiation. Rather than vision, I would use a plan or concept, which I would see change and transform along with the project. Practical constraints can push us to be creative and resourceful, and to use our imagination. Working in modest conditions, such as the cultural landscape in Croatia, I almost feel trained in transgressing obstacles by using special tactics and collaborating with artists that are willing to go along. Though there are times when all of that can also feel discouraging and exhausting.

GM: How do you define the relation between artist and curator? Where are the conflict lines? Is curating artistic work or a service to the artist and his work? There have recently been some examples of artists being invited by institutions to curate major shows and of curators producing their own art. In what way is the line between authorship and curating shifting/fading?

BB: I like to think that artists and curators are accomplices. I also find artistic interventions in museum collections and displays very inspiring, rather than seeing them as a sign of conflict. I like the unexpected encounters that happen with collections and institutions. For me, the position "artist as curator" has always been inspiring, both historically and today. I am very much intrigued by and admire such practices.

GM: What is the role of institutions in your practice? Where does the boundary lie between curatorial and institutional responsibility?

BB: One of the main roles of public institutions—besides their engagement in the production of knowledge—should be the very self- awareness of their responsibility to the public, the ethics. That constant awareness puts them in a privileged position, giving them access to different resources like public infrastructure, spaces, collection, but also the duty to maintain the idea of culture as an accessible public good. Institutional responsibility lies in creating spaces and methodologies for reflection where different voices meet, exploring new languages of art and its contradictions as well as relations with social tissue, building committed relations, making bridges between generations, and supporting the local scene and helping it grow.

GM: What will be the main challenges for a curator in the future? How will curatorial work change?

BB: All that is solid melts into the air...

The challenge is to cultivate not a collective unity, but a collective multiplicity

Paolo Bianchi
in conversation with Gerald A. Matt

GERALD A. MATT: What is a curator? Can you define your understanding and practice as a curator?

PAOLO BIANCHI: In recent years, exhibition makers have eagerly introduced the terms 'curating' and 'curator'into public discourse for their own self-description. This is not infrequently done with the intention of bringing more attention and recognition to their own profession. According to the Duden dictionary, the weak verb 'curate' refers to the actions of those who, as curators, oversee an exhibition and are responsible for its organization. Derived from the Latin word *curare* (to take care of something, to provide for something), the curatorial activity is particularly condensed around the aspect of *cura*: care, diligence, and circumspection of putting space and things together.

The activity finds its continuation in the publication of an exhibition catalogue, in which essays,chapter texts, descriptions of works, and illustrations give documentary form to the curatorialproduction of ideas beyond the period of the exhibition. The core task, however, remains to show works and narrate content. The corresponding maxim for the action could be: show and tell. Without the categories 'show' and 'tell', there is no curating. The gesture of showing is the minimal condition of curatorial action and complements itself to a curatorial triad: the curator as a subject of showing (who) offers a subject (what) to an audience (whom).

Curating is the form and expression of these three elements being brought together. This also means that the meaning of things is not inherent in the objects but is only revealed in the "dialogue" between the person showing, the viewer and what is shown. This is where the element of surprise comes into play when the interpretative intentions of the exhibition makers and the meanings of the exhibited objects coincide with the presumed meanings of the visitors.

My goal as a curator and art mediator is always to try to ensure that the artifacts and artworks on display are perceived as "affective things" that appeal to the viewer's mind, body and soul. In this way, the arts become an important part of our self-description and self-expression. The 4th Industrial Art Biennial in 2023 in Istria/Croatia, curated together with my colleague Christoph Doswald, also follows an affect-loaded path with the title we chose, *Landscapes of Desire*. The term 'landscapes' reminds, for instance, of a colorful snowy landscape by Edvard Munch. In the connection with hoping, longing, and wishing, we also wanted to suggest that there is a human desire to reach new horizons. We are convinced that people are always looking for new and utopian landscapes because in this longing is the desire for a better and more fulfilling life. As a curatorial duo, we associate a stimulating feeling with the word 'landscape' (also as an image of the soul and body). If our setting is successful, then unexpected and different perspectives can emerge in people's imaginations. A good example of this is the word "Dreamland" that the German-Syrian artist Manaf Halbouni realized in meter-high letters on the roof of a cinema in Labin. When looking at this work, the land of dreams appears closer than it seems.

GM: How can curating be relevant to the challenges we face today and in what way does it differ from previous models?

PB: The curators who have established themselves in the art operating system since the 1990s are described as invisible directors with a distinctive signature who appear both theoretically and practically, visually and discursively. Traditionally, they have their places in museums, where they are responsible—as directors—for the entire program, or—as curators—for an individual collection. Or they have established themselves as freelancers, mostly to mediate contemporary art and culture outside the official structures, to realize thematic exhibitions, or to set the trends as global creative nomads for biennials. Exhibitions of this kind can provide an overview of the work of a single artist, illustrate a particular style, practice representational critique, or be thematically set (for example, on music, fashion, or media).

In the meantime, curatorial qualifications are offered in many places. Increasingly, curators are in charge of putting together inspiring programs at film and book festivals. Traditional journalism has also been infected with the curatorial virus through user-generated content. In social networks such as Facebook, the imperative "Curate yourself!" takes into account the *Zeitgeist* of adding one's own self-presentation and display through images and texts to the moment of creativity—as an expected readiness for "exhibitionism", for being comprehensively visible on display.

Ideally, curating promotes artistic innovation, practicing new forms of production and organization in network constellations and generating alternative structures of creative- economic and social value creation.

Curatorial practice unfolds at a high level, mostly in designated places of contemporary influence (such as the former turbine hall of today's Tate Modern in London) and garnishes itself with effective-sounding titles, themes and theses. Exhibiting as the oldest medium of presentation history also conveys the hint that showing always comes before naming. Presenting an exhibit (through curatorial practice) takes its place before any other possible form of representation (through art historical documentation). The sequence of exhibitions forms and itself writes art history. In exhibitions, not only do works and things enter into relationships with one another, they themselves relate to one another and thus hand down certain ways of reading art.

GM: Was there a personal hero, a curator whom you admired? Was there a show which you consider to be a milestone for curatorial thoughts and practice?

PB: For me, the name Harald Szeemann (1933-2005), the year 1969, and the Kunsthalle Bern are of great significance for the beginning of a curatorial turning point. Szeemann's position as a prototype and role model is justified by the exhibition *Live in Your Head: When Attitudes Become Form*, subtitled *Works–Concepts–Processes–Situations–Information*, which has been described as "legendary". Szeemann chooses a new form of staging in which presentation is not based on a chronology or chapter sequence. Instead, the works on new art forms such as installation art, land art, environment, and happening enter into an extremely exciting dialogue through the curator's conception.

As director of documenta 5 in 1972 in Kassel, he, at the time a freelance curator and founder of the Agency for Intellectual Guest Work, for the first time, establishes a thematic orientation for the world's largest exhibition of contemporary art: *Questioning Reality - Visual Worlds Today*. He intends an event with a political-critical background and provocative approaches. Non-art and pictorial contributions from the environment of psychiatry come to the exhibition and trigger a controversial debate among the public. In the first concept Szeemann plans a radical departure from the museum principle, away from a static exhibition and towards the presentation of creative processes and developments. However, this first concept remains unrealized for financial and organizational reasons. The second implemented concept places the exhibition's focus on the tense relationship between art and the parallel visual worlds of non-art, social reality and political propaganda. When Harald Szeemann talks about "individual mythologies" in Kassel in 1972, this attitude corresponds to the renewed interest in Outsider Art at the Venice Biennale in 2013.

There was archaeological reminiscence, also in 2013 in Venice. The Fondazione Prada even presents the exhibition *When Attitudes Become Form*, which has been reconstructed with about 80 percent of the works from Bern at that time. An already curated event in the history of the exhibition is now being re-curated—curated by Germano Celant in dialogue with Thomas Demand and Rem Koolhaas—for a new experience. A wonderful and unforgettable event with side and long-distance effects on everyday life.

GM: Can you describe a personal curatorial work and project you are really proud of and also a project which didn't really work out?

PB: Inspired by Harald Szeemann's *Der Hang zum Gesamtkunstwerk* in Zurich (1983), I started my own project *Lebenskunstwerke LKW* in Linz (1999) and *LKW - Kunst in der Stadt 4* in Bregenz (2000). I was interested in the guest workers between art and life, also slightly disparagingly called life artists. For them, the goal is not a "free art" as it is taught as an academic subject. The goal is, on the contrary, to make art and life freer.

As we enter the 21st century, we can increasingly observe new courses, new orders, new units as well as new hybrid cultures, new media networks and new crossovers. The old vision of the *Gesamtkunstwerk* as an interplay of different arts is experiencing a renaissance, for which the term *Lebenskunstwerk* seems more appropriate to me.

In a *Lebenskunstwerk* there is—without gigantic bluster, without grand gestures of rebellion, restless, independent and intangible—a pleasurable interaction of life & experience, art & culture as well as work & work. It is a real, not just simulated, free association of free individuals, which promises an increase in the intensity of life - existential risk included.

In the *Lebenskunstwerk* (abbreviated *LKW*) the three layers of life/art/work enter into communication with each other, are projected onto each other through performativity (action, reflection, interaction), so that precisely a *Lebenskunstwerk* emerges.

On the one hand, we have the truck, which transports goods from A to B. On the other hand, we have the work of art. The truck drives around building blocks, for example. War material. Relief supplies. Refugees in a refrigerated container. Or works of art as self-contained, transportable objects; there is no exhibition without a truck.

On the other hand, we have the artwork of life (truck); its "course of things" is not linear, but non-linear. It avoids single-minded straightforwardness and leads through irritating detours. The concrete truck is about things and objects, about having; the artistic truck is about the act of experiencing and letting happen, about a state of being. The truck is not a tangible and visible possession, but simple being and doing. In the *LKW*, the focus is less on the finished creative product than on the process character. Someone enters into the creative happening and is in a continuum that cannot be possessed. Here, art and creativity are perceived as living experience, fleeting experience and irreversible development. In the truck, moments of openness to deviation, to the unplanned and hitherto unavailable emerge, nourished from the sources of unconscious forces.

The artist Augustine Rebetez (*1986) is the most recent example of artistic creation that pleads for a dissolution of the boundaries of art. If passion and creativity become a shared good in the artist's environment, then it is logical that the *enfant terrible* of the Swiss art scene is currently building his artists' house and museum with a sculpture park: *La Maison Totale*. In Rebetez's life artwork, the living of art finds a comprehensive expression in experiences and performances, in space and time, in spirit and feeling. In this way, the world of art remains in constant contact with our existence—in the sense of an aesthetics of existence.

The project *Lebenskunstwerke LKW* should also have been shown in Biel. It failed due to a temporary financial bottleneck at a museum there. Otherwise, I have been able to bring all planned projects to a successful conclusion.

GM: You worked for years within the field of art in public space. What is the special challenge of art in public space for a curator?

PB: The artistic and curatorial design of public art (or art in architecture) can certainly be described as a supreme discipline in the exhibition business. After all, it requires specific thinking and acting in contexts that face the challenges of complexity, and a practice that transcends disciplines and their representatives (the list of protagonists is long).

The function of the curator of projects in the context of art in the city is that of a master of dialogue who, through the phenomenon of art, enters into a relationship with all these groups as well as with the social and media public.

If the art scene expands from the studio and the white cube to the city and its public, this takes place, in the successful version, with a high dialogic tension component in 'public affairs' (*res publica*). Starting from *res publica* ('res' means the thing and the event, 'publica' the people), art in the city stands for a process in which it appears as an intervening event in a civil society.

In the anthology *Art and the Public* (2015), the editors are not so much concerned with art in public space, but rather "with the public (in) art". Cited is the neologism 'publicum', which denotes an open-held place of passage and turnover, a specific point where art and the public converge, an in-between space where properties, contents, or perceptions enter into an exchange with one another.

Above all, the curatorial role in a "public art" process corresponds to that of an instigating developer, moderator, and (over)mediator. The curator, as a mediating impulse-giver, strives to soften existing front lines, and links the different individualities and identities of all participants with the specific content of stubbornness that is immanent in art in public space.

GM: Must art in public space be different from art in museums?

PB: If art is to actively participate in the public life of a city, then it is a matter of designing a public sphere or agora in which an exchange between heterogeneous user groups can take place—a place for opinion formation, expression and transfer of opinion. If the task arises for the curation of an entire city, the arts are of particular suitability thanks to their differentiated approach to the public sphere. They activate a third life between the inhabitants and buildings, putting the difference in the center—the in-between. The publicly accessible work of art as a vital presence in the city or village is a thing in between, and the in-between (*inter-esse*, inter = between and esse = to be) is one of the meaningful qualities of an aesthetic human being. The first efficient thrust for public art projects is thus generated from this in-between, which provides an *allmende* for conversations beyond arguments about taste. These conversations/dialogues provide resistant impulses, initiate open-ended processes, reveal critical backgrounds and thought structures of art.

Artistic interventions do not necessarily offer a better or more reflective approach to the city or village than the impulses that urban planning initiates under different premises. However, when art gets involved in a creative and intervening context/process, conventional assumptions and holdings are set in motion - which can result in failure and misunderstanding, as well as generate unexpected events. In Zurich, the failed *Nagelhaus* (2007) by

Thomas Demand and, in turn, the surprisingly successful *Hafenkran* (2014) by the artist collective Zürich Transit Maritim exemplify this.

Probably the most radical and stubborn artistic setting in the field of art in public space comes from Piero Manzoni (1933–1963), who is hardly known today. With works such as the *Merda d'artista* (1961)—(allegedly) 30 grams of artist's shit in a strictly limited edition - or the *Socle du monde* (*Pedestal of the World*, 1961)—a pedestal that elevates the world to a work of art—Manzoni created icons of recent art history. With his *Socle* (which is actually not allowed to be shown in museums, but only in the open air), he has declared the world, with everything that crawls and flies on it, to be a readymade. No one else has ever thought and practiced this in a more presumptuous and ultimate way.

Manzoni relies on the total function of art by amalgamating reality and imagination. For him, the world does not need its own form of representation, but only a pedestal: as a work of life-art, it is already in a perfect state and needs no duplication.

GM: Can you describe, based on one of your curatorial projects, the path from the first idea to the exhibition? What are the most important steps in developing and executing a project?

PB: As *Homo curare creativum* I actually find my "form of play" in all projects less in working off a reality, but in evoking an agile sense of possibility. As a thoughtful "experimental designer" my presentation gesture is never decidedly directed against something, but organizes itself for others or in conscious dissociation from others. More than in museum-like space-time orders, I am interested in orienting myself to relational fields and aggregate states. The formulation of a meaning-giving process of conceptual selecting, assembling and showing is essential. What becomes important for me is the moment of transition, where artworks are understood not only as isolated artifacts but as segments of a visual continuum, thus formulating a thesis about art - which either finds acceptance or rejection. The *Höhenrausch* project on the rooftops of Linz (2009-2021) was exceptional both because of its exposed location and the all-around positive reception it received from the public and art critics, who spoke of an "outdoor spectacle" but praised the playfulness of the interventions.

As a curator, I cultivate an explicit orientation towards the "New Exhibiting" (see volume 186/2007 of the journal *Kunstforum Int.*), which logically also includes a clear turning away from simply placing, disguising, filling up, and delivering the exhibits to be presented. It makes no difference whether the arrangement of the works is thematic (e.g. color, form or material), according to persons, artist circles, or chronologically. What is important is the intention to carry out the realization with a certain radicalness, but not without the necessary precision. Only in this way does it become possible to present the differentiation and contrasts within an epoch or a *zeitgeist*. Or to bring together things whose presentation in one and the same space would break aesthetic or moral boundaries (for example, next to the religious motif of the cross, Karin Sander's presentation of the red Google Maps sign on the church in the Croatian town of Raša).

For me, curating is always also an attempt to offer the audience a practice field of their own seeing and experiencing, before previous (art-) historical knowledge directs their gaze. The degree to which a curatorial work is successful depends on the extent to which the curator is able to reconcile the weight of a theme with the complexity of what is being shown. Ideally, theme and realization merge into an unstrained whole—an exhibition from one cast. Not to forget the time factor. The limited duration of exhibitions significantly increases their appeal to the public. If you miss an exhibition, you will never see it again.

GM: How do you define the relation between artist and curator?

PB: The collaboration between artist and curator offers learning material for both sides. When the artist sees the world through the eyes of the curator and the curator sees the world through the eyes of the artist, both will recognize something they would never have discovered on their own. The dialogue brings forth something new. The "brilliant" idea of one individual is abandoned in favor of a common path.

GM: How independent is an independent/freelance curator? How dependent is a curator employed by a museum? How different is their work and self-understanding?

PB: Ideally, both are united by the same aesthetic attitude, namely that an exhibition acting according to curatorial principles should not only put something up for discussion but should also add a thesis to the content. The idea that the exhibited things have the potential to speak for themselves does not redeem reality. Since the things do not speak—and if they did speak, they would say many things and much more—the exhibition practice needs a guideline or direction. What is fundamentally important? Which voices are to be listened to? What exactly is it about when a teapot is on display in a showcase?

This mediation is necessary because the more authentic a thing is supposed to appear, the more it is alienated from itself in the act of exhibition. This is based on a curatorial paradox in which the exhibitors take things out of an ancestral context and present them now in a new one: something, for example the urinal from 1917 by Marcel Duchamp, is supposed to be exactly what it is, but for this very reason it becomes something completely different—and yet remains physically what it is. Despite everything: the exhibited changes with the way it is exhibited, probably not in its entity and identity, but in its effect and performance. An exhibition without context is not an exhibition because exhibiting in its pure form does not exist. Curators are context-givers.

GM: What will be the main challenges for a curator in the future? Will it be more collective, or will individualism come back?

PB: Art has a more than rich history to offer for the promising movement, from the cult of genius to group intelligence: from the building lodges of the Middle Ages and the hierarchically structured painters' workshops, from the Gothic to the Renaissance and Baroque periods, from the colorful and heterogeneous Lebensreformer colony on Monte Verità in Ascona to the corporate identity of Andy Warhol's New York Factory. The most recent example is the artist entrepreneur Olafur Eliasson with his Berlin studio, which has over 50 employees.

While a rapid growth in collective processes and group formations among artists can be noted from about 1900 onward, little is known about how collectivity has developed in the context of curating. It is worth noting at the outset that exhibition making, as in film production or architecture, is a process based on the division of labor with many participants—from art, design, mediation, scenography, technology, management, and communication. Consequently, curating always takes place as an activity in a swarm.

In the course of the 20th century, two curatorial subject forms emerged: the museum curator integrated into an institution and a free unattached exhibition maker. At this point, we should again mention Harald Szeemann, who decisively influenced the development towards the "free curator" in his time. When Szeemann was awarded the first installed position of Secretary General for documenta 5 in Kassel in 1972, he formed a seven-member working group. However, financial reasons meant that this had to be reduced to three people: Arnold Bode, Jean-Christophe Ammann and Szeemann. 50 years later, documenta 15 (2022) will now be curated by the Indonesian artist collective ruangrupa. This expresses the fact that roles can no longer be clearly assigned: artists function as curators, just as curators appear as artists.

This movement, from single-intendence to working in teams, groups, or collectives, is bound to gain in importance. The forerunner of this development was the exhibition *Get Together. Art as Teamwork* (1999/2000) at the Kunsthalle Wien, it directed attention to the nineties and to the dynamics of an artistic paradigm shift. It showed how both the organizational form and the collective work results in the art business can combine a personal optic with a perspective that allows and promotes the plural. This was done with works by Art & Language, Atelier van Lieshout, Jan Fabre & Ilya Kabakov, Rosemarie Trockel & Carsten Höller, and others.

Consequently, the show was curated by an "open team" around Marion Piffer-Damiani from Bolzano. This was a temporary multiple authorship and experimental collaboration of equal talents who practiced cooperative individuality in the medium of the exhibition. The credo formulated by Piffer-Damiani in relation to the exhibited collective works also reads programmatically for the work of the curatorial team. While individual artists usually proceeded linearly according to their own dramaturgy, teams would prefer a parallel procedure: making things together, adopting ideas from each other, and striving for collaborations with a new play structure, in order to activate a collective intelligence in this way.

As one of the curators involved, I still remember well the brainstorming for the title to the exhibition in the office of the then Kunsthalle director Gerald A. Matt. In the uninhibited thought process of a brainstorming session, the wealth of input exploded. Suddenly the John Lennon song *Come Together* by the Beatles appeared without further ado, as if in the act of a common inspiration. It was also clear that a slightly different expression of sympathy was needed: "come" became "get".

Finally, with a view to the future, we would like to point out an essential factor in collective-creative work: diversity. This is about the interaction of singularly acting persons, including the diversity of their differences with regard to different life realities and worlds. A multi-perspective view allows us to connect all desires with each other. For a contemporary artist or curator collective, it is essential to foreground the diversity of the various members—with their different hopes, perceptions, experiences, ideas, whims, etc. The challenge is not to create a single collective, but rather to create a collective that is a whole. The challenge is to cultivate not a collective unity, but a collective multiplicity.

Art must be politically and aesthetically challenging

Bernardo José de Souza
in conversation with Gerald A. Matt

GERALD A. MATT: What is a curator? Can you define your understanding and practice as a curator?

BERNARDO JOSÉ DE SOUZA: From a historical perspective, the role of a curator has always been an everchanging one: over the last two hundred years or so, curating has shifted from being the endeavour of aristocrats and connoisseurs; the reverie of avant-garde artists; the manifestation of dilletante minds from the most diverse backgrounds, ranging from architecture and theatre to politics and literature; the result of extensive investigative efforts made by art historians; the product of professionals emerging from contemporary academic courses whose ultimate purpose is to shape the very praxis of a curator; to blatantly being the outcome of market-oriented displaying of art by art fairs and collectors alike.

Nevertheless, from a personal and contemporary approach, I'd say curating entails curiosity, the capacity to articulate matter and thoughts driven by a critical understanding of what art has come to mean in the present and has meant in the past, bearing in mind the respective temporal and conflicting sociocultural contexts. For this reason, there shouldn't exist one single understanding of curating, but rather a myriad of curatorial efforts driven by the urgency to make sense of artistic practices in their constant pursuit to reshape or reappraise the world through aesthetical, material, and political means.

In this sense, contemporary curating demands reassigning meaning to symbolic and material culture, unravelling semantic economies and epistemologies, as well as alternative patterns of thinking. By mediating the political and aesthetic debate, proposing other narratives and new topographies of visual tropes—thus creating a landscape of its own, which exists in parallel to the one experimented outside the curatorial frame—hopefully one can lure the audience to enter a different dimension of reality. That's the beauty of curating, devising a heterotopic space which engulfs the spectator in a phenomenological experience, one capable of reconfiguring both the tangible and the intangible worlds.

GM: How can curating be relevant to the challenges we face today and in what way does it differ from previous models?

BDS: As I said, curating is a constant exercise of reframing things—not only artworks but also architectures, bodies, histories, and temporalities altogether. By rearranging the world in the ephemeral arch of time of an exhibition (to be noted, I'm referring to the role of curating exhibitions only), a breach between the past, the present and the future can be opened, therefore creating a particular time-space relation which allows for artists and the public to collectively repropose belief systems and reassess the very political nature of present times—and conversely of historical accounts. And whenever grasping the lingering effects that the western totalizing narratives have exerted over human history, curators can counter-fight the noxious discourses which have insufflated today's poisonous political and cultural atmosphere. Henceforth, a contemporary curator should not only be able to dismantle dominant discourses and colonial narratives but furthermore to entice the audience to formulate other possible ones by politically navigating towards the past and the future at once.

GM: How do you see the changing relations between curators, artists, collectors, galleries, museums, and critics? Was there a shift of power and influence?

BDS: Well, there have been constant, tremendous shifts in the way those agents interact with one another over the course of time. To focus exclusively on the imminent present, I'd say the artworld has increasingly come to resemble the one of fashion, since it responds to an ever-expanding crave for novelty. In brief, this means the market (collectors, galleries, and some curators alike) ignites an insatiable drive for the next big trend or name, and as a result, a plethora of very young artists are constantly being thrown into the carrousel of commodities that sets the contemporary artworld in motion. Conversely though, many great artists in their mid-careers fall into oblivion, while deceased ones, who had never enjoyed their much-deserved visibility, are reappraised by gallerists who so avidly dig into their debased states in order to bring to surface the "archaeological" findings of the art history of just yesterday—often motivated by the market rather than by the altruistic purpose of rewriting history.

As far as museums are concerned, they have become more dependent on funding and donations coming from patrons and collectors who not rarely enter this mutually beneficial relationship expecting increased interest in the artists and artworks belonging to their private collections. Some curators alike, indulge in following this very modus operandi, making safe and profitable artistic choices so as to enjoy the visibility produced when one enters the merry-go-round of the art system. Last but not least, in much the same fashion, art critics (well, they rarely exist these days as their work has been delegated to curators) are eager to write good reviews about whichever artists might give them the kudos to pursue the next step in their curatorial careers.

GM: Can you describe the path from the first idea to the exhibition based on one of your curatorial projects? What are the most important steps in developing and executing the project?

BDS: My group exhibitions usually begin with a pressing issue, a recurrent theme that unceasingly haunts my imagination—it could derive from an artwork, a book, a newspaper article, a film, a relaxed conversation in a bar, a psychoanalytic session, a dream, or even from the mere observation of life unfolding before my eyes.

Afterwards, I'm fully driven and captured by the world of art and literature: that's when my collection of mental images and readings come to surface, connecting existing artworks with their actual creators, prompting a diversity of questions and the exciting possibility of commissioning new pieces for the exhibition. And as the conversations with artists begin, the original idea is reformulated, other books are opened, new conceptual issues emerge, and very concrete material elements come into play, rearranging the whole scenario. The exhibition space is crucial for the development of my ideas: a curatorial project only acquires shape on material grounds; they inform my practice as much as the artworks I see or the books I read.

Generally, once there is a designated space in mind, there is also a pretty accurate notion of the available budget. At times, this information comes prior to the flow of ideas for the show but it all depends on whether you're working by an invitation or simply delineating a concept for a possible future exhibition—and based on how the venture was kick-started, the whole process might be inverted.

Once there is a clear idea of what to do, what to show and where, I become a producer of sorts, operating as a political agent, trying to maximise my choices, making possible the impossible, establishing partnerships or fundraising. If there is a team working with me, it's time to orchestrate the show collectively, whereas if there isn't, I become an "expert" in whatever problems may arise: the paint to be used, the technology to be hired, the device to suspend the artwork, the material to darken the room and so on. Whether you are alone or not, surely all these practical constrains will reconfigure most of the exhibition. Then comes the time to review previous writings, reshape ideas and make sense of the project intellectually, and to install the artworks: a moment to revise the positioning of certain pieces, as well as how one will experience the exhibition.

When all of it is done, there comes the question of how to make the project public: the press, the public programmes, the handouts or publications, the advertising of the exhibition, the maintenance of it, and so on. Lastly, the opening: a moment to congregate and celebrate with the artists, the team, and the public, but also a time to understand the choreography of the audience within the exhibition space and around the artworks—and the last opportunity to reposition the artworks as well.

On a different note, curating solo shows will require another type of intelligence, as most of the ideas come from the artist, and the curator becomes a collaborator, one that embarks in a world whose features are previously known—unless you're commissioning a new work. In such kinds of shows, you are asked to make sense out of a landscape where the tropes are a given: elements to be recombined or rearticulated, repositioned and reinterpreted alongside the artist (if the artist is alive, of course).

Also, it is important to mention that the whole process will change depending on the nature of a curatorial project: destined to take place in a museum, in a gallery, in a project space, in the virtual space etc.

GM: Is curating always a struggle between vision and practical constraints? Can you give an example?

BDS: Absolutely. Curating is always the result of contingency, be it one signalled by institutions, or be it one met in quite informal project spaces. Political, institutional, and economic factors undeniably inform one's curatorial decisions when it comes to making an exhibition.

In regard to material constrains, having a comfortable budget means, for instance, being able to commission new artworks, shipping pieces from afar or even the possibility of organizing extensive public programmes and publications. From an institutional perspective, though, it might imply not being able to present a specific artwork given the lack of climate control or having to tone down the curatorial discourse in order not to defy the political views of the institution. This is all to say that there is a multitude of factors either informing curatorial decisions or challenging one's capacity to overcome such material or political dilemmas.

Given my personal experience, scarcity has always produced the most wondrous and unexpected results; whenever forced to find alternatives, one is ultimately led to foreign territories: replacing the known with the unknown, the safe with the unsafe, the established with the transgressive, the upscale with the feasible. And in respect to the political commitments imposed by institutions, well, that could be seen as a trigger for the use of rather insidious intelligence in order to convey a bold curatorial discourse without falling into complacency with the establishment. Curating will always be a political enterprise, both in abundance and in scarcity. One must make allies, either with artists, the public, institutions, collectors or gallerists, though never falling into the trap of subsuming the curatorial to private interests.

As an example of both political and material constraint, I'd mention a show I organized while directing the Department of Cinema, Video and Photography of the Municipality of Porto Alegre, in Brazil. The artist in question was Alair Gomes, a photographer whose body of work emerged in the 1970s, and whose object of investigation was the male body—generally surfers from Ipanema beach in Rio de Janeiro. Since there were no funds to publicize the exhibition—though we did have the support of the public transport system to advertise our shows at the back of their buses—we decided to print a huge close-up made by the artists depicting the hips of a man wearing a Speedo swimsuit and revealing his somewhat erect penis underneath. It could have been ammunition for a scandal, but those were the early 2000s, and pundits back then would refrain from causing a major stir around an artwork—that was the time lapse between Mapplethorpe's photographs lawsuit after Cincinnati Contemporary Arts Center's exhibition in 1990 and the neoconservative wave that ensued the years of relative freedom in between.

GM: How do you define the relation between artist and curator?

BDS: As one of trust. Showing someone's artworks means recontextualizing their piece, be it in relation to the space, to the surrounding works or the discursive elements informing the exhibition—not to mention the material conditions of display. A curator should always be the artist's best ally, either proving the means for a project to fully come to fruition, elaborating a narrative about a particular piece or body of works, situating it historically-culturally, or challenging the artist's very practice by creating semantic tension around their work.

GM: Where are the conflict lines?

BDS: In my specific curatorial practice—which generally conceives of an exhibition as one single organism, or a topography of its own, informed by a particular narrative—one of the most sensitive points would be placing artworks within highly discursively charged atmospheres in which the ensemble of artworks becomes as important as the realm of existence of a single piece—although I always try to preserve each artwork's gravitational field. In theory, this could be problematic for artists who are not keen on embracing "contamination" as part of their artistic processes, although, I must say, most of the artists I have worked with not only wouldn't mind my "promiscuous" approach to curating but mostly enjoy it. Afterall, art only exists in context, and in transit.

GM: Is curating artistic work or a service to the artist and their work?

BDS: I wouldn't say curating is artistic work, although it definitely involves creative thinking. Curating only exists in relation to artistic work; therefore it could be understood as a practice devoted to exhibiting artworks and providing conditions for its fruition, at times even taking the work beyond its original grounding—semantic or otherwise.

GM: There have recently been some examples of artists being invited by institutions to curate major shows and of curators producing their own art. In what way is the line between authorship and curating shifting/fading?

BDS: As I mentioned before, only in recent years (circa the 1990s) has curating been established as a profession that emerges out of a disciplined academic formation, which means that the history of curating has always been somehow open to experimentation, and to individuals coming from the most diverse backgrounds. Having said so, I see with great naturality and enthusiasm the fact that artists have been curating exhibitions themselves. To name just one ground-breaking example of this kind, I'd mention the exhibition curated by Fred Wilson at the Maryland Historical Society in Baltimore (1991-93), *Mining the Museum*, where he brings to the surface the colonial practices hidden behind the mechanisms of display that shape ideological discourses in museums—an exhibition that anticipated by almost 30 years the current omnipresent debate about decolonial narratives intruding on the colonial space that the museum has been since its inception.

Once again deriving from my own curatorial practice, I'm very aware that I can be quite heavy-handed at times—some of my shows conceive the exhibition space as a stage, the platform for narratives to unfold through the totality of its many constitutive elements, which means understanding the artworks as part of a world in its own right. Often theatrical, those environments become the arena where artworks collide, co-exist in a dimension that amalgamates singularities into a unifying fictional sphere. And from time to time, I even incorporate pieces which are foreign to the context of art per se, namely furniture, antiques or even plants. Some would argue that I'm using someone else's work to create my own. I'd say I'm providing a scenario, a setting or a context in which artworks can exist and therefore be perceived and understood differently—reframed and reassessed in a different light.

GM: How independent is an independent/freelance curator?

BDS: As the freelance curator does not have to fully adhere to the intrinsic architecture of power within an institution, in theory he/she enjoys more freedom in independent art circuits. However, they experience far more difficulties in bringing a project to the surface—especially given the lack of material conditions that institutions usually provide. In practice though, this so-called independence is rather narrow as one is still dependent on the globalized, institutionalized art world.

Another aspect of the freelance curator's life is the struggle to make ends meet due to the lack of a permanent position, which might lead one to embrace a diversity of jobs that do not necessarily allow them to exercise the critical position one would expect them to enjoy—namely, working on demand for galleries, art fairs or private collectors, thus often operating as an agent of the market rather than as an autonomous thinker (there are many exceptions, of course).

GM: How dependent is a curator employed by a museum?

BDS: Whenever working in a museum, a curator must respond to a board, to patrons and sponsors alike, and to an institution that requires being committed to a very general audience, often implying that the curatorial programme should be conceived with a targeted audience in mind, as well as contending with the "party" in power. However, there can still be room for negotiation, or at least for "outwitting" the political manoeuvring in the interest of more critical openings.

GM: What is the impact of identity politics on the theory and practice of curating?

BDS: This has been an extremely relevant topic in the artworld for more than a few decades now. In positive terms, it could be said that the critique of racism has furthered the whole identity politics debate to encompass other decolonizing efforts made by institutions, including critical readings from the perspective of gender. Nonetheless, in recent years—and here I would stress the confluence of the COVID pandemic and the Black Lives Matter movement in 2020, both signalling a political and economic social abyss—the issue has gained momentum and shifted from being a sensitive debate to becoming an insurmountable political wound; one to be unavoidably faced and discussed in our society, and particularly in the artworld.

GM: Did it change your way of thinking and working?

BDS: I wouldn't say it changed my way of thinking, as these issues have always been present in my curatorial projects; it did make me adapt the way of addressing certain problematics, mostly due to the linguistic turn the whole debate has imposed, both ethically and semantically. If on the one hand decolonial narratives have informed my curatorial thinking from the beginning, on the other, writing about and naming such sensitive social and historical wounds has required reassessing language, and, by consequence, its impact over my curatorial practice.

Besides the linguistic debate, though, there is a far more crucial issue at stake when it comes to revising curatorship as an instrument for social change: the matter of equality. As a curator, one can give artists visibility, but beyond the selection of artworks that may deal with identity politics, lies the question of who to show and which artworks to include in each given project—equity and equality being the main factors here. As a result, some questions never cease to arise: What is your place of enunciation when dealing with such problematics? To which realities are you referring to? And how do you contest dominant narratives and institutions without falling into the trap of reproducing the very lines of what is now a hegemonic woke discourse in the artworld—emanating mostly from the US? One that can easily flatten the debate under a vertical commandment, by the way. There are many more realities of how diverse cultures have experienced colonialism than can be contemplated by one single narrative.

Another aspect of this problematics has to do with how the artworld has been dealing with such pressing issues, and how distinct agents in the "art market"—namely, museums, collectors and even curators—have managed to wash their previous history of colonialism by adhering to a politics of inclusivity based primarily on iconography and far less on alternative art forms or on structural changes in the institutional architecture of power. It also strikes me how the entire debate about non-Western ancestries and cosmologies ended up being conveyed by art institutions mostly through figurative painting—instead of breaking with this very same European canon, which is indeed the framed image, a portable object that serves to perfection the demands of the art market.

Far from diminishing the relevance of such political achievements, my questions are destined to create tension around adamant historical problems that, surprisingly, have been swiftly incorporated by the art market and museums alike—as well as nuanced by these institutions. Ultimately, I'd say the whole identity politics struggle has not only changed my practice but has also made me aware of how eager the capitalist system is to overturn change and establish a Lampedusan reform of sorts: "Everything must change for everything to remain the same". It remains to be seen how far this fight will be taken forward—or if it'll indeed change the atavistic colonial dynamics of art institutions.

Moreover, identity politics should be addressed in conjunction with other concurring issues such as scarcity, material culture, climate change, the capitalist system, poverty, technology, amongst many others, as they are all mutually embedded, together shaping today's politics. Engaging with identity politics in isolation runs the risk of atomizing the debate and fragmenting the political subject, orienting them towards an individualistic ideology of the self, which could neutralize the emancipatory potential of such social battles.

GM: Must art be moral? What about art and its values?

BDS: Art must be politically and aesthetically challenging—and by 'political', I mean it should challenge current discourses in their respective time of existence. There is no such thing as transhistorical art, one that resists the political scrutiny of time (there may be one under today's light, but perhaps not in 50 years or so). Values change, as does morality, and the highly transgressive art of yesterday might be seen as heavily reactionary today. Take the likes of Mapplethorpe, Jean Genet or Fassbinder, for instance. The former would rent prostitutes for a few bucks in order to produce his strikingly beautiful black male nudes; Genet would write about exclusively male worlds; and the latter would quite often objectify women in his somewhat misogynistic films, if one assumes the current understanding of identity politics. These were all (gay) artists who systematically challenged the status quo, and were perceived as revolutionary in their time, but arguably today could run the risk of being considered distasteful and even reactionary vis-à-vis some contemporary discourses and positions. And the same could apply to the likes of Visconti or Pasolini, who were both communists, by the way, not to mention Fellini and Bergman, talking exclusively about the history of cinema.

GM: What is the role of institutions in your practice? Where does the boundary lie between curatorial and institutional responsibility?

BDS: They were designed to reproduce a history that dates back to the colonial era; they were created with this very purpose and every element brought into their interiors tends to function as a reminder of that history. To defeat such a purpose, institutions must permanently revise their programmes, their architecture and power structure. Instead of consolidating knowledge, they should deconstruct patterns of thinking. To that end, the responsibility of both curators and institutions should be creating enough tension to bring longstanding narratives to a halt. As much as a curatorial project must stand on its own and be solid enough to propose dissonant discourses and realities, it should always be on the verge of collapse. The inner nature of a museum is to produce a cohesive narrative, but since there is no coherence in the outside world, the institution should reflect upon the political aporia of our times. Uncertainty rather than stability. In a museum, one should always navigate troubled waters.

GM: What will be the main challenges for a curator in the future? How will curatorial work change?

BDS: I believe the main challenge will consist in articulating narratives and curatorial projects which are not merely a reproduction of an algorithmic discourse of sorts based on pre-digested notions of the political debate. If a curator always plays safe, by the book of political correctness, the curatorial risks becoming institutional, conservative, and even reactionary—although it might appear otherwise given the rather new "normative" narratives produced by the so-called leftist ideologies of today. On the left bank of the political debate, as much as in art, there must be tension, never consensus. That's how the boundaries of convention can be broken. Moreover, beyond discursiveness, the curatorial endeavour should also entail the capacity to reconfigure and transfigure the very mechanisms of displaying and seeing art, thus challenging the epitome of its colonial architecture: the museum.

Finally, as far as predicting the future goes, I'd say no one should dare to foresee beyond the misty horizon of days to come, as has been proven by the series of both natural and political phenomena experienced in recent years. In a split second, we might just happen to be faced with an entirely new political, social and technological landscape—one we must respond to, and inexorably change.

Desire and reality are in fact two permanent sparring partners in curating

Christoph Doswald
in conversation with Gerald A. Matt

GERALD A. MATT: What is a curator? Can you define your understanding and practice as a curator?

CHRISTOPH DOSWALD: Although the term is now used inflationarily (food, wine, fashion, books, etc.—hardly any current subject area is safe from curating), I do not want to limit my broad self-conception of this field of work. For my idea of curatorial work, it is important to think about affiliations, build bridges, create connections—in short, to put art in dialogue with the world and vice versa. Of course, it's fun to imagine art in a white cube, to tease out the autonomy of artworks in the laboratory-like contexts of an institutional setting. I, too, have done that with a series of sometimes retrospective, monographic exhibitions. But in my opinion, these are often purely academic exercises. It seems to me that it makes more sense to show art where it can create an element of surprise—in places not necessarily built for the presentation of art. It is important to me to make encounters with art possible for people who do not normally go to museums. That is why, over the last 40 years, I have also dealt in many ways with marginal zones of artistic practice—including locations in companies, in public spaces, or in schools and cooperatively run buildings—and played with contexts that are not inherently specific to art.

The claim of social relevance is not new, but should be practiced more often again. Of course, a good curator will not engage in propagating the majority appeal of art because of this broad target group. The challenge of art in non-art locations lies in the mediation, the communication, the credibility of the artistic action. A good example of this practice is Thomas Hirschhorn, with his rigorous artistic approach: he spends 100 days in a multi-cultural suburban neighborhood in Kassel where he lures young people with little cultural background into his *Bataille Monument* and infects them with new ideas. Or Heinrich Gartentor, whose *Island in the City* in Münsterhof lowered the temperature of Zurich's overheated city center with green art for a summer.

GM: How can curating be relevant to the challenges we face today and in what way does it differ from previous models?

CD: Curating means selecting, experimenting, and communicating. In a way, our profession provides a blueprint for the diplomatic handling of unusual, innovative, and creative ideas in culture, politics, business, and society. Curating means, in the broadest sense, being able to facilitate intercultural dialogues, question the supposedly entrenched knowledge, dissolve fronts, break new ground, and take people to places they would not normally venture. Art can mobilize people for action and motivate them to jump over their own shadows. Art is a wonderful field for experimentation and a way to think the supposedly impossible and then act on it. Brazilian photographer Sebastião Salgado, who made a fortune with his pictures of the world's misery at Magnum, used the money to launch a project to reforest the Brazilian rainforest. The Swiss artist Julian Charrière undertook dangerous expeditions at the risk of his own health—to Bikini Atoll, for example—to report on the dystopian effects of the atomic bomb tests that were carried out there until well into the 1990s. Giving such artists a platform and helping them communicate their ideas to audiences outside the art world is critical to transforming society. And in contrast to the earlier social demands of art (e.g. the Dessau Bauhaus or the Russian Constructivists), this is not a top-down activity, but an approach that relies on the curiosity of mature citizens and their capacity for dialogue.

GM: How do you see the changing relations between curators, artists, collectors, galleries, museums, and critics? Was there a shift of power and influence?

CD: There have always been shifts in the tectonics of these fragile fields of activity. They are related to changes in economic and social contexts. When I started as an art critic in the early 1980s, the global media landscape was still highly diverse. There were several daily newspapers in every small town and several professional journals in every country. All these media were in a very healthy economic situation, so the fees were sufficient to make a good living. As a result of the digitalization of the media, that business model has vanished into thin air. Along with it, the livelihood of the art critic has also disappeared—the profession hardly exists today. The same can be said for galleries: the globalization of the market through art fairs and digital trading platforms has destroyed the basis of locally operating art dealers. This, in turn, has affected collections and artists: collections composed of local artworks can no longer be found; everything follows the global mainstream.

And because of all these developments in the last 20 years, the relationships between the actors of the art system have understandably changed. Whether this is good or bad? It's a difficult question. But it can be stated that the world of art has become both richer and poorer as a result of globalization. So, we can see more art quickly, but it appears more uniform and streamlined. The aspect of the financial viability of projects adds to this. Here, the shift towards the mainstream manifests itself particularly clearly. Because the art system has become an integral part of the global entertainment industry, it is interesting for commercially active sponsors. It goes without saying that these financiers have a vital interest in the broad communicability of exhibition projects. And so it happens that difficult, unwieldy artworks are hardly ever shown. The same can be said about the influence of private collections, which also pursue an agenda that does not necessarily further the development of art in terms of content. In personalities such as François Pinault or Miuccia Prada, these fields of interest overlap. And with the current generation of Asian NFT collectors, new—frankly quite disturbing—facets of these interacting gravitational fields are once again revealed.

GM: Was Harald Szeemann replaced by François Pinault?

CD: Good question. Harald Szeemann is celebrated today as a free spirit, a hero of independence, and a pioneer of curatorial freedom. But that falls far short of the mark. Because Szeemann's legendary exhibition *When Attitudes Become Form* can be seen—despite its visionary curatorial realization—as a sponsorship project financed by the US multinational Philipp Morris, which implicitly propagated the dominance of American culture, politics, and lifestyle. As we know today, the U.S. government used many channels to spread the capitalist values of the "white Anglo-Saxon Protestants". And culture, or art, was an important carrier of messages in this purposefully developed campaign—subversion with culture instead of gunboat politics. When exponents of the European fashion and lifestyle industry today build museums, finance exhibitions, and run galleries and auction houses, it is an analogous approach. With the help of art, messages can be conveyed—political as well as consumerist ones.

GM: Are young artists taking over the role of curators?

CD: The realization that the global exploitation industry described above leaves little room for the new, the young and the unknown, resulted in frustration, and then in the 1980s, a self-help movement developed in the art scene: the off-spaces or artist-run spaces. In this decidedly non-commercial setting, artists exhibited their colleagues and showed art that had no place in the aforementioned exploitation system of entertainment and consumer industries. In such art labs, young female artists act as mediators, indeed to a certain extent as curators. Whether this ultimately results in professional employment in the field of the art system depends on many aspects, including accidental ones.

GM: Was there a personal hero, a curator, whom you admired?

CD: The curator generation of Jean-Christophe Ammann and Harald Szeemann had a formative influence on me. I was impressed by how they talked about art, and how they exhibited the works. *The tendency toward the total art work* by Harry at the Kunsthaus Zürich in 1986 was of an incredible curatorial force: how he managed to integrate individual works into a dramaturgically precise narrative without them losing their independence was impressive and left a deep impression on me. On the other hand, I had never encountered anyone who could talk about art and artists as intensely and credibly as Jean-Christophe. Fortunately, such moments of happiness still occur today when a colleague develops a truly compelling exhibition project. I was recently in Geneva, at the Musée d'art et d'histoire. At the invitation of the director Marc-Olivier Wahler, Jean-Hubert took on the challenge of working with the museum's collection and developed a charming yet highly intelligent exhibition from the disparate and encyclopedic collection—a mix of armory, ethnographic artifacts, religious objects, exotica, and art. *Draw Your Own Conclusion* questioned traditional museological dogmas and concepts, skillfully skipped time and space, and was also great fun! A few weeks ago, I received the catalogue documenting the exhibition. It was a disappointment because the exhibition was so great in its spatial and energetic presence that it was impossible to pack the experience between two book covers. That is the fascinating art of curatorial work.

GM: Can you describe a personal curatorial work and project you are really proud of and also a project which didn't really work out?

CD: In the late 1990s, there was a great sense of optimism in the Swiss art scene. But this was hardly noticed by the public. Then, when I organized a large-scale survey exhibition in the summer of 1997, it became instantly clear that a new generation of artists was at work here, one that was pushing the old image of Switzerland into the background. *Nonchalance*, first shown at the Kunstmuseum in Biel and then at the Akademie der Künste in Berlin, exhibited a completely new kind of energy that played with the advent of digitization, the broad significance of pop culture, and the looming globalization. *Nonchalance* was the first joint appearance of this new generation around Pipilotti Rist, Thomas Hirschhorn, Ugo Rondinone, Sylvie Fleury, Christian Marclay, Daniele Buetti, Lori Hersberger, to name just a few.

Somewhat outside the classical art world was an exhibition project I realized in 2001: *Happy—the Promise of Advertising* took place in Bern at the Museum of Communication and examined the influence of visual culture on social values. My intention was to bring about a broad discussion about perception in the context of the millennium, which I only partially succeeded in doing. The starting point was the idea of delegating part of the curatorial competence to the audience. To this end, I had an opinion research institute carry out a broad-based survey to evaluate which advertising images showed a particularly high level of congruence with the social ideals that were current at the time. People had thousands and thousands of images and, in dozens of workshops, condensed this pool into an image archive consistent with their personal value set. This was essentially the basis for the basic structure of the exhibition, which I then expanded with precise counterpoints. For example, there was a cabinet that contained a mini exhibition of Cuban propaganda posters. Or a 10-minute film montage of TV commercial fragments. And on the then-prehistoric Internet, ran another participatory project which gathered input on the topic from the World Wide Web surfers and projected those messages directly into the exhibition. The exhibition was great, but an overload for visitors and the media.

GM: Can you describe the path from the first idea to the exhibition based on one of your curatorial projects? What are the most important steps in developing and executing the project?

CD: There is no script, every exhibition is different. Therein lies the challenge, and the fascination with curatorial activity. In monographic projects, the artists play a formative role. The exhibition concept develops from studio discussions, and from the intended groups of works. It is a matter of sharpening what already exists, of focusing your view.
For thematic shows, I take a more comprehensive approach, investing a lot of time and energy in research to clarify what my colleagues have already

done on the one hand, and, on the other hand, to develop the necessary foundations for my own exhibition, to find exhibits and to develop thematic fields. Exhibition design also plays an important role in such large-scale projects. As a rule, I like to work with architects in order to create a suitable spatial framework for the content structure I have in mind. This collaboration is also exciting for me because the architects are, so to speak, the first visitors to the exhibition and can give me important tips in their feedback. I have already successfully adapted concepts on the basis of such feedback.

However, I really failed with a project with the Icelandic artist Ragnar Kjartansson, which was planned for the Zurich Reformation jubilee. We planned to do a sound performance in the three Reformation churches in the old town. During one night in September 2018, from sunset to sunrise, a non-stop recital of the Creed would have been performed simultaneously in the three churches—with strings and choir. We were able to convince the three parishes to join in the project. We were able to raise a large amount of money needed to pay the statutory rates of the musicians and singers. But we failed to find enough personnel for the performance. This is because the labor law restricts working time for musicians. The performance, which lasted several hours, would have required several hundred performers, and they could not be found in a small country like Switzerland.

GM: Is curating always a struggle between vision and practical constraints? Can you give an example?

CD: Desire and reality are in fact two permanent sparring partners in curating. A classic conflict of goals. The art of curating, in my opinion, is not to let the growing experience rob you of the desire to tackle even unrealistic projects. It is important to think the supposedly impossible. When I invite artists, I hear the question "What's the budget?" more and more often. My response: "Wrong question. Think about the content first, we'll talk about money later."

Currently, I am preparing the 4th Industrial Art Biennial in Croatia with my colleague Paolo Bianchi. Money is extremely scarce there. But we are trying to treat this scarcity of financial resources as a creative challenge. The Spanish artist Lara Almárcegui deals, in short, with the economy and ecology of the built world. Since Istria has been an important supplier of building materials for thousands of years, we invited her to develop a project. Now, at the port of Pula, a monumental installation made of white stone, which comes from Istrian quarries, is being built. The material was used to build Venice, which can be reached by ferry from Pula. When Lara came up with the proposal, we had no money to realize the project. But because the idea was so plausible, the quarry owner had already agreed to do the work for free. If I had told Lara that we had € 2,000 available per each work of art, the project would not have even been conceived of.

GM: How do you define the relation between artist and curator? Where are the conflict lines?

CD: I often like to work in contextual situations, and love to create new site-specific works together with the artists. That requires openness and willingness to discuss things. Dreaming and thinking up scenarios are critical faculties. Finding the right balance is not always easy and can also lead to conflicts. The artists have to develop just as much trust as the curators.

GM: Is curating artistic work or a service to the artist and their work?

CD: A bit of both. It also takes a curator's imagination of content and space to create a good exhibition project. But unlike working artistically on a particular work, the curator is also obligated to put himself or herself at the service of the work. The curator is ALSO an enabler, a mediator, an advocate, and a communicator.

GM: How independent is an independent/freelance curator, and how dependent is a curator employed by a museum?

CD: I can't say much about that since I've never been permanently employed by an institution. But it is definitely easier to maintain a certain degree of independence if you don't always work with and in the same contexts. I really appreciated working in the noughties with Eric Mangion at FRAC in Marseille as a curator-at-large. I had an institutional connection but no administrative obligations. I had a similar arrangement with the city of Zurich, where I directed the program for art in public space for almost 12 years. This suited my freedom-loving and curious personality. I have a fascination for the exploration of new contexts and environments.

GM: Are there two different art worlds: the art world of museums, big collectors, star curators, auction houses, and big fairs—and the other art world based on smaller biennales, and independent art spaces and curators, as Robert Fleck once argued? Is there also a gap between curators serving one or the other world?

CD: The dichotomy of the system that Robert has addressed is obvious at first glance. Here—the materialistic collector culture with all its ramifications, there—(as a reaction to it) the non-commercial platforms and systems. But these two worlds by no means function autonomously. There are points of contact, overlaps, dependencies. Significantly, the art system exhibits an enormous capacity: it is able to incorporate the marginal, the independent, the underground and the outsiders. The *salon des refuses* becomes officialized within a short time. This is also true, by the way, for most curators, whose livelihood is, after all, paid work.

GM: What is the impact of identity politics on the theory and practice of curating?

CD: In the 1980s, my involvement with so-called alternative culture was very important. For my attitude to life at that time, there were only few points of contact in institutional art and music. And that's why we were very political ourselves, because there was no other way to get cultural freedom. I worked in the Shedhalle and the Rote Fabrik in Zurich, where we showed contemporary art that is now established but had little chance of being exhibited at that time in the established institutions like Christopher Williams, Pipilotti Rist and Francesca Woodman, to name just a few examples. We saw ourselves as cultural-political actors; and in the same way, the current generation sees itself as curators standing in their time. This only becomes problematic when bubbles form from it, and when for dogmatic reasons no exchange is possible anymore.

GM: What is censorship in society and what is it in the art world (if there is a difference) today?

CD: When I recently curated an exhibition in Istanbul at the Pera Museum, I experienced politics interfering with art for the first time in a long time. The Pera Museum had invited me to develop an exhibition from the Press Art collection of Peter and Annette Nobel. The collector couple, with whom I have worked for more than 20 years, have a fantastic collection focused on art with printed media. The exhibition included a work by the Swiss artist Sabine Hertig—a huge collage of newsprint, almost six square meters in size. The picture showed a small house surrounded by a gigantic wave—a metaphor, so to speak, for the enormous mass of information we have to deal with in today's globalized world. The artist used newsprint from around the world as raw material for the collage, which she used with purely formal critiques. By coincidence, she also used a front page of *Le*

Monde, which reported on a PKK funeral. In a six square meter picture, just three square centimeters containing a PKK flag were enough to prompt an accusation of propaganda for a terrorist organization. Madness!

GM: Has Art to be moral?

CD: No, why?

There is no such thing as good or bad art

Okwui Enwezor
in conversation with Eva Karcher and Alexander Mühlauer

EVA KARCHER AND ALEXANDER MÜHLAUER: Okwui Enwezor, let's talk about money. You were born in Nigeria, on the border with Cameroon. Your father was a building contractor, so quite wealthy ...

OKWUI ENWEZOR: ...well, there were three meals a day (laughs).

EK & AM: When you were four years old, the war started in Biafra. Your family lost their home.

OE: Yes. We belonged to the Igbo ethnic group and fought for Nigeria's independence. It was a cruel war of secession that cost more than a million victims. I share this very basic experience with my family and the citizens of Nigeria. The three years of flight have left an indelible mark on me.

EK & AM: In 1983, at the age of 20, you went to New York. Why there of all places?

OE: Because the city had no contact with the old colonialist metropolises. It was not contaminated. London was too aristocratic, too dusty, too narrow for me and my generation. In New York, on the other hand, there was contemporary art, performance, fashion, music, debates on racial issues and feminist activism. I benefited from this creative storm. I also didn't have to tell anyone about my origins.

EK & AM: Have you experienced discrimination?

OE: Haven't we all in one way or another? New York was an adventure. I lived everywhere, in Queens, the Bronx, Manhattan, Brooklyn. I had no fear and a certain chutzpah when it came to prejudices against African culture.

EK & AM: Do you consider yourself courageous?

OE: Yes, in the sense that I take risks when I want to implement something that I deeply believe in. If you take a risk, you don't follow a strategy, it wouldn't work.

EK & AM: Do you sometimes dream of Nigeria?

OE: Oh, that's a tricky question, because it's about memories. Memories are fragmented and fragile for all of us. Because I don't actively speak my mother tongue, I often feel like I'm living outside my memories in a way. Because memories become sharper in your own language, I think. I left Nigeria 32 years ago; that's a long time. But there are intense memories.

EK & AM: Which ones?

OE: Of different seasons. For example, those from the end of November to February, when the dry, cold, hazy winds came from the Sahara. Or of familiar people in my environment, for whom I was no stranger. Who didn't look at me suspiciously. I miss that.

EK & AM: Do you still speak your mother tongue?

OE: Yes, there are always words mixed in between the English sentences. When I think, I also think in my mother tongue, Igbo.

EK & AM: You lived in New York for a long time, now in Munich. Do you have something like a center of life?

OE: I still have an apartment in New York. But the center of my life is now clearly in Munich. When I started at Haus der Kunst in October 2011, it was important to me from the very beginning to be present on site.

EK & AM: Giving up the nomadic life might be difficult for you.

OE: I may be constantly on the move for work, but I'm not a nomad! I don't like the word because it implies fleetingness, constant transition.

EK & AM: But isn't that what we are all increasingly forced to do, to be constantly "on the move"?

OE: Nomadism means nothing other than a migratory economy. We have to come to terms with the fact that we are moving more and more in constantly changing short-term communities. We often don't realize how fragile and vulnerable being on the move makes us. Today we have to move around to find creativity, it no longer comes to us. Contemporary art becomes a compass for our historical consciousness. Sometimes I think I live in Germany outside of history because I don't speak the language. That's exciting, but also a little unsettling.

EK & AM: Why is that?

OE: I'm afraid of losing my roots. I'm constantly thinking about what it means to move from country to country, from Nigeria to America to Germany. I am constantly moving between different spheres. It's the respective atmosphere that teaches me to adapt to a country.

EK & AM: And how does that work in Munich?

OE: Every weekend I'm here is like a short vacation. I now have a few rituals. On Saturday, I go shopping at the Viktualienmarkt or eat a vegetable curry at the Goldene Bar here.

EK & AM: How much free time do you have for yourself?

OE: I'm certainly not a "nine to five" person. In my free time, I do nothing! I withdraw, don't plan anything. No program. My idea of free time is not to travel. I realized this recently when I was in the Caribbean with my 13-year-old daughter and I really enjoyed myself. Snorkelling, diving, surfing, that's not for me. Because it's prescribed de-programming. I don't like being told how to relax.

EK & AM: You mean the delusion of self-optimization?

OE: That's terrible! It kills all spontaneity!

EK & AM: And now, please, spontaneously: What do you like about Munich?

OE: Hmmmm (smiles). A friend once said to me, and he was serious: what he likes best about Munich is that there are no demonstrations and no strikes. Hahahaha (laughs). That's definitely good for the economy! What more do we want?

EK & AM: How do you feel about German society?

OE: The euro crisis is also affecting Germany, even Munich - there's no doubt about that. More and more people are fighting for their existence, for their future. We absolutely need to discuss this situation much more, and if you ask me where, I mean: right here, in the museum.

EK & AM: What role does money play for you as a curator?

OE: You have no idea how often we talk about money here at the museum! There are so many different budgets that we have to coordinate, so many ideas about questions of value. But we can't value money like in the financial industry because we can't make a profit. Our capital is cultural.

EK & AM: Can you measure that?

OE: Culture is qualitative capital that cannot be measured in numbers. I doubt that Munich would be an attractive city if it didn't have this diversity to offer. A place only becomes complete through its spiritual, emotional and intellectual qualities - through theaters, concerts, museums. That's what our money should be working for.

EK & AM: Nevertheless, we humans are trying to quantify everything more and more.

OE: Statistics on tourists, hotel occupancy, things like that. But we shouldn't be at the level of empirical facts when we think about the productivity of money, but at a more speculative level. It's about the quality of our imagination. We need to debate this much more often.

EK & AM: You mean equivalents to money that cannot be measured, such as creativity. What role does the non-profit status of an institution like the Haus der Kunst play here?

OE: The point of non-profit is civic engagement. When citizens get involved in their culture, they identify with it. This is a currency that is much more valuable than pure money. Because it generates critical thinking, ideas, research. A philosophy of productive debate. This is the stuff that culture is made of and that we produce in our company. The idea of the public arises from civic engagement. It is not something that is simply there. It is created. That's what we work for.

EK & AM: How did you learn to work like this?

OE: I'm self-taught, and that's the reason why I have such an insatiable hunger for ideas. I learned by seeing and by meeting artists, not by studying art. I studied literature and political science. Then I became a writer, researcher and curator - and I still am.

EK & AM: What are you fighting for?

OE: We need a more generous civil society. That's what I'm fighting for. And for people to understand that what we do here is not entertainment.

EK & AM: What do you have against entertainment?

OE: Nothing. The exhibitions we put on should be fun, perhaps even enjoyable. But that's not why we do them.

EK & AM: Rather?

OE: I want to make Haus der Kunst one of the three best exhibition venues in the world. To do that, I need productive friction. I believe that the museum is there to allow disruption, to shake up our apparent certainties, to destabilize habits and comforts. That's the role of culture and art, that's why people go to museums.

EK & AM: Does good art always have a political dimension?

OE: What is good art? There is no such thing as good or bad art. I reject the category "I like or dislike". I don't choose art that I like because art is not a matter of taste. I'm interested in works that create tension and friction. Because they trigger reactions and dialogs. It is crucial to involve the audience in the conversation, because at this point a political dimension emerges. How much you enjoy art depends solely on how active you are yourself! That is elementary.

EK & AM: Even in the age of the Internet?

OE: Even more so!

EK & AM: To what extent do you digitize your museum?

OE: That depends on the artistic language. Not every work can withstand digitization. But we put everything online that is suitable for communicating our content, because we want to make visitors aware of what we are doing here. We prepare them virtually for a physical experience in the museum. We also invest a considerable amount of money in this.

EK & AM: What does luxury mean to you?

OE: For me, luxury is access, not possession. I am not an acquisitive person. Luxury has nothing to do with how much things cost. It has to do with a sensitivity for craftsmanship, for unique works with a specific character that require great care in their production. The word "bespoke" doesn't just apply to suits, but also to genetic design or software codes. I am interested in this kind of highly complex luxury.

EK & AM: You also seem to have a certain weakness for fashion.

OE: I admit that. I like shoes by John Lobb, Edward Green and Marcello—and my Nikes. And one of my favorite suit makers is Carlo Brandelli, the creative director of Kilgour, the tailor on Savile Row in London. For me, style is an expression of myself.

Interview by Eva Karcher and Alexander Mühlauer. Reprint of the interview from 25 April 2014 with kind permission of Sueddeutsche Zeitung.

We are more than just a spectacle

Okwui Enwezor
in conversation with Catrin Lorch

CATRIN LORCH: The scene has moved on and you are still at the lagoon?

OKWUI ENWEZOR: You remain responsible for a project like this. This is not an event that you open and then run away. I am very involved in the discussions and performances. And projects like the exploration of Harun Farocki's work, for example, are still ongoing. We have organized a two-day symposium and would like to leave behind an atlas of his oeuvre. Although we can even report a discovery - "White Christmas" was thought to be lost and has now turned up in an archive - we are not yet finished with the work. But the audience is also changing: it's no longer just Europeans and Americans who are coming.

CL: It is said that the number of visitors is not very high.

OE: That's not interesting for me, I don't look at numbers. Venice as a city has always been tough competition for the exhibition. Unlike in Kassel, for example, where the tourists who come to visit the Documenta are reliable, there are so many distractions in Venice. Then there is the long duration - we have extended it by a month. For this reason alone, there are many collaborations, an extensive education program for schools and universities. We are more than just a spectacle.

CL: But that's exactly what many critics were aiming at: that your exhibition wanted to be too much at the same time. And that you were catering to the art market - the entire Baselitz installation, for example, was sold directly from the Arsenale halls to collectors such as François Pinault. You commented on this by saying that you couldn't escape the market today.

OE: The market is there. But I don't wake up in the morning and worry about the market. The market is not new - and art has been in bed with it for so long. The structures we have would never have come about without the market. All the great American museums, the MoMA, the Getty, the Frick

Collection, they were founded by collectors like the Rockefellers or the Carnegies. And shaped by the art dealers of the late nineteenth century. We learned about these connections in our studies, they have been researched and proven. The relationships between collectors, dealers, advisors and museums are complex - and none of these areas can exist without the others. But you have to be discerning enough to realize that I have worked exclusively in the non-profit sector my entire career. And as a curator, it's time to recognize the work that galleries do. I don't see any contradiction in galleries possibly covering transportation or travel costs. Before curators even select their artists, they have already maintained archives, stored and restored works and established contact with collectors. I see this collaboration as a productive exchange. Does it really undermine the independence of the museum if a gallery grants it a discount on purchases? Or does that not serve the public?

CL: But doesn't the market have an influence when it makes itself useful in this way?

OE: I'm not going to give up my intellectual independence for a few discounts. And the only thing that counts is that I put together the strongest program possible here at Haus der Kunst, for example. We don't show Hanne Darboven just because we can afford it. Or because there is a market for this art.

CL: But in order to realize an exhibition like the Biennale, you were dependent on cooperation with gallery owners. For transportation, insurance, installation. Smaller biennials such as Kiev or Moscow - or the Skulpturen projekte in Münster - take a different approach and allow artists to realize works locally in order to avoid the market.

OE: That's nonsense. I've done exhibitions in South Africa and other places where there's no money. Nobody invests in exhibitions there, so you don't have to worry about it in Münster or Moscow like you do in Venice. It's an old strategy from the nineties to let artists travel to work with their backpacks. But I don't think that's sincere. In Moscow, for example, you have completely different problems. There is incredible censorship there. The ideological compromises you have to make in such an illiberal context are unimaginable. The market is actually less involved than many other patrons, but they are accepted without question: After all, who created the British art miracle? The British Council with its clever funding policy. Behind the Nordic Miracle are sponsors who had an interest in art. The

Goethe-Institut is one of the most influential players of all. We overestimate the influence of the market and don't look at this soft power, which sometimes also has ideology in its luggage.

CL: At the Biennale, the Armenian pavilion was awarded a lion. In Istanbul, the Dilijan Art Initiative distributed brochures in which it proudly advertised that it had not only sponsored this presentation, but also twelve artists who produced works on the subject of the Armenian genocide as part of the Istanbul Biennial. Do you mean such projects?

OE: That's exactly the point - I call it curatorial cross-dressing. I'm not going to have the Armenian agenda implemented in my biennial. It's about intellectual integrity, we have to make the best program, not the most extensive one. There are so many organizations that want to bring their concerns into the public debate, many morally justified concerns and a lot of money. I accept that, but I don't have to work like that. For a large biennial, you have to work with a large number of partners - especially with institutions like this. In the end, gallery owners and collectors are the least of the problems.

CL: But the public is rightly interested in the question of who exerts influence on the programs of museums and exhibition venues.

OE: We should be much more interested in the influence of board members and circles of friends. Why does the MoMA in New York show private collections? We need to be vigilant about who controls the field, who the really powerful players are. And as public institutions, discuss where the funds come from. The cuts we have had to accept in public museums in recent years are dramatic. But the fact remains that in Germany you can work independently of politics. That's not even a given in Europe. When I started here, many people asked me how I was going to get on with the conservative government in Bavaria. But neither here in Munich nor in Kassel, during the preparations for Documenta, have I ever been bothered by politicians or authorities. That is - relatively speaking - an enormous amount of freedom. Even in Europe this is not a matter of course; France, for example, is full of zombies who all know that they will be gone as the undead if the government changes - or if you dare to say, "I'm not Charlie". This free place of thought is invaluable.

Interview by Catrin Lorch. Reprint of the interview from 22 October 2015 with kind permission of Sueddeutsche Zeitung.

Manifesta is like a transition agency

Hedwig Fijen
in conversation with Jürgen Weishäupl

JÜRGEN WEISHÄUPL: Hedwig, you founded Manifesta in the early 1990s and its first edition took place in Rotterdam. What was the original vision behind this nomadic biennial — and how did it evolve as Europe and the world transformed around it?

HEDWIG FIJEN: Manifesta was born in a moment of historical transition. After the fall of the Berlin Wall, Europe was re-imagining itself. There was an urgent need to reopen cultural dialogues between East and West that had been frozen for decades. Eight European countries envisioned a new platform — not fixed to a single location, but able to move, respond, and engage with different contexts.

Mobility was essential. It reflected the growing freedom for young artists: they might be born in Sofia, study in London, and work in Berlin. Yet the established biennials — Venice or documenta — functioned mainly as late-career celebrations. Manifesta instead wanted to champion emerging voices, to create a laboratory for experimentation, and to show perspectives that were still unfamiliar to Western Europe.

In the first decade, we focused intensely on creating a dialogue with Central and Eastern Europe in collaboration with the newly formed Soros Centers for Contemporary Art, ensuring artists and curators from both spheres were working together for the first time. But as the geopolitical landscape shifted - the immediate optimism after the Cold War disappeared—so did we. Manifesta expanded into an interdisciplinary model — integrating architecture, urban research, film, music, design — and always remaining site-specific. We introduced new practices such as Citizen Assemblies and Public Surveys, becoming more accessible and changing the monolithic position of curators into a democratic line-up of Creative Mediators. We commission up to fifty new works each edition, which has been especially transformative for artists working in more fragile cultural ecosystems.

Another major evolution concerns the legacy. Since Manifesta 9 Genk in 2012, we systematically evaluate our impact — qualitative and quantitative — in partnership with universities. We want to act as a catalyst for lasting change, not a temporary spectacle. And for that, collaboration with public administrations became essential. We call this *engaged autonomy:* remaining independent and critical while working closely with those who shape cultural and urban policy for the long term. This is how we can help redefine cultural infrastructures and even put cities on the map — as we saw in Palermo and Prishtina, where more than one-fifth of Manifesta's visitors traveled there *specifically* for the event.

In 25 years, our methodology has continuously evolved. We embraced collective curating early on, then participatory practices, and more recently a transdisciplinary approach. The challenge ahead is to keep reinventing ourselves without losing sight of why Manifesta exists: to imagine and test new forms of living and creating together and to act as an incubator for cultural change in cities inviting us.

JW: Looking back across those 25 years — a period in which Manifesta has arguably been on the front line of innovation in the biennial field — which moments do you consider the most significant successes? And what proved most challenging?

HF: One turning point came after Manifesta 5 San Sebastian in 2008. We consciously moved away from the idea of a biennial as a cultural marketing vehicle. Even though Manifesta 6 in Cyprus did not materialize as planned, its ambition — *"How to turn a biennial into an art school?"* — marked a philosophical and pedagogical shift. We became committed to knowledge production and learning, not simply representation, and to creating a cultural incubator for long-term implementation.

The second major transition was our decision to work directly with European cities on their most complex urban and social questions. A nomadic event cannot simply arrive, exhibit and leave. Instead, we ask: *What does this city need? Who has been unheard? What symbolic interventions can spark long-term change?* During Manifesta 11 Zürich in 2011, for instance, we collaborated with ETH and Professor Tom Emmerson to build a floating wooden pavilion to reflect on our current ecological issues. From Palermo to Marseille to Prishtina, architects and urbanists now lead our pre-biennial research — mapping geography, sociology, ecology and cultural policy. No other biennial does this kind of holistic groundwork, which turns into knowledge production used for the second phase of Creative Mediation.

Because we reinvent ourselves every two years in response to a different urban context, Host cities now commission Manifesta as an *incubation engine.* Some critics worry this risks compromising our artistic autonomy, but I believe that in general change cannot happen from isolation inside a white cube. True transformation demands negotiation — without surrendering criticality.

Of course, not everything succeeds. Manifesta 6 Nicosia, which was intended to take place on both sides of the Green line in 2006 on a divided Cyprus, taught us how fragile geopolitical contexts can destabilize our cultural projects. But even failure can be instructive. We have kept our autonomy intact through reciprocity: Host cities support Manifesta and in return we contribute with a lasting value.

JW: Today, biennials exist everywhere — large, small, hyper-local, global. What role do you think these events can and should play in the future? What advice would you give to someone starting a new biennial today?

HF: First, I think the term *biennial* itself has become somehow overloaded — tied to artistic consumerism, tourism, and gentrification. We need a new vocabulary that reflects what cultural events can achieve beyond marketing cycles.

Still, biennials can play crucial roles in commissioning new works, creating new networks, imagining new infrastructures and create alternative urban solutions — especially outside traditional cultural centers. They can help shift policies, enable international exchange, and provide resources for artists to create new work. They can also bridge disciplines and generations — from literature and performance to architecture and activism — and mediate between different local institutions, civic authorities, and communities.

But sustainability is key for us. We are rethinking mobility and the carbon footprint of global art production. We aim to be radically local: staying longer, collaborating with resident communities, and investing in existing materials and infrastructures. We're building lighter, more agile cultural networks that can strengthen local ecosystems rather than extract from them. Ninety-five percent of both our teams and our visitors are local.

Anyone designing a biennial today must start with one question: *How does this community benefit from a cultural intervention and how can this genuinely help transform cities and practices on the long term in close collaboration with local actors?* If the answer is clear, then a biennial can become a strategic cultural and artistic instrument, rather than a recurring event in search of relevance.

JW: Listening to you, it's clear you believe art — or culture in the broadest sense — is a change-maker in society. Does that imply art must also be moral?

HF: I don't define Manifesta's work strictly as a contemporary art platform. It is contemporary *culture based;* a space where artistic, architectural, ecological, and social practices intersect. Whether morality is a requirement is not for me alone to declare. But I believe in taking responsibility and stimulating discussions about certain values, social equality, frameworks and pedagogical models.

We must involve the voices of those citizens and communities who live in the places where we intervene. Cultural institutions have too often operated at a distance from people's real lives. When communities help shape their neighborhoods — their public spaces, their green environments — culture becomes meaningful and empowering.

We are not the United Nations, of course, although we were collaborating with them for Manifesta 14 Prishtina in transforming an unsafe abandoned railway into a Green Corridor. We work on a modest scale, but always with a participatory logic. Rethinking curatorial authority, reimagining institutional roles — these are ethical questions as much as cultural ones. And each edition of Manifesta pushes us to deepen that reflection.

This conversation was conducted by Jürgen Weishäupl for the Industrial Art Biennale in Labin in 2020 and first appeared on YouTube.

I talk with people

Jonathan Fine
in conversation with Gerald A. Matt

GERALD A. MATT: When I was speaking with Hans Ulrich Obrist, we were talking about exhibitions that were relevant to his view on the arts. He addressed two exhibitions, which were also important to my career: there was the *Gesamtkunstwerk* exhibition by Harald Szeemann and the *Magiciens de la terre* exhibition at the Pompidou Centre, which was one of the first projects that brought Western contemporary art together with objects and art from outside Europe. Some people criticized it because they said it was just a continuation of what we were talking about—that the ratio of the artists they brought in from Africa and Asia was totally different from the contemporary artists from Western Europe and the United States and the Western world. While others said it was important because it was the first time that there was a view on people outside of Europe.

JONATHAN FINE: Well, first of all, it wasn't the first time. The first one I know of was Alfred Stiegltz' Picasso-Bracque exhibit at his gallery 291 in New York. Stieglitz showed Picasso drawings along with African masks. This sort of sets off a whole tradition of asking what relationship art forms from around the world have with each other. So, the *Magiciens de la terre,* for me, represents a position taken in a field that started much earlier. It's interesting that Stieglitz himself was working not just as a gallerist but as an artist in what was a non-accepted medium at the time—photography. And yet it is through his gallery, importing contemporary art that he's seeing in France and in Europe alongside works from Africa that he's also seeing in France, in Europe.

But I think for me, if there are two key exhibits, the first was the Primitivism exhibit at MoMA (*"Primitivism" in 20th Century Art: Affinities of the Tribal and the Modern*, 1984). Like Stieglitz, it displayed works by African artists, exclusively so-called traditional African art, and works by modern European artists and attempted to say: we're going to display works of art by European artists and show possible works of art from Africa that may have inspired them or may show some sort of formal similarity to them. And that was a very troubling approach because it again made the work of non-European artists food for the development of "high" European art. It reproduced a hierarchy in which African art and Oceanic art are art but only really if they exist in relation to Modernism and modern masters. The second thing that it did was it ignored all of the developments in art from Africa and from Oceania that had taken place since the early 20th century. Because it turned around and said African art is these masks. African art is these sculptures. Artists on the continent of Africa or in Oceania who were working in other media that acknowledge the globality of art discourse and creative discourse are somehow inauthentic.

GM: For example, the work of Yinka Shonibare wouldn't be authentic enough, especially as he deals with Oscar Wilde or he deals with European history, so this is not what would be considered African.

JF: Right. So, at the same time, as it claimed to be arguing for a valorization of African art, it was only really a valorization of a certain kind of very narrow African and Oceanic creativity, and then only as a sort of inspiration for Western artists. I think *Magiciens de la terre* tried to do that very differently, right? I mean, it tried to break that mode. It tried to say: No, there's a much greater breadth of African art and many more African artists. And it's a much wider and deeper field. And there is a much more complicated dialogue going on. So, *Magiciens de la terre* was one strong answer to the approach taken in the MoMA show. I think, though, that *Magiciens de la terre* on the whole nonetheless fell into the trap of primitivizing artists from Africa and recycled a lot of stereotypes. I mean, just the title itself, "Magicians of the Earth", it's a fantasy that creativity grows from the soil. It's not a human endeavor. It is not work or practice or study, or inspiration. Creativity is, you know, what artists from Africa just breathe, it's what they know, their rhythm and so on. And I think, you know, African artists often have different connections to things in nature or certain materials or certain connections between ways of living based on their own experience, cultures, their backgrounds and education; but at the same time, it's also terribly insulting.

GM: I remember that there were artists making coffins (Kudjoe Affutu). And in their opinion, they made coffins. But the European curator told them that, in fact, they are making art. Or Keïta, for example, the photographer, simply took photographs for people's everyday use. I think we have the same phenomenon with photography too. I mean, Weegee didn't think that he was making art. Others told him then. So, there is a certain kind of paternalism.

JF: Exactly. It's paternalistic, it is very paternalistic. And I think there was a strong reaction, particularly among African artists, who were already involved in the global scene and many African intellectuals against *Magiciens de la terre* precisely because it was perceived, I think correctly, as paternalistic.

GM: But how did this debate or these exhibitions influence your work as a curator? How do you try to avoid this kind of paternalism?

JF: The first large exhibition I did was *Beyond Compare,* which I worked on together with Paola Ivanov and Julien Chapuis at the Bode Museum a few years ago. And I can't speak for them, but for me, it was a rejection of the position of *Magiciens de la terre* and the position of the MoMA Primitivism show. I wanted to show that works of art from Africa and works of art from Europe can be brought into a dialogue that's not purely a formal one, but also an intellectual dialogue. And that this intellectual dialog can be situated not outside of time, outside of history, but in the very specific historical processes of European contact with Africa, inter-African contact, the development of things within Africa and colonialism and the colonial encounter. So, it was conceived. At the time I thought: if you make history apparent in an exhibition, if you show connections that are not just perceived but also real, then you can find a way out of the kind of paternalism that *Magiciens de la terre* and the MoMA show can be accused of perpetuating. So, one example that I loved there was—I'll give two—we displayed a small bronze by Donatello next to a small bronze from the Benin kingdom, and they're only a couple hundred years apart. One was a princess or a goddess, it's unclear which, a shrine figure raising her hand. That's the Benin piece. The other was a *putto* by Donatello that Bode identified and purchased for the collections in Berlin. And superficially at least, they hold similar poses. But that gives you a way into asking what are African bronze or brass casting traditions and the European bronze casting traditions? How are they related? Because they're not too distant in time. Both works show incredible mastery of their medium, but under different premises and with different aims. And you see that there's an incredible agility and ability to work with this medium in Nigeria and an incredible agility and ability to work with the medium in Italy. Two different ends for different purposes in different ways, and a very different aesthetic vision from these two superficially similar objects. So, the pairing of the two raised a lot of questions. For me the Benin piece was better than the Donatello. It showed greater formal mastery. The artist was interested in creating certain kinds of reflective surfaces, creating certain kinds of details, creating certain kinds of expression;

whereas the Donatello was very cursory in his use of surfaces, and more interested in capturing a movement in a moment of time. But that's part of the aesthetic encounter. And that's part of the intellectual encounter when you see these works next to each other. It's an encounter that was not made possible, I would argue, in the MoMA show, in the *Primitivism* show, because the relationship between the pieces was already preordained by the curator. So, if I think about my curatorial practice, it's not to determine entirely in advance what questions I'm throwing out there, but to create visual statements that challenge viewers' understandings of the world and also to challenge viewers' understandings of the objects. But I will say there were two weaknesses of the show in Berlin. One is, we misjudged the moment a little bit. The show was a big success, but it opened not long after the moment when the colonialism debate had just gotten off the ground with Bénédicte Savoy's "noisy withdrawal" from the scientific advisory board of the Humboldt Forum. And our show wasn't only about colonialism or the provenance of the objects. It was about what different connections can be made between them, how they illuminate and come out of colonial contexts. And so, a lot of the questions we got were about whether we were not open enough about the problematic histories of the objects. I think, in retrospect, we could have done more. Been more explicit. But that really wasn't what the show was about. My hope was that because Benin objects were at the very entrance to the exhibition, in other words, it was impossible to see the exhibition without encountering them, and in each case, we talked about the history of the plunder of the Benin Kingdom by the British in 1897 in each entry text. So, it should have been hard for a visitor to miss that colonialism and injustice was one theme that ran through the exhibition. But in retrospect, I think that wasn't clear enough.

Another weakness was, we didn't work with contemporary artists. So, the question of how the contemporary plays a role in this global endeavor we call curating and art curating wasn't present in the show. And I think it's a mistake that I wouldn't make today because it's important for me to remind people that, particularly with African art (and I come at this as a scholar of African art), that African art isn't just historical; it isn't just what was made 100 years ago, 150 years ago, 300 years ago. It's also what's being done now. It's important because, and this goes back to your initial question about ethnographic museums—most ethnographic museums in the German-speaking world stopped collecting around the time between the First and Second World Wars. The collections and the museums are not primarily *historical* museums—we're contemporary museums, even if strange contemporary museums. We're contemporary museums with historical collections, and the historical collections outweigh the contemporary ones in the collections, in the things that were collected during the past.

GM: You are now working on an exhibition for next year dealing with science fiction, where you maybe take into account what you said now and bring contemporary art and ethnological objects together. How do you deal with the debate and effects of identity politics? Who has the right to talk about whom and what? Can or how can European or Western museums talk about art coming from other continents and cultures?

JF: I think it's less a question of right. And more a question of practice. A museum like this one must take the legacy of colonialism seriously. I don't see that as a choice. And as I see it, one of the central points of colonialism was to take away the self-determination of the people who were colonized. In other words, colonizers sought to rule, control, and exploit people in other parts of the world. Sometimes, it was as close as Poland if you're looking at Germany, Austria or Russia with the partition of Poland. Sometimes, it's as far away as China or Indonesia. But it's taking away self-determination. And so, to me, it's less about who has the right to say what than about what approach you take to showing things. And I think that's why you see now so many curators in ethnographic museums saying that they want to work cooperatively. And what I hope they mean is that they alone don't want to make the decision about what to say or how to say it, but they want to create a space within which the self-determination of presentation, of topics and of speech returns to the people from whom it was taken in colonial contexts.

GM: Could you share some thoughts concerning your science fiction show?

JF: Well, the science fiction show is about the future because, I think, as a contemporary museum we also have to look to the future. In essence we have asked how different artists and artist-activists from different parts of the world have taken the tool kit of science fiction and other speculative fictions to confront the problems of the present and to imagine different, hopefully better, futures. We've suggested different thematic clusters of works and discussed those clusters with the artists who we're working with to see if they also make sense to them. And then with each work, we present an artist's statement. So, it's less about us saying what the work means than it is about working with artists to cluster ideas that cohere around a particular theme. And about the artists saying what their work means or what it means to them. So—and I think you can see that with the George Nuku exhibit (*Oceans. Collections. Reflections. George Nuku, 2022*) as well—that it's not so much the museums saying what Māori culture history is, but it's the museum working with an artist who identifies as Māori to create a platform within which visitors themselves can experience from his point of view with his creative works what he wants to communicate about Māori culture.

GM: The curator doesn't talk, but invites people to talk about themselves?

JF: No, I talk with people. We talk with people, right? It's dishonest to say we're silent. Because we're also a voice (often a determinative voice) in that curatorial mix. And I think often the challenge is to find a way to engage in the process without being the person or group who entirely controls the process. And I think as we move forward, there are going to be different models of artistic practice and museums that are going to be developed. Some of them are already being developed. Tal Adler who worked with us at the Weltmseum Wien, but who has also been working at the Humboldt University in Berlin, has created a kind of matrix of things for collaborations with artists where he says, in an ideal world, the funding for the project doesn't come from the museum, which then engages the artists, but both parties work together to find the funding for a common project. This gives the artists a greater degree of control and voice than if the museum alone provides the funding.

GM: Right, but then the artist must still be alive.

JF: Yes, the artist must still be alive. And the question then comes up, what do you do with artists who are dead, right? For contemporary art that is a problem. At the moment, we don't have that too much. Most of the artists who created the things in the museum are either long dead or they're still alive and we're still working with them. We have one case in the science fiction exhibit where an artist died, I think of COVID, and we're showing his works and there we're working with his estate. But that's always tricky because heirs don't always have the same view as the artist him or herself.

GM: To give an example, if you want to bring together, let's say, contemporary Cuban artists with the work of Wifredo Lam.

JF: Difficult.

GM: Lam is dead. So, the dialogue is not possible at all. Maybe there are letters or personal documents, but your position as a curator is quite different.

JF: Yeah, and it's a challenge. And I think it's going to be interesting to see how cutting- edge curatorial practices that take the artist's voice seriously come to terms with historical figures. And sometimes historical figures were revolutionary, and sometimes historical figures were reactionary, and sometimes historical figures, like Picasso, were a combination of the two.

GM: What's your background as a curator? When did you know that you wanted to be a curator working with art? Was there an initial experience?

JF: I would say I started quite late, and it wasn't clear to me that I wanted to be a curator. I trained as a lawyer and as a historian. And then at a certain point in my legal career, I decided I had to do what made me happy rather than what made me money, which I think is legitimate. I was fascinated by the fact that so many museums in the United States and Europe were simply getting African art wrong? I mean, how was it that in the 1990s or the year 2000 we were still discussing "primitive art"? At a point in time when everyone around the world had cell phones and computers, and in many ways, if you went to Africa, people's technological practice was light years ahead of the technological practice in Europe. I mean, it took Europe and North America a long time to wean themselves off landlines for telephones. In Africa, they leapfrogged the landline generation and moved straight to cell phones and smartphones. So, it was fascinating to me how museums and collectors constantly got the question of Africa or African art wrong, and then how they developed a certain fascination for these objects that were clearly a very small percentage of what people working creatively in Africa were making.

GM: You started quite late, based on your historical studies?

JF: Well before I became a lawyer and before I studied art history, I wanted to know: in what ways did colonialism change our world? And I came to that question after reading a book by Klaus Theweleit called *Männerpantasien*, which was translated into English as *Male Fantasies*. Theweleit talks about the way that the experience of many people who later joined the *Freikorps* in Germany had been shaped in the Namibian wars and in Germany's colonies. So, for me, I saw a very clear cultural connection between colonial racism and colonialism and the later politics of the *Freikorps* and the genocidal racism of the Nazi Party. And I wanted to ask, okay, how did that work, not just in a European context and how did that reflect back on Africa? And whenever I started looking at African art, I was struck by how incredible the objects were that I was seeing in museums, how stunningly beautiful and powerful they were. But on the other hand, how this whole incredibly messed up history—racism, colonialism, violence, the art market—was just not dealt with, or discussed. And so, I wanted to get into how history affected the way museums thought about African art. And initially I would say my view of African art remained quite narrow, even though I thought museums were getting it wrong. And that's why when I was a lawyer and I was just not happy practicing law, I asked myself, what can I do that makes me happy, I decided, okay, I've got to go back into art history.

GM: A brief answer to the question: what is a curator?

JF: What is a curator? A curator is a person who tries to tell stories through physical and esthetic experiences. I said physical because, I think, what the experience of an exhibition or a film or something like that requires is the viewer to open her or himself to an immediate aesthetic and intellectual experience. And that's often also physical. Going into a museum is physical. Going into a movie theater is physical, going into a gallery is physical. It's not just something you can do on the Internet. People try it, but that's a different kind of consumption, that's a different kind of logic.

GM: How can curating be relevant to the challenges we face today? Let me make it more concrete—in 2017, the French President Macron, said in Ouagadougou in Burkina Faso that there had to be established a new relationship between France and the countries of the African continent. And he talked about temporary or final return of the African heritage to Africa, and he spoke about a "nouvelle éthique relationnelle", a new ethic relationship.

JF: I mean, it was very interesting for me to come to Berlin and see that as a criticism because, and this may sound a little bit odd, ever since I studied at Cambridge and at the University of Chicago, in my early twenties, I understood myself to be part of the post-colonial moment. One of the very first intellectual encounters that really challenged me was when Gayatri Spivak came to the University of Chicago—I think it was in 1988—to give a version of her pathbreaking written intervention *Can the Subaltern Speak?* which is a direct engagement with the questions of voice, agency, history and post-colonial theory. So, it was very weird for me to, sort of, as someone who's thought of himself as interested and engaged in the post-colonial moment to come to Berlin, to then be in the position of working in an institution that had not yet adapted to the post-colonial moment more than 20 years later. And I think we've seen, with the coincidence of Black Lives Matter with Rhodes Must Fall in South Africa, that the impulse to reassess and change how narratives about where we are now and how we got here are constructed is critical. But it was very strange to see that happening in in Germany so late and in a sense so incompletely. And I have to say I still think redefining a post-colonial relational ethic primarily through art and museums is very strange, because art is only one aspect, and one small aspect, of what defines and continues to define colonial and neo-colonial relations. I would argue it may be one of the most important symbolic aspects of redefining relations, but it is not the most important economic or political aspect. And so, pushing this discussion into a discussion primarily about the ethics of art and museums and away from economics and politics feels very odd to me.

GM: I agree. But this is a phenomenon that you see also in other fields. Everything which cannot be solved is put on the shoulders of the arts. The arts must be politically correct because no one else is.

JF: Yes, and onto museums, which are not really well equipped to do this. We are not the Ministry of European and Foreign Affairs. So, to say that a new relationship with Africa is to be created through exhibitions in the Weltmuseum or, in Germany, that the Humboldt Forum should be the embodiment of a new relational ethic, is a very strange position.

GM: How do you see the changing relationships between curators, artists, collectors, galleries, museums and critiques? Whas there been a shift of power?

JF: That depends on the kind of museum, and on the field. I mean, we in Austria are incredibly privileged that we're not entirely dependent on private patrons for our daily work. We sometimes regret the fact that we don't have the massive budgets that some museums in other countries have. On the other hand, it affords us a kind of independence from private collectors and, in a sense, politicians that we wouldn't otherwise have because there is a strong tradition of artistic and intellectual independence—*künstlerische Freiheit, Freiheit der Wissenschaft*—from which we still benefit. So, how has the current debate changed what we do? I would say we exist in an incredibly privileged position because the state gives us the vast majority of our budget and we have to get the rest through visitor numbers, and we're not dependent on private donors to the same degree as other museums.

GM: I'd like to address the fact that private collectors now build museums, sometimes bigger than the state museums, and through their collections, have a great influence on prices and artists. And this has also a consequence for museums, including state museums, which buy art and are dependent on the art market so strongly influenced by those collectors. They also engage curators and pay for critiques. A big challenge for the independence and authority of museums and curators?

JF: For the *Science Fiction(s)* exhibit, we're showing some works from some prominent artists represented by prominent galleries. I've found that the galleries are very flexible in working with us. In part, I think, because it adds a new dimension to the importance of their artists if they have been shown in public institutions. But I'm very sensitive to the question of whether we should be dictated to by galleries and/or private collectors. And I would hope very strongly that that does not lie in our future. I have to say, in some cases it makes me a little bit sad because there are some works that I think we would love to have in our collection, but we can't afford them on our acquisition budget, which is very limited. And at the moment, you know, Austria doesn't have the same tradition of *Mäzenatentum* (art patronage) that the United States does. So, there isn't really the same group of people I can go to and say: "Hey, you know, could you give us the funds for this contemporary work by this artist, which would be fantastic."

GM: Exhibition making is dependent on these changes now. High prices for artworks mean high prices for transport mean high prices for insurance, so costs go up and make things more difficult.

JF: Yes, and I think it's high time that museums ask themselves how and why they show certain things. I mean, I think when I reflect back, we lived in an age where we'd go through blockbuster exhibitions, where works of art from museums from around the world would be gathered in one place, and we'd all know that the conservation demands were incredibly high and that everything had to have an art transport and be shipped by air. And the effects on the environment were extreme. And I think what is the challenge that we're going to be facing now is going to be how to re-imagine and reshape our curatorial and exhibition practice to take account of the Anthropocene, the limits of what could or should be done given the environmental crisis that we're living in. And it's not entirely clear what the way out is, right? Because if you have tons of people flying to Paris to see the Mona Lisa, is the environmental effect of all those planes worse than transporting the Mona Lisa on one flight to Washington D.C. and having people in the United States just fly to Washington D.C.? I think there needs to be a lot more thinking about how to really address exhibition making in an age of climate crisis.

GM: That sounds great - exhibitions getting more local. You can see local artists and when you go somewhere, you see what happens there rather than the repetitive international standard. But this also means getting provincial.

JF: Yeah. So that's also a danger—provincialization. I think we're going to be confronted with increasing questions about what you transport, when, how and why. I mean, for example, for *Science Fiction(s)*, we made very deliberate choices together with the artists about what would be transported, how it would be transported, who would fly here for certain things and who wouldn't and for what reasons. So, we were thinking about the climate effects of this exhibit, the time we were doing it. We also thought about that with the Nuku exhibit. I think the question may become: can you curate from a distance? Not can you lone from a distance. Because although we curate largely from historical collections, you can still send prints digitally and you can produce them digitally in other places. You can send films digitally. You can show them in other places. I think we're going to see a shift towards more digitally dependent media in the future. And I think—and this takes us back to the beginning of our conversation—because I think we are heading toward a deeper re-contextualization and reinterpretation of the objects in the already existing collections. I wouldn't say they're provincial. The premise of your question is right. Do the objects have to move for something to happen not to be provincial? I think not. What has to happen is that the way people view them, curate them, consider them, contextualize them, has to change. You can work with a very unassuming object, but if you're embedded in a whole series of non-provincial questions, it can open worlds.

GM: Will you invite artists to produce in the museum?

JF: We're already doing that. I don't know if you saw the George Nuku exhibit. He also created a canoe from Plexiglas for the permanent collection. And he did it here. And he did it with people here. So, it was less about transporting objects than about bringing George here and having him work with people here, which immediately de-provincialized what was going on.

GM: Was there a personal hero, a curator you really admired?

JF: Yes, I would say two. I would say Okwui Enwezor was one of the most brilliant curators whose work I've encountered. And the second—and this is going to sound a little bit weird—is my dissertation advisor, Chika Okeke-Agulu who often worked closely with Okwui. I think of the conundrum of the MoMA show *Primitivism* and the *Magiciens de la terre* show. Okwui just demolished that as a set of false antinomies and said: look, there's phenomenal modern and contemporary work going on in Africa. And when you look at it, you see the history of the Continent in totally different ways and you see the history of the colonial encounter in totally different ways, and you see other histories and other contemporary concerns as well. And through his incredible dynamism, his incredible connections, his incredible eye, he put his vision in the center of world curatorial practice. I believe the reason we're living in an age of global art can, to a large extent, be traced back to Okwui Enwezor's interventions.

GM: Was there a show which you consider to be a milestone for your curatorial thoughts and practices. You already mentioned some.

JF: With a distant view. Good or bad?

GM: Good. But also, something bad can be important, a milestone.

JF: I would say the Benin show that Barbara Plankensteiner did, which toured to Chicago in 2007, and which for the first time, took on the question how you talk about and present works from the Benin kingdom, given their colonial past, collaboratively with people from Benin. And I think that's one of the reasons why today Barbara Plankensteiner is really a giant in my museum's sector.

GM: Can you describe a personal curatorial work which you're really proud of, a show which brought all your ideas together?

JF: No. No, because I think I'm constantly looking at what we're doing and what I've done and reevaluating it and thinking what could have done differently or maybe shouldn't have done or maybe should have done more of. I hope that doesn't sound too self- critical or self-deprecating, but I mean, I think, you know, we don't stand in one place and neither does the world. Things don't only have one meaning that is fixed at one point in time. We're always looking back and reevaluating what we've done. I will say this, I think for me, one important moment was acquiring a drawing by the Nigerian artist, Uche Okeke, who was a key figure in Nigerian modern and contemporary art history, for the Ethnographic Museum in Berlin, with the help of a very generous patron, and then putting it on display. It was a tiny, tiny exhibit. It was one work and one text about Okeke's use of line and how he developed it waiting to come to Germany on a scholarship. And for me, that was my first curatorial statement that historical collections aren't the end of the story. We need to talk about how historical objects were collected but not lose sight of modern and contemporary art and modern and contemporary artists.

GM: How do you get from an idea to an exhibition? One has a lot of ideas, many of which are discarded because they don't really work.

JF: Well, discussions. The genesis, for me of the *Science Fiction(s)* project lay in a discussion I had with Ute Marxreiter, whom I knew from Berlin. I wanted to do something about monsters and about how monsters are a projection of fears, and then to look at who's afraid of what, when. And she said she was working on something related to science fiction. And I said, oh, that's actually fantastic, the more we talked about it. So, the idea, I would say, came from Ute and then we developed it over months through some very intense discussions, especially with the other members of the team at the Weltmuseum. But how do you know whether an idea can work? I think I'm going to paraphrase the United States Supreme Court Justice Potter Stewart about pornography: "You know it when you see it." I think anything can be an exhibit, but you know it when you see it, if it's a good idea. Does it challenge people's expectations of what they're going to see? Does it give them a new way of thinking about an issue that they're maybe already grappling with? Does it open up new perspectives? And is the art itself exciting? And as soon as I talked with Ute light bulbs went off for me, and I think light bulbs went off for her. And as I talked about it with other people, I realized light bulbs started going off for them. So, it was something that many people had thoughts about. And the question was, which thoughts form the core ideas that the artists and we want to work on.

GM: What is the impact of identity politics on your practice of curating? Are there any tendencies to censorship? Does it hinder you? Or more polemically, must art be moral?

JF: Does art have to be moral? I can't answer that. Does identity politics hinder me?

GM: You could also ask: does it help you?

JF: I think the question you should ask as a reflective curator is: who am I likely to anger and why? And is that something that I want to do? There is a place for outrage, for outrage's sake. I think identity politics and political correctness as terms are one way of pushing and making the question of respect and recognition sound negative. I couldn't do an exhibit like *Science Fiction(s)* without talking about the question of cultural appropriation. And if you look at the poster, you can see that for the artist, Nicholas Galanin, the question of cultural appropriation is important. It has been important for many indigenous artists. And you could say bringing up the question—that's identity politics or political correctness. Or you could say, hey, that's something that artists who are doing really exciting work are thinking about and we need to understand why they're worried about it. And frankly, I think when you look at the appropriation of unmarried Hopi women's hairdresses and costumes for the biggest science fiction franchise that has earned the people who did it billions of dollars, none of which, or very little of which, has flowed back into the communities from whom the inspiration was taken, you should ask yourself: Is this really right? Is this the world we want to live in? Especially that when those artists then turn around and try and use some of the stuff Hollywood has made, they often have to ask permission from huge corporations that became huge by taking things that the ancestors of the artists made in the first place. So, is political correctness a hindrance? No, I think, it's actually an opportunity to explain how the world works.

GM: Would you curate an exhibition about the view of European culture on American Indians and title it "*Winnetou*"?

JF: It's interesting, I'm not sure that I can answer without a detour. I would say there was an interesting exhibit in Berlin at Haus der Kulturen der Welt called *Spectral White*, and I loaned a couple of personal objects to the show, because I had a couple of works by a Nigerian artist in the first half of the 20th century—Thomas Onajeje Odulate, who made caricatures of British colonial figures. The point of the show was to look at what Africans and people in the Pacific and the Northwest Coast thought about their colonizers. What was the image of "the white"? And it goes back to a work by a German intellectual, Julius Lips who left Germany and ended up at Columbia University in the thirties. It was called *Savage Hits Back*. It was about the view from Africa about what Europeans looked like. So, if we are looking at each other, would I do a show about European views about Africans or Native American people? Yes, probably, but with Native American artists and curators. To me, it would not be interesting to do that exhibit to just show what "white people"—in quotation marks—think of people who identify as Native Americans. We are surrounded by that every day. You can see it in advertisements, in Karl May books, and pretty much everywhere you look. The question that is more interesting, I think is, what's going on and how does it feel from a Native American perspective? And how do you tell those stories without putting the white people in the middle of it? That's a more interesting challenge, and I think that's where many curatorial projects fail. For me, *Spectral White* was interesting, but only really half successful because it still put the white German guy who had to flee to Columbia University in the center of the story. He was still the touchstone for the organization of that exhibit. This takes me back to another exhibit, which really struck me negatively. It was about Fichte, the ethnographer, and it was called *Love and Ethnology*, also at Haus der Kulturen der Welt. It was trying to get into the lives of the Black queer people in South America, in the Caribbean, in the United States who encountered Fichte. What was their sexuality about? How did they view ethnography? But it told the story again using the German guy, and it put him in the middle. My reaction to that was, if you're talking about Black queer people from the 1980s and 1970s, a lot of them are still alive. Go and interview them. Ask them what they think of it. Why do I want to know what a German guy thought about them, even if he may have been an interesting guy? If I want to know what's going on in Black sexual cultures in the Caribbean, the Americas, North and South, I'm not going to ask the white German ethnographer what he thinks about them. I'm going to just ask the Black people what they think. And some of them are probably even in Berlin, you know. So, I just don't understand the impulse to put a white person in the middle of a story that's not about white people. That just makes stories that aren't about white people about white people. So, to the extent that political correctness and identity politics say to you, hey, wait a second, whose story are you telling, and why are you telling it? Who are you putting in the middle of it?

GM: Back to the moral responsibilities of curating. A show of Leni Riefenstahl's work, being aware of her involvement in the third Reich and her view on Africa, in your museum, thinkable?

JF: Oh, absolutely. When I worked at the Ethnological Museum in Berlin, and the Berlin museums were offered the Riefenstahl *Nachlass* (estate) and they took it, one of my colleagues, Paola Ivanov, started to work on getting a project approved with colleagues from East Africa to critically examine Riefenstahl's photographs and other collections. to. And Riefenstahl collected lots of "ethnographic" stuff from East Africa, including phallic shaped gourds. So, there's not just the Riefenstahl work from the Nazi era, there's her work from East Africa. And for me, would I show that stuff? Yes. It's fascinating to me to see what kind of connections there are between Riefenstahl's images from the twenties and thirties and forties and her photographs from the fifties, seventies and eighties, you know. The continuities and differences bear a lot of thinking about. So, I mean, unfortunately, you picked a bad example. It's easy, yes.

GM: Okay. We'll leave that. My last question: What will be the main challenges for a curator in the future?

JF: The main challenge for curators in the future is going to be how to deal with the green transformation that we must undertake and how to rethink museums as institutions and the practices of curation and exhibition.

GM: Thank you.

This interview took place in February 2023 at the Weltmuseum in Vienna.

Good curatorial work means good eyes

Yuko Hasegawa
in conversation with Gerald A. Matt

GERALD A. MATT: What is a curator? Can you define your understanding and practice as a curator?

YUKO HASEGAWA: A curator is working not only as a researcher, but also as an exhibition maker and something like a catalyst. We look at what is happening in the art world. We are taking part in making art history as a part of a commitment. The curator's role is also to create a public space. The curator must be a thinker, a researcher, something like an anthropologist, also a place making designer, the designer of an experiment.

GM: How can curating be relevant to the (social, political but also cultural) challenges we face today?

YH: Because the world has been changing very quickly, the curator must be a good observer, more an ethnographer, and also a sociological researcher. But we have also to be experts of art history. And we have to have our own criteria of art and in a world which has been changing very quickly, we have to construct art history, so-called global art history, also in terms of the multi-modernisms in modern history.

Even if we agree that there is a kind of art history, each one of us has a different narrative, a histoire. History is something like a story. It is also very important connecting the past and the present and reflecting the contemporarness. The curator should be a good translator of the artist. Artists are using their senses, their sensory languages. Normally we get just pure information. But there is no particular thread to understand the world. The curator has to make proposals of one perspective, to make a mapping, like artist editing.

Artists use a wide ranch of information, use all kind of resources to give certain ideas to the people. Therefore "Sensory learning" is very important, because people have to use all kind of senses, also intuition, also imagination.

This year I made a lot of research. I was writing and working with so-called research-based artists and gave a home to a kind of art and research, which is metaphorical, also abstract, and poetic. It's about accepting the results and perceive them by different senses. In that way, a curator is not only helping with the production, but also create an opportunity for the audience of how to get in touch with the art works. It is important to make this kind of large-scale translation, of interpretation, of facilitation. This can be a Space to work , a symposium, a book. A curator can be everything. A curator has to ask how to create this interface to transmit artistic ideas to the audience and he has to give the audience an opportunity to think about themselves, also to sense themselves. Audience creation in that way is a one of the most important contemporary topic for curating.

GM: How do you see the changing relations between curators, artists, collectors, galleries, museums, and critics? nowadays, curators often work for private collectors, artists and collectors curate, critics are involved in curating for collections and museums.

YH: I have recently given a lecture about criteria and missions of the October people in 80s, 90s. Critics accuse them of two things: One is curatorial politics. Second is public art.

But don't forget, the critics job is quite limited because it's without any engagement, without any kind of actual practice. If they are observing, talking about it from a distance, this distance is not enough. Many curators are doing many different things, starting without any kind of theoretical consistency.

But in general, the critics are powerful, whatever they publish is much stronger than what we say, what a museum says.

Private institutions founded by a rich collector, or a company also have the same role.

And even if some parts of the art world get too expanding, too dominant, we can also critizise them, can keep up a critical point, but that means work and engagement. The Power of the dominant Players can be balanced.

If the big galleries are showing only spectacular artists to make money, this is in my opinion out of time. I am watching all these economical developments and activities in the arts, this liaison between money circulation and art product circulation.

But only being critical is not enough, you have to be more efficient, pragmatic and strategic in the some time, you have to make an impact or facilitate something to push these powers into another. Even if you don't have much power, or money, you can talk about your ideas, through your work and by the internet also with young people.

I am also doing a lot of projects even in rural places. I just went to rural Taiwan. A lot of forgotten places and people are kind of waiting to become activated by art and creative impulses. There are a lot of potential resources, cultural resources, and also natural and social resources. I deeply believe, that art works in curatorial projects can be a catalysator for change. That's why I also work with a lot of public projects. This means with my constant practice and conviction I can contribute to that change.

GM: Coming to the history of curating: Was there a curator whom you admired? A personal curatorial hero?

YH: Yes. My personal curator hero is Harald Szeemann. I just studied all of his curatorial works, like the famous exhibition at Kunsthalle Bern "When Attitudes Becomes Form". This was a starting point. He studied certain materials, and he also did a very good performance by himself. And at documenta he looked at all kinds of materials and supported experimental artworks. But he said, those institutions and exhibitions, like the documenta and international art exhibitions are there to protect artists thoughts and should also serve artists experiments. This is one legacy which I consider is important for me. He also expanded the mode of art definition because he was talking a lot about things of daily life and made further exhibitions with very anonymous people who had their own kind of memory objects. The memory object could be one with a strong message to understand curation. And he also curated outsider art. Those projects are amazing. And all his exhibitions and the processes were expanding the realm of curation.

He created such a wonderful job. At the Venice Biennial he just republished and left space for other people. All these kinds of practices are very important for me. He was a wise man. He had very strong ideas. But his identity was Hungarian. His family migrated, and he grew up in Switzerland. He did these kinds of exhibitions and talked about what is Swiss art and the history of Switzerland. This is almost as important; he took responsibility to create art history. For all these things, I highly respect him.

But my new hero is Bruno Latour. He is more important nowadays. He is a mentor. And he passed away very recently, so sad. He just told me about the whole science. This kind of scientific and political history could be very important to consider these days. Because this creates a totally other dimensions and another discipline to look at the function of art. I read about his exhibition which he made at ZKM, and I also made research about this exhibition. I missed to see the exhibition, because of the Covid situation, but I worked with him at the same institution, at ZKM. I made an exhibition next to him, he made an exhibition about a research topic. We followed our own curatorial practice and we exchanged. So, in this way it is very important what he told about the role of translation and the role of activating people's curiosity, also towards an ethical mind to answer the situation. Because of his scientific knowledge and this connection, he is another kind of mentor for me, the first is Harry, the second is Bruno. Yes, those two.

GM: What are you working on right now? Is there a show that you are curating at the moment?

YH: I am working on several projects. I just finished the Taiwan biennale. The Taiwan biennale was going to happen two years ago, but then it took place last year, because of the Covid situation. Even if it is very difficult to get international guests, I really liked to make the exhibition.

My issue was the idea of social common capital. It means infrastructure, social infrastructure, natural environment, information, also the memory and experiences of people, all this kind of social capital, it is also a curator's job to activate theses aspects of potential capital.

So, I worked with Taiwanese people in the second biggest city, Kurate. I also worked with the Taiwanese universities to create new Human Resources.

It is a quite exciting to curate in the forest, the university and other diverse places like the promenade in the city.

I just wanted to work on the idea of social common capital as I am coming from a 21st century art museum, which I built, which I created. It is now an important museum, on a local, not so much global Level. Important for me is how a museum can bring art to the people. Matching those kinds of ideas, I am starting a garden project. Therefore I am just working with people who have a garden or deal with a garden to make a new kind of ecosystem. And I make connections with other institutions around, also historical institutions.

To bring many visitors to the museum and share artistic ideas with them is only one part of success. But real success is to create a sustaining network. And an important issue is to encourage your own system to be an example of a functioning ecosystem and also invite people to think about it. So I am working on a new ecology exhibition including a garden project based on theory and radical pedagogy. Radical pedagogy is very important for me, as a keyword, because it means translation, also visualization of what is happening, and transforming ideas to people. I highly respect ordinary people. They are living with a strong kind of curiosity, they already created their kind of micro-ecology.

In that sense my teaching is as important for me as my curating. For years, I taught a master course for students, and I taught at the university of fine arts. There were only 7 or 8 students in the master course, and they all come from different countries. Some of them are from Korea, Taiwan and China. They went to Europe and stayed there to learn. But what they learned doesn't work in Asia. Thats why they came to me.

For me it was very interesting to discuss with them. What's their kind of perspective for a new art system, for institutions, collections, art and the work with artists and public. We Asians have highly evaluated local craft, daily seen objects. We don't have any kind of strong distinction between art, applied arts and crafts. That's our specific focus.

A critical point for me is capitalism and materialism, also this strong Western individualism. It was also a root of the disrapture of 2001, when the Twin Towers were destroyed. As I am a Buddhist, I am so much thinking about creating a kind of coherent situation. So we have to create a new kind of future for us.

GM: What does Identity politics mean for a Japanese curator?

YH: I would make it even more precise: What does Identity politics mean for me, a Japanese woman. Japanese are Buddhists, I am Buddhist, a woman, a human being. In this country it is not so easy to survive and to be accepted, because it is a male dominated situation. I don't want to say, I am a minority, even being a woman and come from a peripheral area. But I have a different voice coming from a different position.

So if somebody needs orientation, I can present and argue my certain point. I just curated a biennial, I created a museum, a museum, which is a very democratic museum. These are all political positions. We don't just promote art. It's all about how we can make strong citizen through the power of art, and it is also about creative resources. For me making an exhibition is political action. I also stand for a strong criticism of the dichotomy between subject and object as well as human society and nature. What I try to do with my work and ideas, is to make some adjustments, a kind of comment, a reorientation from my point. This is my mission.

GM: Also the Art World now use the category of "global south". Is "global south" a category for you?

YH: I am a very open person to accept other proposals. Those kind of terms are working for some parts. For instance when you look at post-colonialism, and how Okwui Enwezor applied the word post-colonialism, it really worked. Now we are in a post-post-colonial situation. If we use the term of the global south, yes, we are the local south, there is power and people, and the north is not any more the dominant power. Using the Term "global south" for some time period, that is working. But it's also a kind of stereo typed word, it becomes a cliché. Sometimes it worries me. We are constantly using new cultural categories, using a new kind of special term to indicate a certain kind of current position. If we look at the "global south", south is south, geopolitically south. But the "global south" has a very different kind of situation. It's not an entity. So, we have to be very careful before we continue to use the term.

GM: How do you see this relationship between curator and artist? Is curatorial work a service to the artist? Is it more a dialogue? How did the practice between curator and artist change?

YH: Here I am observing two aspects. One aspect is simple and very basic. Good curatorial work means good eyes. The curator finds an artist and provides an opportunity to present their work. But there are also closer collaborations. If we are working on a big exhibition, like a biennial, we have a certain budget, often a great venue and an opportunity for the artist to create new work. This is a real collaboration. The exhibition process becomes a real collaboration. it's not only that the artist is showing their own proposal or an existing work. There are a lot of conversations in between base on a real collaboration to produce new work and a new project. It is also often concerned with the transformation of the environment, the idea to give a transformation idea to the community.

The other aspect is, in post-Internet times, which Boris Groys addressed in his thoughts, curators and artists are making contents. Those are the kind of contents they share through the internet. Curators also edit these resources, art works and information. We curators are very much content providers. That means, curators' and artists' work is very similar, is getting closer. Even the artists are interpreters of a complicated information situation, they visualize it , they receive it through their senses. A curator's work is to map it. We give a certain kind visual map to the people to digest. So all this is like about translation and Interpretation.

So it's not surprising that now many artists make a commitment to curators and also work as curators. Some of the artists are highly research-based and work in a very conceptual frame. These artists often quite balance visions, themes, and selection of art works and make an interface to transmit an idea to the people. I looked at Pierre Huyghe's curation in Japan at the Okayama Art Summit. He just invited artists , who know him very well.

But what's really different, we curators, freelance or curatorial, whether in an or outside of an institution, are taking responsibility for society.

GM: You are curator and director of a public museum. What is the difference between curatorial responsibility and institutional responsibility?

YH: If you become director, you have a totally different kind of role. First there is the administration, the responsibility for infrastructure and for the staff. And you have to create a museum's identity. As a curator you have to more make things happen. You create artistic content. As a museum's director, you have to do both. It's a big responsibility. Curatorial practice is sometimes the same like an institutional role, but I don't think many curators are concerned about that.

Institutions have to work in a way which (and that is my theme) make people grow. Institutions have to be a kind of school, as they have to be a laboratory and a memory box. There are a lot of different functions an institution has.

My thought is that institutions are sometimes very idiosyncratic, like a personality. This doesn't apply to big museums, but certainly is part of the character of a progressive institution for contemporary art. Being relevant means being idiosyncratic. Things are very synthesized. And curators' or directors' personality also shapes and reflects an institution into the.

The work of independent curators is a different responsibility for art, artists and society. For me it includes a correction of art history. If you invite a young artist, you make him part of art history. You take a responsibility for the past and the future. Your choice is a kind of correction. You just decide that it makes sense to choose this artist to be connected to the future. This correction is a gift, also in consequence for institutions. Also, the citizens, the interested people will be the owners of that correction.

GM: My last question is: What are the main challenges for the curator in the future? How will our work change?

YH: I think nowadays the word curator is very popular, too popular. Because there are curators of the arts and curators of many other things, for which the word curator, curatorship, curationis is used. Lots of the art works and not only art works also other objects and information are being curated. This object orientation, is just indicating a certain kind of phenomena. Material and information are almost the same. In that case the curator's role has become more diverse, it's expanding. So, I cannot define what is curatorial work. But if I can say, we really have to work for the society, that there are not only human beings, but we also have very much to take care of interspecies, conversation, dialogues, that are non-human. Nature and things around us, like plants and animals. We create a new humanity including those kinds of non-humans. Our curatorial work shifts towards this direction. It is definitely not enough if we only talk about human art history and human art works are human.

It's a museum's job to put life and society up for debate from a wide variety of moral perspectives

Max Hollein
in conversation with Reinhard Spieler

REINHARD SPIELER: Welcome, Max Hollein, to our Sprengel Talk. Thank you very much for taking an hour to talk with us from New York.

MAX HOLLEIN: With pleasure. Thank you very much for the invitation.

RS: You are director of the Metropolitan Museum in New York, the Met. You have taken on one of the most challenging posts one can have in the museum business at a time that couldn't be more challenging. We know you from Frankfurt. You then spent two years in San Francisco, and for two years and a half now you've been at the Metropolitan. How are you doing in New York? How is the Metropolitan Museum doing?

MH: We are doing quite well. When we were able to reopen the museum to the public at the end of August last year in 2020, we were euphoric, as was our audience, who came back. Apart from all the new challenges, however, normality gradually set in. This also became evident in our exhibition program. We opened four major projects in the last five weeks, a Goya exhibition, an exhibition on Alice Neel, Carol Bove' sculpture on the façade of the Met, and Alex Da Corte on the roof. Of course, we had, and still have, to face very different conditions and challenges. We are still not fully staffed at the museum. Eighty percent of our staff work from home offices. And our audience, of course, is primarily local. There is no international tourism in the city of New York yet, and tourism from the U.S. is just starting to pick up a bit. You can see that in Central Park, where the horse-drawn carriages are running again, because no New Yorker would take them to go through Central Park. In that respect, things are moving forward. Our focus during the pandemic, indeed to this day, has been to preserve and protect our institution and its mission as best we can. However, the challenges and changes of our time pose fundamental questions for us, for the museum in general, and for the Met in particular: What is our role in a changed world? How do we deal with it? How can we use it positively for our museum?

RS: How is your capacity rate at the moment? What is possible daily in terms of visitors to the museum?

MH: Before the pandemic, we had over seven million visitors a year at the Met 5th Avenue, the Cloisters, and the Met Breuer. I expect we'll end up at 2.8 to 3 million visitors this first year after the pandemic, well below 50 percent. We don't have a problem with the regulations limiting the attendance. Normally, we can accommodate around 55,000 visitors a day. Currently, the limit is 25 percent of that, around 15,000. We are not reaching that at the moment.

RS: Are these individual visitors, or do you also allow groups?

MH: We currently don't allow guided tours or organized groups. There are no tourist groups in New York either, they are all individual visitors, especially New York audiences, and within that audience, of course, our Members. We are an institution that is unique in New York and faces a special challenge. We have a pay-what-you-wish policy for New Yorkers. The tourists pay the full price, while New Yorkers pay significantly less on average. That's why the current period is having a greater impact on the Met than on, say, MoMA, Whitney or Guggenheim.

RS: You said in an interview that the Met will emerge from the crisis as a transformed institution. What will the changes be? What will the institution look like in a few years?

MH: In fact, during the pandemic, our audience increased enormously, namely the audience for our digital offers, and this happened regardless of generation. I remember Frankfurt, where we also had a very intensive digital offering, but it was only used by younger groups of people. That has changed completely. There were no longer age differences. I noticed it with our funders as well. Our trustees and some donors, for example, an 85-year-old lady and board member suddenly started making zoom and virtual calls. I myself didn't know what Zoom was, a year and a half ago. That has spread tremendously and so not only our audience, but our reach has expanded massively. And that is going to continue. For me, it is not so much about having more visitors as a result. It is important that the Met becomes not only more international, but also more multi-local. We did virtual openings during the pandemic with enormous success. At the Goya opening, 35,000 visitors attended. So, we will continue to celebrate openings at the Met virtually around the world in the future. Think of symposia and expert discussions and the time and money they require. All these projects will take place much more virtually in the future. As a result, they can also be staffed with the best people and attended by many more people, so to speak. For our lectures, for example, we now have twenty times the attendance we used to have, just to mention one of the changes. It was also important that during the time it was closed, New Yorkers realized what the Met meant to them and how much they missed this museum when they could no longer visit it. So, again, we are going to be a museum for New Yorkers even more of than before. What has changed significantly, however, is the mission for our museum. We will increasingly be a place of debate, of discussion about the big issues, including social issues, a place that gives voice to many. That is what our staff demand, that is what our patrons demand, that is what our audience wants, and that is what we ourselves demand. In this respect, the role of museum within the overall structure of a society is changing. It is also a question of ethical values, which sponsors you work with, which topics you take on, and much more.

RS: I find it very interesting what you are saying about becoming a museum for New Yorkers again on the one hand but also being globally oriented on the other. You have already built up the digital museum in Frankfurt and were the absolute pioneer in the German museum scene. Do you see another quantum leap now? How digital should and may the museum become?

MH: It is different for every museum. The fundamental question is how you define 'museum' and what your expectations are. With our 1.5 million objects and 200,000 square feet of space, we are primarily, of course, a museum for a visit here in New York. At the same time, we are also a museum that works around the world. We do fellowship programs in India, we do excavations in Egypt and in Turkmenistan, we do rescue missions in Syria, and many other things. So, we see ourselves as a museum—both physically and digitally—that covers and offers a whole range of other tasks beyond a visit and direct interaction with the artwork. All our digital offerings are not aimed at getting more visitors from New York, but we rather want to share what we research, what we experience, what we develop with as many people as possible. Having, in many cases, the best collections of objects outside the country of their origin and culture, it is enormously important for us to be in dialogue, to be accessible, to share—locally at these places as well. And in that sense, the "hyper-local museum" is an essential development. As a global institution, we are also hyper-local. For example, we make programs that are only in Chinese and have been developed specifically for a Chinese audience. That is where digital offers become indispensable. Just as Netflix has very specific digital offerings for a very local audience, a museum like the Met must always think and work in local contexts. That starts with the time. For example, if we do all our programs at 7 p.m. New York time, no one in Europe can attend. Or only night owls.

RS: If you try to be active from China to India to Syria, that also leads to a whole complex of moral questions. This also touches on questions of identity and, above all, questions of provenance. Do you feel pressure on the Met? We are currently discussing the Benin bronzes in Berlin. When you think about your huge collections of non-Western art, do you satisfy certain demand through your international presence, or do you awaken it in the first place?

MH: On the one hand, our policy is not only to be as accessible as possible, but also as transparent as possible. Internationally, we are a museum that—despite the enormous number of objects—makes most of the information and most of the objects available and researchable online. In that sense, our internationality has nothing to do with the kind of feeling that we have to give something back now.

The big difference between the Met and museums in Belgium, France, England, but also in certain cases in Germany, is that our collection and our collection history have no colonial origin. The Met was founded 150 years ago. At the time, we didn't have a single object. And there was no building either. There was just this typical American can-do mentality. A lot of New Yorkers went to Paris, visited the Louvre, and then probably decided in the café next door to do the same thing in New York and then got going. That means our collection has developed differently, grown differently.

Nevertheless, we are of course deeply concerned with questions of looted art, provenance, and how we deal with different origin stories. We also have cases of restitution now and then. Recently, we restituted a golden sarcophagus to Egypt that we had acquired less than 10 years ago. As it turned out, it came from a looted excavation. For us, it is enormously important that we are committed to the idea of the museum, and that the Met is a global and encyclopedic museum which enables greater understanding and learning from one other through the coming together of cultures. I am convinced that not every work of art can have its artistic, missionary, or spiritual impact only at the place of origin of its creation. Nor do we see ourselves as an American institution, precisely because the Met is in New York and New York is a "crossroads". You have to remember that 140 curators work at the Met. Many of them are not Americans. Our curators speak 80 different languages.

RS: Let me refer to the identity debates and also the moral discussions, which are much harsher in the U.S. than in Germany. For example, Gary Garrels at SFMoma had to leave after 20 years of work, after he had sold Mark Rothko in order to buy art by black artists and then said that he would still buy art by white men in the future. Longtime Guggenheim curator Nancy Spector also had to leave for similar reasons. Now you are a white man at a multicultural museum that the Met is. Do you feel this kind of pressure? And if so, how do you deal with it?

MH: The pressure you mention is something we all feel and should feel. It's not a purely American phenomenon either. I am Viennese, Austrian, I studied there, then went to the U.S., worked there, then I went to Frankfurt. I got to know the situation well on this side and the other side of the Atlantic. I think what distinguishes America positively as well as negatively is the escalation level always going immediately from zero to a hundred. What develops slowly in Germany happens immediately in the United States. As a result, these issues immediately become prominent, even urgent. They suddenly concern all areas of society and also make things happen. And that is sometimes very good. The topics that American museums are now dealing with are also becoming relevant on other continents. What is specific to the U.S. is that certain events—like Trump's presidency, but of course also the Black Lives Matter movement, and the economic and social consequences of the pandemic—have caused reappraisal and a reckoning with history. It is about the history of racism, systemic racism in this country. I asked myself for a moment if I was the right person at this house, the right director? Also, because my knowledge about it was underdeveloped.

However, I realized that the knowledge of my American colleagues was just as suboptimal. Of course, everyone knew something about Martin Luther King, but hardly anyone outside the black community was concerned with pervasive racism more deeply. From that point of view, there is a sense of urgency. And debates and some decisions that may seem overblown may be judged differently six months later. Nevertheless, *grosso modo*, it is about important changes, decisions and priorities that are important for this country. They are also important for our institutions, but ultimately, they are of global significance. And this is not just about racism, but also about ownership, engagement, communities, diversity and equal rights.

RS: One of the first cases of cancel culture in Germany that I remember was the demand to take down a Balthus painting. How do you deal with cancel culture demands?

MH: First of all, as far as Balthus is concerned, nothing is being taken down at all. In principle, however, any form of debate is good, including a debate about Balthus. That is part of the debate about a work of art, about an artist, about an oeuvre, and of course it also shows the complexity of society. I also spoke out quite clearly at the time and rejected the idea that every work of art should be morally edifying. For me, one of the most impressive works of art is *Salo* by Pasolini, a film that is deeply disturbing and for that very reason takes a profoundly different, yet moral, perspective. It is a museum's job to put life and society up for debate from a wide variety of moral perspectives. In social media, however, the volume of discussion is often much greater than the discussion itself—to the extent that we must respond accordingly through those same channels. But that doesn't mean we have to democratically vote on which artworks to buy or show. It is only right that the museum and the artworks themselves naturally trigger a discussion—and should trigger a discussion. We have two huge paintings by Kent Monkman that we commissioned to hang in the Great Hall of the Met. They tell a different story of Native Americans. We were fully aware that this was going to generate a lot of discussion—and anything less, I have to say, would have been a surprise even to Kent Monkman.

RS: I would like to talk about the development of the Met. We were impressed to read that you are planning a new building for contemporary art, for which you still have to raise an incredible 600 or 700 million dollars. How big should a museum be? How meaningful is it to make a huge museum even bigger? Would it not make more sense to create a separate institution for contemporary art that could be much leaner, more agile?

MH: Two comments on this. We are not getting any bigger. And that is based on a rule that was imposed on us but turns out to be a blessing in the context that you are talking about. The last major expansion of the Metropolitan Museum was in the 70s followed by a decision made jointly by the City of New York and Central Park that the Met would not grow an inch further into Central Park. All we have been doing since then is reallocating space within our museum. And since I have been here, I have been pushing vehemently to make sure that we present our collections in the best possible way. That means that we are going to renew a quarter or a fifth of our total gallery space over the next ten years. And we are going to spend over a billion dollars on that. It is based on the understanding that the collection itself—and also the context of the collection—must absolutely remain alive. It is not just about making exhibitions out of collections, but about re-presenting, changing, and re-contextualizing the collection. It is not an easy undertaking; and we are not alone in that. If you compare us to other great other houses like the Prado, the Hermitage or the British Museum, you won't see this kind of ongoing transformation in any of them. We are certainly the house that continues to acquire the highest number of works of art. We buy about $50 million worth of artworks a year, and we continue to receive gifts of the same intensity. In other words, the Met continues to be a very dynamic, perpetually changing institution, yet one that remains within its spatial confines.

RS: At the same time, this also means that you cannot show many of the objects.

MH: Yes, that is true. We are a constantly evolving institution, also in terms of our collection. And that is still important to me with regard to contemporary art. I believe that one of the Met's great strengths is that we can represent the entire history of art and culture under one roof. And we have also always oriented our collection policy towards contemporary art. Neither the Louvre nor the Hermitage collects contemporary art. The Prado is now once again in a dispute with the Reina Sofia about who is allowed to do what. At the Met, that was never a discussion. For us that means, it is very important that contemporary art or modern art is not shown in a satellite institution somewhere else. And there are already very good contemporary collections in New York. If we were not in New York and not in Paris, the Met's collection would probably also be the best contemporary collection in the city. It is enormously important to show the contemporary part of the collection in context with our other collections. And only we can do that to this extent and quality, hence our conviction that there should be no separate building for our twentieth- and twenty-first-century collections.

RS: The Met is a universal history museum that unites all world cultures. In the past, however, the cultures of this world were viewed through the mono-perspective of Western glasses. You said that we need multi-local perspectives, different narratives. Still, how many different perspectives can you work with when you are working in one location with a limited amount of space? Do you do that with changing presentations? How do you deal with that?

MH: Yes. For us that is indeed the central task. However, I don't think we will be able to diversify our collection in the next 500 years in such a way that we are no longer a Eurocentric institution. That is simply part of the history of the Met, or even the history of American collecting. We have these focal points, of course, and at the same time we are intensively expanding our Native American Art collection and have also hired our own curator for that. But nonetheless, our holdings of, for example, European Sculpture and Decorative Art, will always be stronger than our collection of Peruvian Decorative Arts of the same period. To make the history of the objects legible and to communicate connections is key. We have already done that with the British Galleries, which we just reopened. On the one hand, it is a celebration of British art and culture, but on the other hand, it is also a history of British colonialism, a history of slavery, of economic exploitation, a history of mutual influence of cultures. So, you can tell different stories through a differentiated form of presentation. I'd like to mention the example of one of the most important films for me: *Rashomon* by Kurosawa. There is a story, a fact, that is told in four different ways, each time the same thing, but from a very different perspective. And that is what we must do as well.

RS: Would a museum of stagnation be a concept for you? A museum that does not grow, a museum that does not keep opening up? Could maybe even a museum that shrinks be a utopia for the museum?

MH: That is conceivable. It is a form of museum that can certainly be propagated when thinking from the collection. We also know this from private collectors. A stronger focus—or indeed, reduction—can be an absolute strength. I am thinking of the Kolumba Museum in Cologne, for example. I think that is a valid type of museum. Absolutely. For the Met, that is not an option because of the way we are conceived, the way we think and act. When I came to the Met, one of the big surprises for me was how acquisition-driven this institution was. And that comes, of course, from an ideology of this house that was founded 150 years ago without a single work of art. You should look at our capital stock. We have 4 billion in capital assets. On the one hand, half of our operating budget is covered by interest, and on the other hand, about one third of our capital assets are available only for acquisitions. That means they cannot be used for any other purpose. It would be impossible for me to say as the director of the Met that we won't continue to acquire anything from now on. We are obligated by the mission of the institution to continually develop, improve and, also, to enlarge the collection.

RS: On the 'deaccessioning' keyword: we have heard that you have to and want to sell works, on the one hand because of the crisis, because visitors and revenues are falling, but also to finance structural expansion. What is your basic position on this? It is a delicate subject.

MH: It is very important to really understand this correctly. American museums have been disposing of works since their beginnings, including the Met. Deaccessioning is a completely normal process in the American museum landscape. We are no exception to that. Since I have been at the Met, there have been seven sessions just on deaccessioning artworks. Deaccessioning is not a reaction to any crisis. American museums believe strongly not only that a collection is continually evolving, but that you can continually improve it. Divesting certain works from the collection is part of that. For example, we are always disposing of duplicates in photography and prints. We'd also sell a Canaletto, for example, if we have 18 other Canalettos from the same area and it is certain that this work will never come into the gallery and has no great significance for research either. We have a clear deaccessioning policy. However, the American Association of Museums, the AMD, has provoked a discussion by suggesting that it is permissible to use funds from deaccessioning not only for the acquisition of new works of art, but also, for example, for the salaries of the staff responsible for the collection. I, too, think that it is right as a temporary measure. And at the Met, we too would and will consider that. But so far, we have not done anything like that. It is important to see that we spend about 50 million a year on acquisitions. If we had excess revenues from deaccessioning funds that we spent on staff salaries every year, that would be a justifiable temporary measure for me.

RS: How do you raise 600 million dollars at a time when there is a pandemic? Would deaccessioning also be considered to fund a new building or rebuild?

MH: No, absolutely not, deaccessioning must not be accelerated for this purpose. No more must be disposed of than in a normal collection clean-up process, which, as I said, is a professional and existing process in all American museums that has been going on for decades. What the American Museum Association clearly says is that during those two years, funds that you keep generating through the normal process anyway, which you do not use for acquisitions, you can use for salaries. But that is not a way to fund large capital projects. Is a 600-million-dollar building fundable now? I do not want to answer that now. We have seen that the capital markets, particularly U.S. capital markets, have flourished tremendously in the last twelve months, which means that the assets have not shrunk; they have grown, especially among people who are involved with us. The question is: what are the priorities for patrons and for American philanthropy in the post-pandemic period? I don't think museums are and will be the only priority. That said, our project, which makes our collection more modern and allows us to better face important issues, is my absolute priority. And I am sure our patrons see that as well.

RS: Perhaps one more question about museum funding, which involves a whole complex of moral discussions up to and including the Trustees' Codes of Ethics. For example, the Sackler problem affects not only the Met, but other houses as well. How to secure funding while also adhering to moral codes? Or, to put it polemically, stay clean or tighten one's belt?

MH: I was always impressed by the American museum system, how American museums are funded. It is not just how resilient, but how diversified their funding is. I have worked very well in both systems, and German museums are still in a very good position thanks to public funding. That is a great achievement of German culture and the German cultural landscape. Nevertheless, in Germany you are often dependent on only one funder. When politics change or when budgets are cut, you feel it immediately in Germany. It is not like that in America. For example, Trump's presidency had no impact at all on our funding. On the contrary, if we lose a funder, or if we distance ourselves from them for ethical reasons, this can be compensated for in our system of 150 major funders and another 5,000 medium-sized funders, and 20,000 small funders. This is an expression of a pluralistic funding system that reflects a myriad of special interests. The great task of a director in America is also to cultivate these funders, large and small, their passions or several of their passions. In doing so, one must be careful to retain as many patrons as possible so that from the concert of differences, one can continue to shape and develop the institution without being dependent on particular interests of individuals. That is great art, so to speak, and it is easier to do that in a city like New York or Boston or even Los Angeles or Chicago than in Boise Idaho.

RS: Two short questions. One is specifically about the United States. How present is Native American art relative to others? And has that developed differently even during your tenure, perhaps?

MH: Yes, we have increased its presence and, also, the understanding enormously. We have created a separate curatorial position just for Indigenous Art. We have integrated Native American Art very clearly as part of our collection in the American Wings, where we also depict and tell the American story of the last 250 years through works of art. And we have included a large collection as an endowment. This also includes bringing Indigenous artists into the canon of voices of contemporary art. There is a lot of catching up to do, but that is exactly the path we consistently take.

RS: And as a final question, which artworks does a Metropolitan director have in his office? What do we see behind you there? Did you set that up yourself or was it taken over?

MH: I like to furnish my office with works of art myself. Behind me, there is a Jackson Pollock from the phase where he switched from the figurative to the completely abstract. You can still see some Mexican Muralist influence. And then there is an Indian Chola bronze and an Egyptian deity watching over me.

RS: Thank you very much and all the best to you in New York.

MH: Thank you very much. Thank you for the invitation.

This interview is an edited version of a Sprengel-Talk between Reinhard Spieler and Max Hollein first published on the YouTube channel of the Sprengel Museum Hannover on 25.3.2021.

Exhibitions don't emerge in a vacuum

Verena Konrad
in conversation with Gerald A. Matt

GERALD A. MATT: What is a curator? Can you define your understanding and practice as a curator?

VERENA KONRAD: I refer to the Latin word *curare*: to take care of, to look after something. As a curator, I take care that a project succeeds—a project, whose contents and context I have ideally formulated myself. When I began my curatorial practice, I contributed to the success of projects in the sense that I sought to make a contribution to the process of identifying ideas and formulating questions about and approaches to a subject or a phenomenon as well as to the process of production. These were generally concrete exhibition projects. Essentially, curating is about hermeneutics and communication. It's about wanting to understand something oneself and about discussing this. And then, in a second step, it's about how one can disseminate findings and positions so that others also have access to artistic perspectives and works, and also to scientific knowledge.

Today, my work in this area has changed to the extent that I'm often only responsible for helping to establish the wider context of an exhibition, while my colleagues develop the details in discussion with me and with the many other people who are involved. For me, some of the key requirements of the curatorial process are to remain open, to weigh up all the arguments and to share one's enjoyment of a subject or of concrete artistic works with others, to learn oneself and to make this learning process and this enjoyment accessible to a wider audience.

GM: How can curating be relevant to the challenges we face today and in what way does it differ from previous models?

VK: The term 'curating' is overused today and, to put it bluntly, often applied to the act of "choosing something". Not that there's anything particularly wrong about this. Hans Ulrich Obrist has described the role of the curator as, amongst other things, that of the "intensifier of taste" and choosing something is a task that is as fascinating as it is challenging and full of responsibility. And yet, the dominance of the term troubles me, because I see curating as a quiet and concentrated activity that requires no platform of its own. For me, it's more about creating platforms for others, for artists and their works, for example, but also for subjects. One result of the professionalisation of the role of the curator is the fact that the activity itself is now subject to critical attention. Authors and scientists have been subject to such attention for some time and it is primarily self-reflective. The act of selecting, of defining the concrete form of a presentation, involves a certain exercise of power, which can relate to public perception or to the specific perception of something in the context of the wider debate or on the art market and can go as far as the potential rewriting of history. Hence, our role is not only to critically scrutinise, and encourage scrutiny of our own work, but also to scrutinise curatorial practice to date and, for example, art historical writing—which I do in my work from a specifically feminist perspective. I've been particularly interested for some years in networking and cooperation between the areas of curating and communication. This is the area where I think that there's most need for development, also for more traditional curators.

GM: How do you see the changing relationship between curators, artists, collectors, galleries, museums and critics? Has there been a shift of power and influence?

VK: I've already seen and experienced a wide range of constellations at first hand. The important thing to me is that I retain the ability to take my own decisions. From time to time I have to pay a price for this in that, perhaps, a certain exhibit isn't made available or certain receptions aren't all that they could be. Curatorial work has a lot to do with networks, yes. What role am I playing—or even not playing—in a certain situation? What is my mission here? It seems to me that the essential thing is to remain aware of all these relationships. I do not see that things have changed in general. I prefer to work with colleagues who are interested in working together too and institutions which support this.

GM: Was there a personal hero, a curator whom you particularly admired? And what were their qualities and achievements? Was there a show that you consider to have been a milestone for your curatorial ideas and practice?

VK: Of course there have been role models. These have been most powerful for me when I've been able to be really close and to learn, not from outside, but on an everyday basis. And their impact has been less about the result than about the way of working. I've learnt from many people and continue to do so. The work with Silvia Eiblmayr has a very important place in my career. I admire her shrewdness and her ability to be uncompromising when this was really important to her. And her ability to recognise issues and set the agenda at a very early stage, as well as to pursue her interests over many years and with such depth, make her an important model for me. I'd really like to achieve this same depth.

Today's role models are often colleagues whose approach impresses me. For example, I value the concentrated and reflective work of Harald Krejci, director of Museum der Moderne in Salzburg, and of my colleague Andreas Ruby at the Swiss Architecture Museum.

GM: Can you describe a personal curatorial work and project, of which you're really proud, and also a project that didn't really work out?

VK: I could name several examples of both scenarios because I've fortunately not been spared my share of self-doubt. Not every concept comes off and sometimes there are really happy moments—these could result from a large amount of good feedback, but also from the fact of having got really close to a phenomenon. Both experiences generate a lot of positive energy. But constructive criticism can sometimes do this too.

Listening to the critical voice within me I'd say that there were four projects in the past few years with which I was very satisfied. The first of these was *Architektinnen*, a public research project that we carried out in 2016 as a contribution to increasing the awareness of the role of women in the technical design professions in Vorarlberg. I believe that this project has a long-term relevance and I am delighted by the impact that it continues to have today. Other very satisfying moments for me were the cooperation with Anna Heringer in 2019, the production *Architecting after Politics (*****S)* with Brandlhuber+ and Christopher Roth in 2019 and a small production/retrospective entitled *Das Beste aus Plus-Minus*, which addressed the subject of architectural criticism in the media. The sense of achievement here came from the cooperation with the participants, from the contents which were very much aligned with my own interests, and from the positive reactions from colleagues, exhibition visitors and guests of our institute.

GM: Is curating always a struggle between vision and practical restraint? Can you give an example?

VK: Yes, definitely. So many decisions have to be taken. There are dependencies, considerations, contexts, limitations and, putting it positively, many possibilities. Curating is a process that, to a certain extent, also anticipates what happens later in the course of the reception of the exhibition, but there is also the level of production. Hence, it is about approaching, understanding and deciding but, at the end of the day, it is also a practical exercise that must be completed by a certain date and, hence, also demands a certain level of pragmatism.

And then, from time to time, unbelievable and absurd things also occur. I co-curated an exhibition in which we showed a work by Jonathan Monk that consisted of neon lettering. We had to hang it far too high up because the fire protection regulations and safety requirements of the municipality didn't allow us to hang it any lower. In the neighbouring federal museum, which is just a few metres away, these regulations wouldn't have applied. Today, at least ten years later, I think that I should have been bolder and had more trust in myself. But I learnt something from the experience. There are certain things that I now sometimes consciously defy in collegial agreement with the production management if I feel that it's appropriate and important to do so.

GM: How do you define the relationship between the artist and curator?

VK: It's a form of collaboration, especially when it involves more than just a one-off meeting. It starts with being inspired by a work or the wider oeuvre of an artist and help to position this so that others can appreciate or get near to it, but I also offer feedback that can sometimes influence future work. The relationship that develops is very personal, because it concerns not a product but a person's work and the perceptions that underlie this work. As the interface between artists—or, in my field, between authors of projects—and the public, I'm careful to maintain a critical distance by involving interdisciplinary project teams and discussing things widely with colleagues.

GM: Where are the lines of conflict?

VK: I've only experienced very few to date, but the presentation of a work is naturally a situation where one ideally arrives at a common understanding. I try to put myself in the public's shoes and to consider what it means when a work is presented in this way and not another. How can I do justice to the work and to the person behind it, but also to the needs of the visitors to the exhibition? Exhibitions don't emerge in a vacuum—they have a political-temporal background and a spatial—but also an institutional—context. As a curator, I've already addressed these contexts in advance through my selection of a personality and of their oeuvre or of individual works. Then, from a certain point, I take joint decisions with the involved artists and give them a huge say while still clearly articulating my own expertise.

GM: Is curating artistic work or a service to the artist and their work?

VK: Of course, curating is a creative activity, but I've never felt that it's artistic. Curatorial work is naturally carried out in the service of an artist's development. However, it also has many other project and subject-related elements such as scientific, media-theory and architectural aspects, etc., so I'd say that my work is principally aimed at an interested audience and seeks to encourage discourse. In this sense, it serves the cultural development of our society and of the individual. I carry out this work with a lot of personal commitment but also, at the end of the day, because I believe that art should be seen, by as many people as possible, in order to inspire and encourage us to reflect and rise above ourselves, but also to politicise, to move, to amuse and to comfort.

GM: There have recently been some examples of artists being invited by institutions to curate major shows and of curators producing their own art. In what way is the line between authorship and curating shifting/fading?

VK: I'm quite sure that there are multi-talented personalities who are capable of doing this. And then it's pure pleasure. I see the focus of an exhibition that was put together by an artist differently—and I have different expectations. It's fascinating to hear what interests other people, what networks they're able to open up, and I see this is as enriching and inspiring, as well as sometimes being a good PR tactic for a museum. I don't have academic expectations here but I'm often, for example, positively surprised by the quality of such cooperation if this is professionally backed-up by a museum. Conversely, I'm happy for all those curators who are artistically talented. But sometimes this is also no more than the desire to experiment, or even hubris. Anyway, you'll never come across me as an artist. That much is certain.

GM: How independent is an independent/freelance curator?

VK: Of course not even freelance curators are truly free. Even those who work freelance are aware of dependencies: financial, organisational or within the relevant network. There's certainly huge pressure when one has to not only finance a project, but also, in doing so, earn one's own livelihood. That said, however, freelance projects can have an impact and take a critical position beyond the confines of an institution.

GM: How dependent is a curator who is employed by a museum?

VK: I think that this varies widely and depends upon the organisation and its leadership. I know institutions where my colleagues are able to work with a huge amount of autonomy and where their expertise is highly valued—and I know others where the opposite is the case. At a basic level, I'm often really amazed that so many people with huge contemplative skills—and I think that this applies to most actors in this profession—are prepared to concede so much when it comes to their own working conditions. Independence exists at many levels. Excellent decisions can be made on the basis of collegial communication and respect, regardless of hierarchies and institutional structures. Institutions can also protect and facilitate long-term research and projects. In my career I've had good opportunities to get to know both scenarios and am careful to give my colleagues space to apply their expertise. The key to a good project is a team that works with enthusiasm and conviction.

GM: How different is their work and self-understanding?

VK: The different working conditions aren't necessarily a reason for having a different self-image, especially as so many colleagues know and have experienced both perspectives. There are, however, incidents that occur from time to time and that have struck me as a freelance curator. For example, the lack of a certain piece of equipment can lead to a different form of networking with other players but also, on occasions, to other decisions, which reflect the background possibilities. In many cases, the insecure livelihoods and lack of respect and resources can eventually become demoralising and generate a lot of self-doubt. For many freelance curators, the opportunity to travel and be part of the international art network also, in reality, represents a huge obstacle. Hence, I only know a few people who exercise this profession at a very high standard for many years.

GM: What is the impact of identity politics on the theory and practice of curating? Has it changed your way of thinking and working?

VK: During my career I've already experienced a number of approaches to this issue. In my own work, I seek to recognise and call out discrimination. At the same time, criticism from others helps me to identify my own blind spots. As a contemporary, I act in the here and now. But as a curator, I also attempt to critically assess political tendencies such as the current debate about identity politics in order to avoid being limited by dogma.

GM: What is censorship in society and what is it in today's art world?

VK: The issue of identity politics arises with increasing regularity in the public debate and I believe that it's important to focus on the underlying issues, on equal opportunities and recognition, but not to avoid discussing such matters out of fear of being misunderstood. Our work is bound up with the process of understanding and communication. It's about encouraging discussion rather than attempting to justify something or offering an opinion. For example, an artistic work can be really fascinating precisely because it triggers such discussion. The key is the contextualisation. I'm as uninterested in curating with velvet gloves as I'm bored by artistic productions and exhibitions that are so cautious and "eager to please" that they've lost all their energy.

GM: Does art have to be moral?

VK: It can be everything, moral or immoral or it can negate this notion completely. As a curator, however, my role is to be able to anticipate how an artistic work could affect other people. The conclusion that I draw depends upon why I want to display a position in the first place.

GM: What is the role of institutions in your practice? Where is the border between curatorial and institutional responsibility?

VK: As I am the director of a small institution, this is perhaps a question that my colleagues and our institutions curator should answer. My self-critical response would be that I clearly allow aspects of the policy of the institution to flow into our work while attempting to maintain an overview. Why are we showing this position in this year's programme? Why are we using our resources for this project and not for another? I always try to answer these questions as concretely as possible. Hence, the policy of the institution primarily plays a role in selecting issues and taking decisions at the beginning of an exhibition project and also as we start to publicise it when the task is to communicate the project. However, while we develop the contents our decisions are rigorously based on the subject and the positions that we are presenting.

GM: What will be the main challenges for a curator in the future? How will curatorial work change?

VK: I think that the selection of subjects will become even more critical. These will become central to our institutional positioning. One major challenge will be attempted interference from politically motivated initiatives and organisations who claim that their positions occupy the moral high ground and who should certainly be given space—in order to address these issues but not their claims to hegemony.

Our collegial cooperation with the area of education and communication will develop as this sector becomes more professional. The resulting digital content—that will also be partly produced by the institutions themselves—will give rise to a new form of media analysis and criticism, which will become an even more important part of our work.

It would be wonderful if images could end wars

Koyo Kouoh
in conversation with Jörg Häntzschel

JÖRG HÄNTZSCHEL: The title of the Triennale is *Currency*. What do you mean by that?

KOYO KOUOH: I am interested in the changing role of photography. In the past, photographs were out there in the world; now, the world is swimming in photographs. We used to seek out images, now they come to us. Over the past thirty years, humanity has produced more images than in all of human history combined. What are the consequences of this for how we live together? How does it change our view of the world? And what images do we project of ourselves? Images have become the currency for human exchange. We no longer send letters, let alone sculptures or paintings; we send photographs. It's no coincidence that the most popular social network, Instagram, is based on images.

JH: To what extent do images define our social status, the value of our lives?

KK: Photography and capitalism are closely intertwined. It is capitalism that is responsible for this flood of images. These images condition us: how we see, how we feel, how we judge. They shape our opinions. They consciously or unconsciously lead us to consume.

JH: How do you put together a major photo exhibition under these circumstances?

KK: For us, it was always clear: The Triennale should offer a moment of calm, a pause, allowing time to think about what is happening to us and the images.

JH: Is that why your exhibition feels so impressively classic? Almost as if there were no iPhones or Instagram?

KK: We didn't want to make the digital image flood the literal subject of the exhibition. We didn't want to replicate it exactly; I wouldn't have found that interesting. We wanted to work against the *zeitgeist*. We want to show the seriousness of photography, its social, political, and aesthetic significance.

JH: How did you select the works?

KK: We followed four paths, four strategies. One we called *Delicacy*. It's not about the delicacy of the subject, but the relationship between the photographer and their subject. A particular proximity, attention, and care. Take Aroma Elewa from Nigeria, who uses photography as a tool for her performances, and who, with a Nollywood and feminist approach, makes Black female voices visible and audible.

The second is *Materiality*. We selected works by artists who expand the possibilities of photography so that it does more than just present an image. They intervene directly in the image, blurring the boundaries between photography and other media. Like Osamu James Nagawaka or Ziad Antar, who work with the physical texture of images. They distort and manipulate images using chemistry and other methods to give them their own texture. In my generation, we still thought that photographs represented the truth. But now we all know that images are constantly manipulated and edited.

JH: What about engaging with the historical genres of photography: portrait, landscape, documentary photography?

KK: It was also about showing the unsettling and disturbing elements in the seemingly familiar beauty of these genres. This applies to the images of Fazal Sheikh, who has been documenting the Middle East conflict through the landscape of the Negev desert for years. These are technically brilliant images, beautiful landscape shots, but as a viewer, you cannot ignore where these pictures were taken.

And then we were interested in what we call 'countermapping'. It's about bringing places and objects that have been invisible to the photographic map. Showing images that capitalism would prefer to hide from us. Like those of Claudia Andujar, who lived with indigenous people in the Amazon for decades and created an extraordinary body of work. She is now 91, but her works only gained recognition in recent years.

JH: What role does politics play in the images? For example, in Paul Yeung's simultaneously creepy and highly comedic series of police officers in Hong Kong?

KK: The great thing about these images is that they look staged, even though they're not. The perspective, the composition, the lighting—all come together perfectly in a single shot. I'm fascinated by such images. They're highly political, but the political aspect stands in tension with their artistic quality.

JH: In a time when everything is shown to death, how can it be explained that vast areas of reality evade representation? There are hardly any images of climate change; most refugees drown in the Mediterranean without any photographic trace. There are no images of global capital flows either.

KK: The forces of capitalism condition us to see the world in ways that awaken needs to consume. At the same time, the same system keeps entire spheres of life and regions in the dark. Alfredo Jaar addresses this in his work: He shows the covers of every issue of the American *Life* magazine from the first edition in 1936 to its cessation in 2004. Only five of over 3,000 cover stories were dedicated to Africa, even though the magazine was so influential in the mid-20th century, almost like television on paper.

JH: Returning to the metaphor of currency: The inflation of images should not be confused with a devaluation of images. There are still images that shock us, and because they are now much more widely disseminated, their impact has increased. One could say, for example, that Putin lost the war the moment the world saw the images of people with bound hands, dead in their own gardens.

KK: I see it differently. It would be wonderful if images could end wars. But we know better. Of course, one of the strengths of photography is that it evokes emotions: joy, pleasure, disgust, shock, outrage. An image like the one you described still shocks people, thank goodness. Every war is a catastrophe, no matter where it occurs. Still, I believe that the oversaturation of images has led to numbness. An image causes an outcry for ten or twenty seconds, then people swipe or click on. It reminds me of the 1980s when the number of television channels exploded. Until then, you watched a program, but now it was click, click, click. That changes how we see and relate to what we see.

JH: Would there have been Black Lives Matter without the image of the police officer kneeling on George Floyd?

KK: Black Lives Matter was present in American society long before George Floyd. The video only amplified the movement. The case of George Floyd was the one that broke the camel's back. There were hundreds of such cases before him. The question we should ask is: What makes an image a trigger? We see hundreds of videos of African Americans being murdered by the police, but then there's one that makes a movement visible.

JH: What makes this one image different from the others?

KK: It's not this one image that's different, it's society that is ready at that moment.

Interview by Jörg Häntzschel. Reprint of the interview "Es wäre wunderbar, wenn Bilder Kriege beenden könnten" ("It would be wonderful if images could end wars") from 19 May 2022 with kind permission of Sueddeutsche Zeitung.

What matters for me is the recognition of Africas diversity

Koyo Kouoh
in conversation with Jonathan Fischer

JONATHAN FISCHER: You have just launched a one-year exhibition series under the title *Who Said It Was Simple*, focusing on personal freedoms, particularly the handling of homosexuality and homophobia. Does homophobia hold a different significance in Africa compared to the West?

KOYO KOUOH: I believe there is no specifically African or European approach to homosexuality, but only a human one. The first part of the exhibition series documents how the media in African countries address the issue. In May, the Raw Material Company will showcase photos, videos, and installations by three African artists on the lives of sexual minorities.

JF: Is your goal to defend human rights?

KK: Yes, and for that, we need an open discussion. In an accompanying text to the exhibition, Nigerian gay activist Ayo Sogunro explains that there are over 250 different societies in Nigeria, some of which have traditionally practiced homosexual acts. And then the Nigerian government decides to punish homosexual practices with long prison sentences—allegedly because they contradict the country's culture. Where does this radicalization of society come from? Who is behind it? It's mainly about political and religious interests. Homophobia is being instrumentalized to control people.

JF: You treat visual art as a medium for global societal critique. Are you responding to the current political debate on homophobia in Africa with your exhibition?

KK: We work on long-term projects, so we don't react to trends. An exhibition like this takes about a year to organize. On the other hand, we are constantly dealing with the consequences of colonialism. This includes homophobia. Many of the related laws we still apply in Senegal date back to the third French Republic. France abolished discrimination against homosexuals in the 1980s, but in Africa, the old policies continue. They have shaped identities that contrast with traditional African freedoms.

JF: The tension between "constructed identities" in Western and African notions seems to be a recurring theme in your work. Last year, for example, you curated an exhibition about the Dutch wax fabrics which are present throughout Africa.

KK: It's fascinating how a history of colonialism, appropriation, and re-appropriation is written here. Why do Africans accept these fabrics, which were neither made in Africa nor by African designers, as "typically African"? Why do people believe in such projected ideas? For me, it's about questioning what is taken for granted and asking what "African" means today.

JF: Don't Western viewers expect African artists to refer back to tribal traditions?

KK: Yes, there are enthusiasts of African masks and sculptures in Europe who deny contemporary art its authentic African identity. To translate: "Stick to your masks and sculptures." This attitude is racist.

JF: On the other hand, contemporary African art is more present in the West than ever before. African curators like Okwui Enwezor and Simon Njami are celebrated worldwide. You yourself curated a fair for contemporary African art in London last year.

KK: What matters to me is the recognition of Africa's creative diversity, from photography to popular music. Hip-hop, for example, ultimately developed from African ingredients. Visit an area 200 kilometres south of Dakar, and you'll hear traditional rap chants. Black Americans spread it worldwide, but this art has been practiced here for centuries. Africa is constantly denied its influence—even in political reporting. Tunisia and Egypt are in Africa, yet it's always referred to as the Arab Spring, not the African Spring.

JF: Didn't the Senegalese Spring offer an alternative to many African stereotypes by showing that democracy and civil courage can triumph over corruption?

KK: In 2012, I curated a photo exhibition in Berlin to make visible our democratic resources. Democracy and a multi-party system have been part of Senegal for decades. When it became clear how corrupt our government was and that President Wade was planning a third unconstitutional term, protests began. At first, there were public debates and political discussions. Even before the Y'en a marre movement brought masses to the streets, politicians, rappers, journalists, and students had been holding actions for two years. But the West paid no attention.

JF: Does the Raw Material Company aim to spark such discussions?

KK: Senegalese people don't need an art centre for that - after all, we had student protests in 1968 that even outshone those in Paris. But I want to take art out of its self-referentiality: Art has more to say than just aesthetics and form. Artists have fine antennas to make societal processes visible—in ways different from commerce and politics. Art in Africa has always expressed critical positions. Many dances and Griot songs are political, and even traditional sculptures often carry a political message. We just sometimes can't read them.

JF: You're well-connected worldwide. Does it still make a difference whether an artist works in Paris, Berlin, or Dakar?

KK: I tend to say no. The essence of creating art is the same everywhere. At the same time, I must admit that it is the African metropolis that challenges people—and with them, artists. Here, more than anywhere else, you have to be present, intelligent, and quick to survive. You're constantly being thrown out of your comfort zone, and that fosters the creative process.

JF: What resources does a Senegalese painter have after graduating from art school to present his work to a larger public?

KK: If he's lucky, he gets into the graduate exhibition at the National Gallery. But then there's a lack of gallery networks that could support him. There are few collectors and buyers of young contemporary art—and even fewer critics who would report on it. The graduate from the art academy will feel very isolated. Visual art in Africa suffers from the separation from other art forms. Traditionally, art in Africa comes in a variety of forms: you're not just a dancer or mask maker, but also a poet, writer, and painter at the same time. There has always been simultaneity. The Raw Material Company aims to help build an infrastructure that overcomes this fragmentation of the arts.

JF: How involved is the state?

KK: In the years after independence, many African artists were supported by their governments to express a new national identity through visual arts. Senegal is exemplary in this regard. Art and culture have a steady budget in the state budget, from which the art academy, cultural centres, or the Dakar Biennale benefit. However, I find the quality of art education problematic. As a former French colony, we have adopted the attitude of our colonizers: art serves to glorify the state. Our last president, Abdoulaye Wade, spent a lot of money building a monumental theatre palace in the city centre. But there is no program to use the theatre. The director and employees manage the building as a pure self-purpose. Similarly, many positions in cultural management are assigned unqualifiedly. This nepotism is the real problem in Africa.

JF: And it is left to private initiatives like your Raw Material Company to propose an alternative program?

KK: With the Raw Material Company, we have created a blueprint for all of Africa. A place of freedom where art can express not just pleasure, but also pain, fear, and social critique. However, the necessary infrastructures are still lacking in many places. That's why, at our last symposium, we had artists, curators, and art officials discuss the building of art institutions in Africa.

JF: Have you never considered working in the West, like your curator colleagues Okwui Enwezor or Simon Njami, to possibly receive more funding and exposure for your projects?

KK: No, it's much more important to me to create an exhibition in a 100-square-meter space here in Africa than to work in a big art museum in New York. We Africans must finally learn to trust in our own size. The aftereffects of slavery and colonialism have deeply ingrained a sense of inferiority in our psyche. Do you know what the name Raw Material Company signifies? That we Africans find everything essential for life, all raw materials, in our own country. And I'm not just talking about gold, oil, or cotton. Art is also a raw material for human development.

Interview by Jonathan Fischer. Reprint of the interview "Homophobie ist eine Folge des Kolonialismus" ("Homophobia is a consequence of colonialism") from 19 February 2014 with kind permission of Sueddeutsche Zeitung.

Art Biennals can work as heterotopian spaces

Gerald A. Matt
in conversation with Kasia Matt-Uszyńska

KASIA MATT-USZYŃSKA: What is the general subject and common curatorial focus of this year's 3rd edition of the Industrial Art Biennial in Labin, Istria?

GERALD A. MATT: I think the title *Ride Into The Sun*, a song by Velvet Underground that we have chosen, gives a general idea of our focus for the biennial. It deals with confidence and disappointment, hope and fear, nostalgia and utopia in society and world facing dramatic changes. The invited artists and their works reflect the decline of the Industrial Age and the advancing digital revolution, its implications for society, and its way of life and work. For me, it was important that the biennial discussed issues and problems related to the effects of the delegitimization and decline of ideology and the uncontrolled omnipresent universal capitalism, as well as the incompatibility of the postindustrial world with its ongoing economic growth and increasing waste of resources with a livable environment and nature—and how these developments change the relationship between human beings and between humans and nature.

KU: How does your concept interrelate with the region of Istria as well as global perspectives?

GM: Through the selection of artists and art works, and the exchange of global and local issues, positions and thoughts. Istria, with its former mining towns like Labin, shipyard, harbor and industrial towns like Pula and Rijeka or pioneering tourist towns like Opatija, as well as other locations, provide the blueprint and a local backdrop for discussing the global problems concerning the dramatic changes in the life and work of human beings today, through a dialogue between artists from the region and those from outside.

KU: Which artistic and social aspects were important to you?

GM: What was very important to me was the framing of the exhibition by major historical and contemporary films. Films like *Earth* by the Austrian filmmaker Nikolaus Geyrhalter dealing with the ecological consequences of the exploitation and industrialization of nature and landscapes, or *River of Fundament* by the American artist Matthew Barney presenting his mythological view on the decaying Detroit and the industrial dream. Excerpts of Godfrey Reggio's visionary film trilogy *Qatsi* about the urbanization and acceleration of our world, and John Ford's *How Green Was My Valley*, underline the show's focus on the extreme social, ecological and economic changes, problems and challenges our world faces today. They create a basis for discussion. I also think that for discussions of contemporary life, mobility, tourism and its implications, film quotations like Piwowski's *Rejs* or Tati's *Les Vacances de Monsieur Hulot* are important contributions. Also, Erwin Wurm's project *Table of Conspiracy*, which deals with problems of communication in digital times and gains new relevance in the corona epidemic.

KU: What was your contribution to the biennial and its theme?

GM: My contribution to our biennial project *Ride Into The Sun* revolves around the dynamics of globalization, digitalization, automatization, the logics of capitalism and climate change calling dramatically into question our world and our way of living and working. The dialectics of reality and utopia, nostalgia and progress, fear and hope, confidence and disappointment and the contradictions between the loss of "the good old world" and the gain of "a new, better world", between demarcation and openness, resistance and change, all of which increasingly determine life and its fractures. The only certainty left is that we live in a world which is changing faster and faster. The familiar old world disappears, and a new world assumes contours and leaves people with a feeling of lost visions, control, identity, home ("Heimat") and prosperity, and with a longing to get back in control. The feeling which the corona crisis has additionally reinforced. The Velvet Underground song, *Ride Into The Sun* incorporates our immanent desire for another, better world and life, a ride that should lead us to a peaceful and prosperous society for everyone, to a more humane world, a world close to the dream of a pleasant Arcadia warmed by beautiful sunbeams, but also a ride which could end in the nightmare of the unbearable hell of the mercilessly burning sun and heat, a world of human and natural disasters. The last mythological attempt to "ride into the sun" failed, Icarus paid for it with his life.

KU: How did you frame this focus? Were there any key works—pillars on which you built your exhibition?

GM: Nikolaus Geyrhalter's film *Earth* is one of these central artistic works. It opens our view on the changing face of the world. The film is an epitaph for landscapes taken over and branded more and more by the traces of machines and human technical interventions. Several billion tons of earth are moved annually by humans, with shovels, excavators, and dynamite. The film observes people in mines, quarries, and large construction sites in a constant struggle to appropriate our battered planet. Another important contribution to the biennial is Matthew Barney's enigmatic and lyrical film *River of Fundament* co-directed by Jonathan Bepler. It is based on a series of Barney's performances. The film follows Norman Mailer (played by three different actors over the course of the film) as he travels through three different reincarnations enduring the seven mythological states of his soul. The plot is loosely based on Mailer's novel *Ancient Evenings*, in which Mailer's body represents three generations of American cars: a 1967 Chrysler Crown Imperial, a 1979 Pontiac Firebird Trans Am and a 2001 Ford Crown Victora Police Inspector. Barney also deals with the myth of Motown, Detroit's rise and fall as an allegory of the Industrial Age and the decay of the American dream. Sequences of Godfrey Reggio's *Qatsi* trilogy with music by Phillip Glass: *Koyaanisqatsi* (Life out of Balance), *Powaqqatsi* (Life in Transformation) and *Naqoyqatsi* (Life as War)—titles based on the Hopi language—helped to frame the issue of the biennial. The *Qatsi* trilogy abandons language and consists of slow motion and time-lapse footage of cities and many natural landscapes across the United States. It presents visionary images of urbanization and the acceleration of urban, economic and social change with its consequences.

KU: Can you describe some of the artists you invited and their contribution to the theme of the Industrial Art Biennale?

GM: In the central venue of the biennial, the Underground City, Lamparna, a former mine and its infrastructures, Scott Hocking presents photographs of his interventions and sculptures. Scott Hock Hocking lives and works in Detroit and uses the city as his artistic stage and its industrial ruins and relics as his material. His work *Garden of the Gods* is an installation built on the collapsed roof of the Albert Kahn-designed Packard automobile plant in Detroit. A handful of Kahn's cast concrete columns remained standing among the rubble, leaving a site reminiscent of both the Forum Romanum and Bernini's Plaza San Pietro. Using the columns as pedestals, the twelve gods of the Classical Greek Pantheon were replaced by Hocking and represented by wooden television consoles found elsewhere. Working like an archeologist, Hocking tracks down the relics of the former glamorous car industry and its mythological spirit. Hocking also shows photographs of his work *The Egg, and Michigan Central Train Station* is a site-specific sculptural installation and photography project created within Detroit's 100-year-old former train depot, vacant for over 20 years. The installation is made from thousands of marble fragments that litter most of the 17-story structure's upper floors, remnants of the once marble-lined corridor walls. The project, built over the course of 18 months, is based on the ancient symbolic meanings of the egg, culminating with the egg's eventual destruction.

Toni Schmale will show one of her concrete sculptures of concrete, *loch ist loch* using materials we deeply connect with the Industrial Age—concrete and steel—creating abstract monuments to human endeavor by the transformation of substances and forms. Claudia Larcher's meditative video *Ore* zooms in from a helicopter view of an abstract landscape and its dissolved colors to a close-up of a battered earth and the traces of the exploitation of its resources. Her *Noise Above Your Heads* intermingles rock formations and architectural features as dystopian and surreal scenarios, referring to Bruno Taut's sketches of alpine landscapes, bunker-like server rooms for data backups of today's banking systems, and a surreal penguin diving through a flooded tunnel. Basim Magdy, in his satirical and at the same time melancholic Super-8-film *13 Essential Rules for Understanding the World,* shows us images from a bouquet of tulips to a moving high up carousel. The ironic and resigned instructions like "Never try to change anything. You can't even change yourself", or "Never claim to defend nature or defend the environment", or "You are an alien on this planet", mirror a disorientated and unsettled world.

In their video work *World Climate Change Conference,* Rimini Protokoll reflects the endless discussions, negotiations and debates at the forefront of the world climate conference in Paris 2015, a testament to the indecision of the stakeholders of the environment and climate politics and its complexity.

Paul Albert Leitner's photographs are the result of long walks through the Istrian towns of Labin, Pula, Rijeka and Opatija, where he photographed public signs and letters, relicts of use and decay, capturing the language and history of public space and its changing functions. As he says: "A walking pace is the best speed for a photographer." His photographs tell us a story of the presence of narratives by their absence and vice versa. In his photographic forays, the strange becomes familiar and the familiar alien.

Agnieszka Polska's sound installation *The Happiest Thought* refers to Einstein's impulse for his general theory of relativity and explores the

Earth's biosphere as it looked before the greatest Perm/Triassic mass death in its history 250 million years ago when up to 90% of the planet's vegetation died out because of volcanic carbonic dioxide. Maruša Sagadin's sculptures add a moment of surreal irony to mankind's attempts at creating and intermingling material and ideas. With another work, a slideshow, Basim Magdy leads us through the dying memories of nature fading away in dissolving colors.

The annex room of the Pula Arena shows works of Mary Reid Kelly. The Pula arena was constructed between 27 BC and 68 AD and is among the world's six largest surviving Roman arenas, a monument to antique life and ideas. Three works by Mary Reid Kelly—all stylized black and white videos referring to Roman and Greek mythology—are shown in its annex. *Priapos Agonists* combines the myth of Minotaur with American everyday sports culture. Like Jorge Luis Borges' portrait of the Minotaur as anti-hero in *The House of Asterion*, the Minotaur of Priapus Agonistes is hopelessly lost in an environment of repetitive space. *The Syphilis of Sisyphus* deals with the desperate Sisyphus-like battle of our society to make nature submit to the ideal and glamour of artifice. *The Body of the Sturgeon* envisions an American submarine at the very end of the Second World War. Sailors on the fictional USS Sturgeon grapple with claustrophobic boredom and entertain each other with ad-hoc burlesque performances—a capsule of an alienated and isolated society far away from common life.

KU: How did you deal with the variety of viewpoints of three curators? Or in which way were you able to keep an individual curatorial position while at the same time realizing the project as a kind of collective?

GM: I think what we share coming from different backgrounds—me, former director of a Kunsthalle and now running an institute providing intellectual and structural services in the field of art and culture, from art shows, lectures, studies to a TV show, Christian Oxenius, a free curator working closely with a very young art scene, and Branka Bencic, a free curator who was just appointed director of the museum in Rijeka—is a mutual understanding what curating can and should be, curating as a means of communication, of communication and bridge-building between artists, public, medias and institutions, a practice of building bridges and understandings between different communities, connecting different attitudes and people. Consequently, the biennial is also based on communication and shared expertise and experience. Based on the people, landscape and history of Istria we developed a theme which gives the frame for artistic thoughts, concepts and works, which deal with global questions and problems rooted in a local context. In the end, all decisions were taken in that common spirit. For me, tourism was an important subject around which I conceived the exhibition at the Sporer Pavilion in Opatija. The Sporer Pavilion was erected in 1900—the heyday of tourist development—for the Quarnero company of Vienna, a Company at the forefront of early tourism. It was expanded by the architect Sandor Neuhausler, who added the large terrace facing the seafront promenade. It stands for the close relation between leisure time, tourism and culture, as it was used as a pastry shop as well as an exhibition pavilion. The pavilion was named after Juraj Matija Šporer, a physician who played an important role in the promotion of Opatija as a seaside health resort. Reflecting its touristic function, Alban Muja encoded the Sporer Pavillion with big letters carrying the word "Hotel", marking the replacement of former economic and social structures by the tourist industry. On the terrace square of the pavilion visitors and trespassers will have the opportunity to interact with a wooden table by the artist Erwin Wurm. The table is bolted on a pallet and provided with two holes and an inscription (*Handlungsanweisung*, instruction of the artist) inviting the public to put the head through the hole and try to communicate under these physical restrictions. Wurm's Installation *Table of Conspiracy* addresses the difficulties of communication due to digitalization and overflow of information as well as to the restrictions of movement and expression by the corona crisis. Inside the pavilion, artists analyze and criticize a society which focuses on endless economic growth and discuss the problematic social, economic, ecological and esthetic consequences of a booming tourist industry. In an interview the artists Rugile Barzdziukaite, Vaiva Grainyte and Lina Lapelyte discuss their opera performance *Sun & Sea (Marina)*, a project which touches upon the issue of climate change, human body, environment and consumerism. They won the Golden Lion at the last Venice Biennale by portraying a relaxing day with all its collateral damage from plastic bottles, toys, headphones to overfilled food containers. They deal with society and its lifestyle which brought about a crisis it cannot fathom. The interview is accompanied by documents and press responses to the Venice project. The sequences of the film *Les Vacances de Monsieur Hulot by Jacques Tati* follow the misadventures of Monsieur Hulot who joins the "newly emerging holiday-taking classes" for a summer vacation at a modest seaside resort. The film excerpts, shown on a TV set, ironically mock the confidence of postwar Western society in the optimistic belief in capitalist production, and the value of complex technology over simple pleasures, *Rejs* (*The Cruise* or *The Trip Down the River*) by Marek Piwowski parodies life in the People's Republic of Poland and, through an absurd weekend river cruise, reveals reality as a hilarious parody of the entire communist system and its ideology. Robert Kusmirowki's

Lindenstraße 35 takes us to the golden travel age of the late 1920s and early 1930s, when Berlin was a world metropolis, and the dream of air travelling was still alive. A historical photo from the early 1930s with the interiors of a Deutsche Lufthansa AG office are his inspiration for the reinvention of the space. In a vitrine, faked photographs of Lufthansa and its beginnings blur the line between fact and fiction and remind us of the innocent vision of air travel around the globe.

Guido Kucsko presents a postcard stand gathering self-made postcards with the images from a journey on the traditional touristic train route from Vienna to Opatija, from the capital of the Austro-Hungarian monarchy to its elegant holiday resort at the Adriatic Sea. The Südbahngesellschaft established hotels along the way, linking transport and accommodation and developing an attractive touristic infrastructure that laid the foundation for today's "turbotourism".

Tanja Prusnik adds her masks depicting the new reality of travelling, restrictions which dramatically endangered the phenomenon of ever-growing tourism as we knew it.

With his work, *Hart und Weich Nr. 2,* Marco Lulic addresses the legacy of modernism in socialist Yugoslavia based on the relationship of form and ideology, and the body and its representation. He recreates the organically formed swimming pool of the Haludovo Hotel, a hotel complex from the 1970s on the Croatian island Krk built by the Croatian architect Boris Magas and financially supported by the Bob Guccione, publisher and founder of the magazine *Penthouse,* a hotel from a time of "hope and glory", where the booming tourism created the illusion of a peaceful reconciliation and cooperation between communism and capitalism. The installation discretely serves as a stage for Dejan Klaraklajic's film *We Don't Sell Hollywood* documenting the opening night of the US-Yugoslavian joint venture between grey socialist functionaries and the glamorous "King of Porn", Bob Guccione. The embarrassing rooster Guccione, the loosely dressed penthouse bunnies, hard drinking communist bureaucrats, curious fishermen and their irritated wives increase the surreal impression of the deal.

Opposite to Lulic's work Erwin Wurm makes an ironic comment on a society of abundance, ignorance, cheap pleasure and food addiction with his sculpture of a person composed of sausages.

Claudia Larcher's, film *#postalps* analyses the fatal contrast and simultaneity between nature, agriculture, goats, tourism and the industrialization of landscape and livestock. The dependencies of the alpine world in Vorarlberg and its inhabitants have created a functionalized artificial world based on economic efficiency.

The architects Wilfried Kühn of Kuehn Malvezzi and Guido Jan Bral were asked to create a new purpose for the abandoned Palace de Justice in Bruxelles. They didn't propose the trendy and ordinary solution of implementing a boutique hotel in the historical building to serve the city's growing tourism demand. In contrast, they developed the idea of freeing the landmark from any new function and leaving it as it is, as an empty monument to itself—a rejection of the omnipresent recycling and transformation of history and architecture. To support his plan he produced a poster, which is shown in the exhibition.

Rimini Protocol's film *Chinchilla Arsehole, eyey* is based on their radio play on control options, verbal attacks, Tourette and the question of what normality means in today's society. It's also, an ironical report about an unusual journey through Germany—a touristic stress test. Christian, who suffers from Tourette Syndrome, drives across Germany, and not everyone responds compassionately to the abusive words and taboos which the illness is able to detect. Albert Leitner presents us, in his work series *Hotelwelten*, his impressions from more than 40 years of travelling and photographing. Hotels, their facades and interiors, salons and bathrooms, entrances and backyards, arrivals and departures, and portraits of the artist himself posing as permanent traveler, consolidate into a wonderfully melancholic picture book of an irrepressible pleasure in discovering himself and the world.

KU: What makes the Industrial Art Biennial exceptional and how does it differ from other biennials?

GM: It's the time and place and the *spiritus loci*. It's the relativity of borders mirrored by the history of Istria and its political, social and economic consequences. A region that stands for a specific change of the relation of life, work and its structures. The artists of the biennial reflect upon and interpret the results and the status quo of the enormous changes from the Austro-Hungarian Monarchy to Italian fascism, Yugoslavian communism and Croatian nationalism, from collective economy to capitalism, and from old industries (shipyards and mines) to tourism and services.

KU: Which significance or role do you see in art for today's society and what can biennials achieve?

GM: The restrictions of the corona epidemic drastically show how important art is to society. All the restrictions of the anti-corona measures imposed by the authorities in the cultural field, from theatres to exhibitions, make us feel that the encounter with art is an essential part of our life. We deeply miss it. To make it short, it is what Christo put in his programmatic and poignant sentence: "The work of art is a scream of freedom." Freedom which is and will be existential to all of us. Biennials are agoras, places of exchange and transfer of ideas, places of mutual understanding and networking, artistic interventions that can work as catalysts for a local art scene. Art biennials can work as heterotopian spaces in the sense of Foucault, "real places—places that do exist and that are formed in the very founding of society—which are something like counter-sites, a kind of effectively enacted utopia in which the real sites, all the other real sites that can be found within the culture, are simultaneously represented, contested, and inverted. Places of this kind are outside of all places, even though it may be possible to indicate their location in reality". Foucault uses the metaphor of the mirror to explain the relation between utopia and heterotopia. The art biennial I believe in represents, in a way, that mirror. It can help to cross social, cultural and political borders and works as a mind and game changer.

KU: What are the chances and challenges of the biennial as an exhibition format—now and in the future?

GM: The increase in art biennials all over the world is in a way the result of globalization, growing wealth and mobility. They bring the art world closer together and not only help to cross the inequality between the different art scenes worldwide but also to strengthen the diversity of artistic expression and practices. On the other hand, the future of biennials at a time of rethinking international lifestyles and travel, and their ecological consequences, I think, the balance between the local and the international must be reconsidered, as well as the relation between art events, artists and the public. Biennials, which function merely as temporary hotspots for an international art crowd coming or flying in just for fashionable openings like a greedy swarm of locusts and leaving back a more or less deserted agglomeration of art works without any relation to the local public and context will have no future. The usual uninspired questions of art jet visitors like "When did you arrive? When are you leaving?" should be a thing of the past. Biennials as places of relevant themes and contextualization, of exchanges between the local and the international, networking of ideas and artists, discoveries of artists and their works without the commercialization and quota pressure will definitely have a future.

KU: What impact will the corona crisis have on art and artists?

GM: It makes life and work incredibly difficult for artists. Art is based on communication and the exchange of different ideas, experiences and practices which are extremely impeded and threatened by the corona crisis and its restrictions on social and artistic life. Now, we cannot foresee the future economic, social and cultural implications of the epidemic. We can only hope that it will help to re-focus on the essential values of life and art.

I believe curators should be educators

Abaseh Mirvali
in conversation with Gerald A. Matt

GERALD A. MATT: What is a curator?

ABASEH MIRVALI: For me, a curator is, above all, a storyteller—someone who builds a meaningful narrative by selecting and engaging with artists, artworks, and ideas. But storytelling in this context isn't linear or didactic; it's about creating a layered experience that invites reflection, resonance, and sometimes even dissonance.

In my practice, curating begins with deep listening—to artists, to communities, to history—and from there, crafting a framework that allows artworks to be in conversation with one another and with the public. The curator's role is not to dictate meaning, but to create the conditions for it to emerge.

GM: How can curating be relevant to the challenges we face today, especially social challenges, and in what way does it differ from previous models or the previous work of curators, 20, 30, 40 years ago?

AM: Curating today carries a different urgency—and a different kind of responsibility—than it did 15 years ago when I started. While the core of the practice remains: building relationships with artists and facilitating the public's encounter with ideas and aesthetics, the social, political, and ethical dimensions of curating are now impossible to ignore.

When I transitioned from politics and public policy to working as a museum director, I was an American of Iranian heritage directing a museum in Mexico. That positionality—moving across geographies, cultures, and institutional structures—shaped my understanding of how context matters. At the time, curatorship was still largely defined by centralized, often Western voices, and the discourse was relatively homogenous. In Mexico, even within Latin America, there was little meaningful exchange with colleagues from Brazil or other neighboring contexts. It was often who you knew—not what questions you were asking—that gave shape to the conversation.

Today, we've shifted dramatically—perhaps even swung to the other extreme—where only curators from a particular region are seen as legitimate narrators of that region's experience. While I believe it's crucial to have a deep, lived understanding of the context one works within, I also believe that multiple voices and points of view are necessary to truly reflect the complexity of our times.

What's essential is ethical responsibility—doing the work, building trust, and approaching communities with respect rather than extraction. Curating in the present moment must be porous, collaborative, and deeply grounded, both intellectually and relationally. Only then can it meet the social and political challenges we collectively face.

GM: You are questioning some results of identity politics, namely that only someone from the same community is seen as entitled to speak about it.

AM: Yes, I think we're living through the outcomes of a necessary corrective. For too long, cultural narratives were shaped almost exclusively by those outside the communities being represented. So, this rebalancing—where authorship is reclaimed—is both powerful and long overdue. But like all pendulum swings, it may have gone to an extreme, where we risk essentializing identity and reducing complex lived experiences to fixed categories of legitimacy.

When I began curating, I wasn't consciously framing my perspective through a lens of "otherness." I had grown up in San Francisco, with an Iranian heritage, but I didn't see myself as outside the dominant cultural discourse—I saw myself as part of it, as someone moving across multiple registers. Only in hindsight, after years of working across the U.S., Latin America, Europe, and the Middle East, do I recognize how much the contexts I've lived and worked in have shaped my curatorial vision.

Living in different cultural environments has allowed me to see how context—social, historical, political—is inseparable from how art is made and how it's received. My focus has always been on doing the work to understand those contexts deeply, and to build exhibitions that emerge from that understanding.

So yes, identity matters—but so does responsibility, research, humility, and curiosity. The curatorial field is evolving, and I believe it's possible to honor lived experience while still allowing room for cross-contextual dialogue and shared meaning-making. That, to me, is the more sustainable and generative path forward.

GM: How do you see the change in relations between curators, artists, collectors, galleries, museums, and critics? Has there been a shift in responsibility or in power dynamics? I ask this in light of your career—you've worked with collectors, directed a museum, curated independently, and are now Artistic Director of a fair.

AM: Absolutely, there has been a profound shift—and a noticeable blurring—of roles across the field. In some ways, this hybridity can be generative: it allows for more fluid collaborations and opens up platforms that weren't accessible before. But in other ways, I see it as a dilution of accountability. The term "curator" itself has been stretched to the point of abstraction. It's now used to describe everything from playlist-making to interior styling, which flattens the depth of what the role actually entails.

Curating—when practiced with seriousness—is a rigorous, deeply intellectual, and emotionally invested process. It requires time, trust, research, and sustained dialogue with artists and audiences. Whether it's a solo exhibition, a biennial, or a modest institutional program, it's about crafting a proposition that is coherent, layered, and resonant. That gets lost when the term is used casually, or when market interests supersede curatorial intent.

In my own trajectory, I began as an institutional director, and that has both opened doors and closed some. It gave me a broad understanding of systems—funding, governance, human resources—but it also meant that I wasn't often seen as someone who could take on a chief curator role. And that was difficult, because I have always been drawn to the depth and challenge of curating. There were moments when I longed to set aside the administrative weight and immerse myself fully in curatorial work.

That said, working across different parts of the ecosystem—from institutions to private collections to art fairs—has given me a valuable perspective on how power and influence circulate in today's art world. There's a responsibility that comes with occupying these multiple roles: to maintain critical integrity, to resist flattening the discourse, and to center artists' voices even within commercially inflected spaces. It's not always easy, but it's essential.

GM: With all the limitations formulated by the director ...

AM: Yes—and having served as a director myself, I've come to appreciate the weight of those limitations. Understanding how budgets work, how institutions function structurally, and what's at stake when those systems are strained has made me a more grounded and empathetic curator.

Often, our brilliant curatorial colleagues haven't had to manage institutional budgets, staff, or governance structures—so when they step into directorial roles without that preparation, it can be overwhelming. Curating and directing are fundamentally different jobs. One is primarily about intellectual and artistic vision, the other about organizational leadership, diplomacy, and financial stewardship.

I've seen this challenge arise repeatedly: curators with extraordinary conceptual clarity are appointed as directors and find themselves at odds with the day-to-day responsibilities—HR, development, board management. It's not a matter of competence but of preparation. Directorship requires a distinct toolkit.

In my case, being aware of institutional constraints allowed me to work creatively within them. If I accepted a project with a limited budget, I didn't overextend—it's not just about ambition; it's about sustainability. Knowing the repercussions of overspending makes you more thoughtful in your planning and more respectful of your team's labor.

I would also add that the context matters enormously. In the U.S., being a director comes with particular constraints: you are deeply anchored to your local community, your board, your funders. You don't have the same mobility or intellectual freedom that curators do. In Europe, by contrast, there is often more space to operate beyond your immediate institutional or geographic boundaries. That distinction fundamentally shapes how leadership in the arts is lived and enacted.

GM: This is why directors stay much longer in the U.S.

AM: Yes, exactly. Building the kinds of relationships required to lead a U.S. institution takes time—and it's deeply tied to the local context. You're expected to be present, to cultivate trust with your board, donors, civic leaders, and local audiences. That embeddedness can be incredibly rewarding, but it also makes mobility more difficult. It creates a kind of institutional inertia—directors stay longer not only because of personal investment, but because their departure would risk destabilizing that carefully built ecosystem.

GM: Let's talk about the role of criticism. Do you think there's less interest in criticism or art texts among the public? Is that partly the responsibility of curators and critics—have we lost the audience through the kind of language we use?

AM: I think the real loss is that we have fewer truly rigorous, independent voices in art criticism today. The shrinking of editorial platforms, the precarity of cultural journalism, and the merging of critique with marketing have all contributed to a vacuum. And while there are still incredibly thoughtful writers and thinkers out there, the space they once occupied—where criticism helped shape discourse and challenge institutions—has been diminished.

Of course, part of the issue is also accessibility. There's a tendency in the art world toward overly coded language—writing that becomes more about signaling insider knowledge than communicating ideas. While I absolutely believe in intellectual rigor, I don't believe complexity has to come at the expense of clarity. We can speak precisely and expansively without being exclusionary. That's our responsibility—not to simplify content, but to create bridges between thought and audience.

There's also a kind of elitism that still persists—where value is often measured by proximity to certain institutions, or by having attended particular programs like Bard, Goldsmiths, or others. And while those spaces can be incredibly formative, they aren't the only path to knowledge or critical engagement. There are many forms of intelligence and insight that come from outside formal academic structures—from lived experience, from cross-disciplinary work, from community-rooted practices.

Criticism, when done well, deepens our relationship to art—it asks questions, offers context, and proposes meaning. But for it to thrive again, we need to widen the field: support writers, diversify platforms, and most importantly, speak in a way that invites people in, rather than keeps them out.

GM: Apropos of learning, was there a particular director or curator you considered a personal hero—someone you saw as a great example of how to do the job well?

AM: Yes—Richard Armstrong was someone I deeply admired, and at one point I even tried quite hard to work with him. What impressed me wasn't just his curatorial eye or institutional leadership, but the way he moved through the field with a sense of grace and steadiness, especially in moments of institutional or cultural tension.

He had the rare ability to balance a strong intellectual commitment with an openness to change. He understood that leadership was not only about shaping programming, but about navigating complex ecosystems—boards, publics, artists, funders—and doing so without losing sight of the art itself.

Watching his trajectory over the years gave me an early model of how one could evolve within the art world while remaining grounded. He wasn't performative; he led with quiet confidence, and he built institutions that reflected both ambition and care. That combination left a lasting impression on me.

In this field, you learn just as much from observing integrity as you do from brilliance. And Richard Armstrong, for me, embodied both.

GM: He was Director of the Guggenheim, wasn't he?

AM: Yes, but before that, Richard Armstrong was Director at the Carnegie Museum of Art in Pittsburgh, and what always struck me was how consistent and generous he was across both contexts. I never saw him behave differently in Pittsburgh than I did in New York. There was never a trace of arrogance or entitlement that sometimes accompanies success. That mattered to me.

There's often a misplaced hierarchy in the art world where institutions in so-called "second cities" are seen as less relevant. Coming from a background shaped by both the U.S. and Europe, I find that perspective troubling. In Europe, there's a broader understanding that cultural production doesn't need to be centralized—Kunsthalles in smaller cities carry as much weight and intellectual seriousness as those in the capitals. That's something I continue to value deeply.

I've also long admired Michael Govan—not only for his institutional vision at LACMA, but for his generosity. Despite leading one of the most prominent museums in the U.S., he has always been accessible, open, and willing to share knowledge. He embodies what I consider a true leader: someone who holds institutional authority without becoming remote. His thinking about what a museum should be—how it should serve a community while staying globally relevant—has shaped my own views on institutional responsibility.

And if we're speaking of figures whose influence was controversial but forward-thinking, I have to mention Thomas Krens. He received considerable criticism for his international expansion strategies at the Guggenheim, but looking back, I think he was simply ahead of his time. Today, institutions like the Pompidou and the Louvre are pursuing similar global models. Krens had a bold vision, and he also had an exceptional eye for talent—he first hired figures like Govan and Max Hollein, who've gone on to define contemporary museum leadership.

Among curators (although she too is a director), Susanne Pfeffer is someone I hold in very high regard. Her exhibitions are rigorous, politically sharp, and conceptually clear. She brings urgency to the institutions she leads, and she does it with an unwavering commitment to the artists she works with. That kind of integrity is rare, and deeply inspiring.

GM: What will be the main challenges for a curator in the future, in your opinion? Will curatorial work change?

AM: Absolutely. Curatorial work is already changing, and I think it will continue to evolve in response to external pressures—economic, political, and social. We're likely to see a more distinct divide between exhibitions that aim to engage critically with the urgent issues shaping contemporary life, and those that seek to offer escapism—pure visual pleasure, entertainment—because frankly, life is becoming increasingly difficult for many people.

The global condition is precarious, and we're seeing that reflected not only in the art but in how institutions position themselves. In this climate, I think one of our biggest responsibilities as curators is to protect the space for complexity and for nuance.

Another challenge is the shifting relationship younger generations have with cultural consumption. Their perception of art and its relevance is different. If we don't invest in cultural education early—if we continue to treat art and culture as peripheral—we risk losing the public altogether. Without informed curiosity, we won't have audiences.

GM: I remember when we were young, it was very trendy to be part of the art world—going to openings, being with artists. People appreciated it. I think that motivation has faded in the younger generation.

AM: I agree, and I think that loss can be traced directly to a lack of education and access. Cultural engagement isn't intuitive; it must be nurtured. It should begin early—before university, before high school even.

And then there's the economic reality. I was marked by the years I chose to work independently. In the U.S., something as simple as going to the movies can now cost $25. That may seem trivial, but it isn't. Culture has become prohibitively expensive. When access is limited to those who can afford it, we perpetuate exclusion.

GM: So, art should be more affordable?

AM: Yes. Absolutely. Accessibility needs to be rethought—it's not only about removing barriers but also about creating entry points that feel open and inviting.

GM: Should curators also teach and be educators?

AM: Yes, I believe curators should be educators—not only in academic settings but within the exhibitions themselves. That doesn't mean diluting the work; it means making it legible, giving context, creating encounters that are both intellectually and emotionally resonant.

When I was appointed Artistic Director of viennacontemporary, I spent a lot of time rethinking the fair's structure—not just the content, but its accessibility. For example, I redesigned the floor plan so that public talks are held in the glass hall, which is visible from the street. People can walk in off the sidewalk and attend without needing a ticket.

I also made sure that the Erste exhibition was placed at the entrance in a way that allows the public to experience it for free. These may seem like small gestures, but they matter. They send a message: this is your space too.

But art is also about joy

Simon Njami
in conversation with Johanna di Blasi

JOHANNA DI BLASI: *Africa Remix—Contemporary Art of a Continent*, your exhibition at the kunst palast museum in Düsseldorf—which will travel on to London, Paris (Centre Georges Pompidou) and Tokyo—offers the most comprehensive insight into contemporary African art to date. But is it not the case that the trend is moving away from such explicit "Africa exhibitions"?

SIMON NJAMI: *Africa Remix* will be the last Africa exhibition that I do. In the past, it was about showing that something like contemporary African art exists at all. At the beginning of the nineties, people like Jan Hoet, who was traveling for his Documenta at the time, still doubted the existence of contemporary African art. Now we can look for new ways.

I originally wanted to call the Düsseldorf exhibition *Out of Africa*. The 'out' was supposed to signal that we should leave the Africa framing, but my suggestion was rejected. In Düsseldorf, we are showing the diversity and differences of Africa. As far as I know, our exhibition is the first to cover the entire continent, not just sub-Saharan Africa, but also the North. We generally talk about contemporary African art, but we know that the history of South Africa has nothing to do with Ethiopian history. Art production is also different. There is no way to write a general history of African art because there is no such thing. I would also like to point out a fundamental dichotomy of contemporaneity in Africa. Two different types of contemporary artists are currently working there. Some work in a national and local context. The others are mostly younger and work in a more global context. But that doesn't mean that they do the same as their non-African colleagues, but they listen to the same music, there are more or less the same things in their rooms, the same books. They follow certain trends, but as Africans they use and master things in a different way.

JDB: What is your intention with *Africa Remix*?

SN: I want to show that African artists are individuals above everything else. There was a time when all productions from Africa were called primitivism. The so-called art of traditional Africa, we might better say objects, was and still is partly regarded as anonymous production. Sally Prize criticized this in her book *Primitive Art in Civilized Places*. The prevailing assumption is that it is not a conscious creation, but a kind of collective or natural genesis. I want to make it clear that today (I don't deal with the old objects in my exhibitions) there are differentiated, highly individual forms of expression. People who expect to learn what African art means in general will leave the exhibition with more questions than answers. They will know what it does not mean. Everyone has their own idea of Africa. I want to deconstruct preconceived ideas of Africa. I want people to go out and say: I know nothing, I know nothing at all.

JDB: *We are all Post Exotics* is the title of a work by Fernando Alvim. It seems to me to be a kind of secret motto of *Africa Remix*. The sentence is written on a white tableau with an integrated mirror.

SN: The word exotic contains the syllable 'ex', meaning outside. When someone looks at Alvim's work, they find themselves within the framing of the work, they become an exotic object of observation. So, everyone, whether Japanese, African or European, becomes exotic at the moment of looking. This means that exoticism no longer means anything and that we are all post-exotic.

JDB: You write in your catalogue essay that "a sweet and sour comedy has been performed in the field of African art for around fifteen years". What do you mean by that?

SN: One of my most successful exhibitions was *The Other Journey - Africa and the Diaspora* at the Kunsthalle Krems in 1996. It was so successful because an Austrian critic wrote so much nonsense about it. He came expecting Africa, he then accused me of withholding something from the public because he found nothing African, only things that artists do elsewhere. He didn't go into the individual works, but wrote, for example, that Abdoulaye Konaté, an artist from Mali, probably has five wives. But he only has one. I corrected this and a polemic started, the ORF got in touch. It was all a game, of course. The result was that a bunch of people wanted to see the exhibition. That's what I call a sweet and sour comedy.

The artists I call the "usual suspects" are able to deal with the misunderstandings and expectations regarding African art today. They play with it. There are still people who think Africans know less than they actually do. People always think they know more. I find that funny and interesting. There are a lot of gaps and Africans are gradually filling them. Yinka Shonibare's works, for example, the ones that made him famous, are very ironic and very intelligent. He simply took the typical African Wax Hollandais fabrics and decorated a Victorian living room with them. Of course, the British were excited, they called it a kind of social commentary, a commentary on history, etc. Yinka said he just found it appealing to relate all the Victorian stuff he grew up with to wax. Of course, there are always people who want to fulfil what is generally seen as typically African. But not everyone who uses tins, raffia, cardboard, all these Arte povera things in their art wants to fulfil Western expectations.

JDB: *Inclusion: Exclusion*, 1996, was a pioneering exhibition in the German-speaking world when it came to the presentation of non-European art. The aim was to break with "500 years of Western hegemony". There was talk of "remapping" and even "remixing".

SN: Yes, but who decided on inclusion and exclusion? Peter Weibel came with a point of view that was already dysfunctional and that's why he had to embellish it with texts and theories. I'm not worried about that. But what worries me is when an African like Okwui uses such post-colonialist theories in his *Short Century*, a post-colonial exhibition, and an exhibition is then no longer an exhibition at all, but a demonstration. When I go to an exhibition, I want to see an exhibition, I don't want to read books or sit there for four hours to watch a video, regardless of whether it's good or bad. The less we know what we want, the more we try to fill it up with ideas.

JDB: Fifteen years ago, the current director of the museum kunst palast in Düsseldorf, Jean-Hubert Martin, officially introduced contemporary African art into the Western context with his exhibition *Les Magiciens de la Terre* at the Centre Georges Pompidou in Paris. At the time, the display was postmodern and decontextualizing: Boltanski next to African coffins. We are now in a phase in which Africans are increasingly "curating" their own culture. The Cameroonian social scientist Achille Mbembe speaks of "African modes of self-writing". How is this expressed in exhibitions?

SN: The only advantage of the new framing, regardless of what we call "African", is that we are starting from a different perspective. Historically speaking, these are new ways of writing stories. This can also be done through photography, which is very important in Africa. It is obvious that an African will not portray an African in the same way as a Japanese or a European. A Parisian will give a different image of Paris than someone who is not from Paris, but that is not to say that one perspective is more relevant than the other. African history has been written for a long period by non-Africans, the images have been produced by non-Africans. Therefore, it has been a distorted, one-sided vision.

Many hands are needed in the process of rewriting history. There are still only a handful of African curators and a handful of African authors. We have a kind of monopoly over the subject matter, which is not good. The aim cannot be to freeze Africa in a single rigid view, but to show how diverse and how contradictory it can sometimes be. Okwui Enwezor's point of view is not mine and Salah Hassan's point of view, if he has one, is not mine either, and yet we are all three Africans.

We are already at a point where European curators can no longer deal with African art as they used to, because they know that there are some people there who can look, write and debate and who have knowledge of European art and art history and therefore know both sides.

JDB: The fact that an African curated the Documenta in 2002 and that more Africans were represented than ever before has not increased interest in African art in Germany, say gallery owners.

SN: You only have to look at the list of Africans who were represented there to understand that no inspiration could come from it. They were all the "usual suspects" who didn't even need the Documenta: Kendell Geers, William Kentridge, Santu Mofokeng, Pascale Marthine Tayou, Georges Adéagbo; apart from one Nigerian whose name nobody wants to remember and who was told to photograph the houses in Lagos according to Rem Koolhaas' theories about sprawling megacities. When I spoke to him, his only concern was getting back to Lagos in time for the weekend to photograph a wedding. He wondered himself why he was in Kassel. It was a simple studio photographer.

JDB: In your essay *Introduction to African Contemporary Art*, you spoke of the field of African contemporary art as a "huge strategic absurd battlefield where everyone believes that all you need to do is be the first". In Germany, we have a situation where some outstanding collector personalities, with their preference for *art brut* in particular, still determine the image of African contemporary art to this day. Is there still this divide in Africa between self-taught and academically trained artists who had a harder time in the West?

SN: Not for me. People always try to put a label on everything. Pascale Marthine Tayou, for example, is self-taught, and undoubtedly an interesting contemporary artist. This categorization is a legacy of ethnographers. When Susan Vogel organized the 1991 exhibition *Africa Explores. 20th Century African Art* in 1991, she differentiated between airport art, self-taught art, international art and all sorts of things. That means absolutely nothing to me. If someone sells things at an Airport market, they are simply an artisan.

The problem with decontextualization and these flag bearers is that when they go somewhere, they want to find something that fits their definition of Africa. They reject what seems too close to their own, as if it were forbidden for Africans to use televisions in their art, when they deal with television on a daily basis. They say: this boy is contaminated by Europe. At *Les Magiciens de la Terre*, there were people from "Third World" countries who were told that you are artists, and they said, oh really, oh thank you. From the West, people like Christian Boltanski, Louise Bourgeois and Nam June Paik were invited, with very cutting-edge works. The exhibition then gave the impression: this is what we do in the West, and this is what the rest of us produce, although completely different trends and people had been thrown together.

In Africa, traveling and visiting studios is still a great privilege. Those who do this and buy have an easy time of it. When museums want to do something, they fall back on collectors. They then hand over their collection for free, perhaps write some text and make up something. That's why I say that Africa is a playground. People still see Africa as the dark continent where anything is possible.

I spoke to a young artist. Someone from Europe who claimed to be a curator, but whose name I had never heard, told him to change this and that in his work. This young man was willing to change his style just because this supposed curator was from Europe. There is a lot of this going on in Africa. That's why it's so important for Africa to develop its own discourses and art institutions, so that people don't follow the first person who promises them an exhibition in Europe, hang up their work in a restaurant or a café and proudly proclaim it at home: We were in Europe, we had an exhibition. That doesn't help anyone.

When the artists gradually organize themselves, they will no longer be so easily enticed. Then Africa will no longer be this empty space where anyone can come and say I've discovered this or that. At the moment, however, we are still living in the age of discovery. That is crazy. It's because Africa has no voice, because it has no museum for contemporary art, apart from a few places like South Africa of course and Nigeria, even Mali has some. That's why the only possible way for artists is to go "out of Africa".

JDB: The Nigerian curator Toma Muteba Luntumbue speaks of an "explosion of an artistic scene", a creative "shock wave" that pulsates from Egypt to South Africa. Does this correspond to your observations during your numerous trips across the continent?

SN: No. The problem is that these people don't travel enough. One of these traps is that an attitude develops where you no longer want to examine things. To say there's an explosion, 500 artists are participating in the art market, that's sixties' jargon, that's a dream. I see normal growth. At my seminars in Africa, I meet young people who ask me, Mr. Njami, what is contemporary art? As if it were a specific genre of art and as if there were a recipe for it. However, these questions that young people are asking were not asked to this extent in the past. What is happening today is not very important, but these questions give an idea of what it could look like tomorrow.

Today there is no explosion, no structures, there is nothing. Some young people are trying to gain experience, they are joining forces, some are opening galleries. There is no state support, everyone is on their own. African artists don't play a role in the global circus. If you look at the global market, you only see a handful of Africans. In Zaire, there are a lot of people selling things to Belgian tourists, but it would be silly to call that an international activity. If I go to Frankfurt or Basel, how many Africans do I see there? If they were global players, you would see African galleries. Or if you look at how many big exhibitions of contemporary African art there are in France: None. Not in Germany either, apart from T*he Short Century*, which was not a German product but came from Enwezor. Chris Ofili was in Venice, but he says I'm British, I'm not African. There was African art in a sponsored pavilion at the Biennale, but not in the curated program. I saw the Chinese, but the Africans were still in their ghetto. It takes time and we shouldn't lie to ourselves.

JDB: Exhibitions are usually dominated by Anglophone Africa. Is it easier for an Anglophone to succeed?

SN: I wouldn't say so. The French invest a lot of money in African culture. There has also been some movement in the theoretical field. You hear more people talking about art in Francophone Africa than in the Anglophone part. However, there are fewer concrete actions. In the Anglophone part, things are tackled more resolutely, people are more aggressive in a positive way. They are active, knocking on doors and trying to make the leap. London gives Black artists a lot of space. In France, you can have the best reviews in the world, and they won't give you an exhibition in any institution. In London, on the other hand, there is a strong Black trend. There are many

Black organizations there. At one point, ten percent of the public cultural budget was even allocated to initiatives of 'Otherness', 'Cross Culture', etc. Jamaicans and Africans live in London, and they all have British passports. Chris Ofili even represented Great Britain at the last Venice Biennale. He has Nigerian roots. The British side seems more efficient. I think Francophone Africa was colonized in a different way, there was all this fraternity stuff, whereas the British were clearer. They colonized and didn't even pretend that there was any kind of symmetry. That probably left a little more energy for people who didn't expect anything to be done for them in the first place.

JDB: You paint a romantic picture of the African artist: "The African artist does not speak. He works, grasps and invents a cosmogony, an order of the new world. With computers, video monitors, spotlights, but always with his soul." What is his silence all about?

SN: In Africa, art still has a lot to do with craftsmanship, with making something. Which is not to say that no conceptual art is made there. But less energy is wasted on showing how conceptual you are or are not. When you do an interview with artists, they let you talk, sometimes with a smile on their face if they disagree. I don't talk to them about art, we have drinks, we talk about life, I get a feel for the person, and every now and then they tell me something about their art.

JDB: How would you describe the emergence of African modernism?

SN: As far as we are talking about art, it is a fixed period in art history, cubism and so on. In terms of the world, it is the present moment. What we call modernism, this global modernism, came to Africa with colonization, the rules of the Europeans came with the fact that overnight people were ordered to use canvases even if they felt no need to.

During the thirties, people like Aimé Césaire and Léopold Sédar Senghor tried to define and create an African aesthetic. That was the Négritude. I think that was the beginning of African modernism. Alioune Diop was also influential. He created the magazine *Présence africaine*. These people prepared the ground for the decolonization phase of the early sixties. They wanted to prove and assert their Africanness. They looked back because they had the feeling that their culture was being denied. They wanted it back. They pigeonholed themselves, said "I'm black and I'm proud", I'm authentic. Négritude was much more of a theoretical movement than a concrete one. It helped people to liberate their thinking. Of course, conflicts were inevitable. When Senghor organized his *Premier Festival*

Mondial des Arts Negres in Dakar in 1966, Iba Ndiaye was asked if he would like to curate the art section. At a certain point, he resigned himself because he said, "I'm not an African artist, I'm an artist." It wasn't enough for him to define himself solely through his Africanness. The generation I call contemporary, people between 20 and 40, the Rap Generation, no longer has to fight the battles that were fought for them. They don't have to fight for decolonization because they were more or less born in free countries. They have other battles to fight. People today are stronger in some ways, weaker in others. I like the way they are weaker and question themselves. In the past, artists had to make themselves socially useful. Those who painted clouds seemed superfluous. Today, questions of identity are at the forefront. The desire for contemporaneity is much more of an existentialist quest than a global one, for example, to liberate a continent, to liberate the world. We turn to art while locked in our studios. We stand in front of a canvas or some other material and ask ourselves what in God's name we should do with it, here and now. And of course, when people come from Zimbabwe, they cannot forget what is happening in Zimbabwe today; when they come from South Africa, they cannot forget that apartheid prevailed there and, to a certain extent, still prevails; when they come from Egypt, they cannot forget that images were forbidden there, that figuration was forbidden.

JDB: What importance do you attach to the aesthetics of "scattering", of visual excess?

SN: It's only one aspect of African aesthetics. When I put Tayou on the cover of *Revue Noire*, there was a debate in Cameroon. The older artists, who had studied at Beaux-Arts, said: "Hello Mr. Njami, we respect you, but we have to ask—how can you call this art?" I gave them my answer and then said: "The young man is here; you can ask him yourselves." Tayou told them that he was no longer interested in canvas and had decided to work with the things surrounding him in everyday life. The older artists were horrified. For them, art was painting on canvas or sculpture—and they were all Africans.

JDB: Installation art as a form that brings its own context with it seems to be deeply rooted in Africa?

SN: Every initiation moment was an installation moment. In a Voodoo ceremony, everything revolves around installation. You have to do "this here, that there", you have to work with the space, there are rules. As long as there were no churches in Africa, it was part of everyday life to place things according to a certain order—a higher order. The people who did this were seers, wise people. I also see artists as seers; they see a little more than we do—or at least, they should. An artist can immerse themselves in various spheres. In Africa, these spheres are very complex, and they're connected to an ancient way of handling things. Today, it's important to put things into their real perspectives.

JDB: The newest cultural export from Africa seems to be horror videos from Ghana and Nigeria. They're being exhibited in museums alongside contemporary African art and traditional mask art.

SN: You just have to look at who's behind it. In Bayreuth, it's Tobias Wendl, an anthropologist and ethnographer. He's not interested in art, but in civilization. When he organizes an exhibition, it's about showing how certain people live, what films they watch, what masks they use. I have no problem with that—as long as it's clearly labelled as a cultural or anthropological show. Then we know what we're dealing with.

I love those horror videos—they're wonderfully cheap, they're kitsch. But I would show them in a different context—for example, at a horror film festival with movies from Bangkok, Cairo, and Ghana. These films are often made in just a week and sell very well. They're funny because they're so badly made, with props falling over. If there are vampires, you can see their plastic teeth. These videos are for entertainment—that's their charm.

JDB: It seems that in the West, art is dissolving into applied sociology, political science, and urban studies—often as a result of engaging with postcolonial issues. How do you see that?

SN: Pierre Restany, the French art critic, said in 1969 that art is dead if it loses its movement, its purpose, and its connection to people. I think it *has* died in Europe. We›re currently in a phase of revival, in a transitional stage where we're trying to redefine what art even is. I think the problem in Europe is that the pendulum has swung too far toward theoretical engagement with art. There's more art discourse than art itself. We have much more of the *idea* of art than art. We're in a time where everything's spinning like a carousel. We need to be on the lookout for something new.

JDB: Why is the term 'diaspora' experiencing a renaissance in Black culture? In Germany, we mostly associate it with the dispersion of the Jewish people.

SN: By its meaning, 'diaspora' refers to dispersion—the scattering of people. In my view, the term is often misused. When someone calls me "diasporic", I always correct them. I'm not a diaspora African; I'm African. I have both Cameroonian and Swiss citizenship. When I talk about the diaspora, I mean African Americans, Cubans, Brazilians—not someone like Tayou, just because he lives in Brussels. He's an immigrant.

JDB: "We must kill the Western model", said Alpha Oumar Konaré, President of Mali, in 1991 at a conference. Do you agree, and if so, what alternative do you see?

SN: Yes. In the field of art, we must remember that "fine art", as it exists, is a Western invention. The mechanisms of art, its vocabulary, are Western. The essence of art is, of course, universal. In Africa, too, we have caves with million-year-old paintings. But the codification of art is European, and we live under those rules. I want to revise those codifications, give them a new meaning.

If you look at traditional masquerades, you see that a mask is meant to dance. So, what does it mean to put a mask in a display case? It's dead. It's an object—but an object that means nothing. Architecture, painting, and sculpture aren't African cultural concepts. Materials were used for specific purposes as part of a holistic vision. In masquerades, music, textiles, sculpture, painting—everything is used. That's why in *Africa Remix*, I also integrate music, literature, design, and film. It's about showing that there is no separation or specialization. In Europe, people are starting to rediscover the need to bring things together. In Africa, that's always been the case.

JDB: What is your *African Exile Museum* about, and what does "post-post-colonial occupation of Europe" mean in that context? Do you believe the approaches of Cultural and Postcolonial Studies are already outdated?

SN: People in Postcolonial Studies are so serious, so boring—they don't have any fun. But art is also about joy. *Race, class, gender*—who still cares about that? While teaching at UCSD (University of California, San Diego), I see people who gained academic footing thanks to these theories but now ignore the fact that the world has moved on. Today, there are no more Eurocentric exhibitions to fight against. Of course, Indians and Chinese now participate in the international art scene.

With the *African Exile Museum*, we want to respond to the process of global mixing. For us, European history is also African history. Europe, in a sense, belongs to Africa—because of the colonial past, but also because many Africans now live in Europe. That's why the right move for us is to "occupy" European territories. The *African Exile Museum* is a process in which we temporarily occupy European museums, art halls, and cultural centres—and dictate the rules to the hosts. Of course, they're friends; we discuss things. The idea is simply to shift perspectives.

JDB: Hybridization and "cultural jamming" were buzzwords in the 1990s. Now, the dividing lines between cultures are again more emphasized. The vision of a "world culture" seems to have faded. How do you see this shift, especially in relation to Africa?

SN: In Africa, these problems aren't really perceived, because people live not in a theoretical space, but in a real one. There are, for example, Muslims who drink whiskey but still go to the mosque. It may sound cliché, but in Africa, the human being still counts. In Europe, there's the stock market. In Africa, barter trade still exists. Go to Lagos with a check and see who will take it.

The biggest challenge Africa faces is the re-evaluation of history. You see the same issue in ex-Yugoslavia or ex-Czechoslovakia. The borders were arbitrarily drawn at the Berlin Africa Conference in 1884, and we must figure out how to deal with that. In general, for Africa and the whole Third World, we're talking about hybrid spaces—not in the abstract sense of postcolonial theorists, but in very concrete terms. Everything is in motion, everything is changing.

If I were to return to Paris in 200 years, I could find my way around easily. If I return to Cairo after two years, everything has changed—the street signs, the buildings. These places are in a self-perpetuating state of transformation. Most of these countries are only 40 years old. They are still experimenting. There are no frozen spaces like in Europe, no old ideas. France never questions itself—not even when Jean-Marie Le Pen makes it to the second round of the presidential elections. People just say, "We had the revolution; we don't need to try anymore. It's enough to say, 'We are French.'" Third World countries can't afford arrogance—no one would listen to them. They have no certainties.

And we were curious. It's not a coincidence that curare is so close to the word curious. I think curiosity is one of the keys. Endless curiosity is key to this profession.

Hans Ulrich Obrist
in conversation with Gerald A. Matt

GERALD A. MATT: What is a curator? Can you define your understanding and practice as a curator?

HANS ULRICH OBRIST: The poet and artist Etel Adnan told me some years ago that the world needs togetherness. This is really interesting in relation to curation, because of this idea of togetherness, of bringing things together, making junctions, as G. J. Ballard once told me. I have often thought the curator is also a junction-maker, somebody who produces junctions, and of course who brings together objects and takes care of art. The Latin word curare, of which curate is derived from, means 'to take care of'. That continues to play an important role. And it is about making junctions between objects. We are in a time when we are not only dealing with or working with objects. We are also working with non-objects, quasi-objects, and hyper-objects, which Lucy Lippard pointed to already in the sixties, that there is a dematerialization of art. Lippard talked about non-objects in that sense. Then Michel Serres coined the notion of the quasi-object, an object, which only gains meaning if we interact with it directly or indirectly. That would also be the whole spectrum of participatory art. Timothy Morton coined the notion of hyper-objects, the weather being an example of complex systems. In a world which is so interdependent, we also need to take that into account. I stick to Ballard's notion of the curator as a junction-maker, making junctions between objects, quasi-objects, non-objects, hyper-objects, and, of course, junctions between people. I bring people together. That is also what our marathons do at the Serpentine, make junctions between people. It is certainly an important part of my work.

GM: When did you know you wanted to be a curator? How did it start?

HUO: That is an interesting question. I think it was a gradual process. I somehow started to be very passionate about art but at a certain moment I realized it was not only about art history but also about today. I think the true epiphany happened when I was a teenager. I visited the studio of Peter Fischli and David Weiss, these extraordinary Swiss artists. They were working on Der Lauf der Dinge (1987), this chain reaction film. And I think for me as a seventeen-year-old being in their studio and seeing the magic of this work in process, that was the moment when it became clear that I wanted to work with artists. It wasn't necessarily clear how, but I somehow wanted to organize exhibitions. At that time the notion of the curator wasn't so widely used. Today the word curator is used everywhere outside the art world as well. Food stands, flower shops, concept stores, and a coffee shop in London; all are curated. The use of this word is amazingly widespread, but back then it wasn't used that much, it was more the idea of the Ausstellungsmacher, an exhibition maker like Harald Szeemann who embodied this notion. When I met Fischli and Weiss and other great artists, I knew that I wanted to make exhibitions. Only later did I realize that the field was much wider, that it was not only about exhibitions. There are a lot of other things curating includes.

GM: How can curating be relevant to the challenges we face today? And in which way does it differ from the time of curators like Harald Szeemann thirty years ago?

HUO: Certain things continue, and other things change. The idea that the curator works with emerging artists and supports practices at the beginning continues to be relevant. Shortly after meeting Fischli / Weiss, I met Rosemarie Trockel. Trockel told me that it is important to look into practices of previous generations, which might have been overlooked. At that time Louise Bourgeois was becoming well known. Trockel said, one should actually go from city to city and see if there are other extraordinary artists, especially female artists, who have been overlooked. So, I went by train from Cologne to Vienna. I was seventeen when I arrived in Vienna, and I was keen to meet artists there, the art scene of that time. I met Erwin Wurm, and at Rima I also met Alois Mosbacher, Thomas Stimm, Hubert Schmalix, Brigitte Kowanz. I also asked them about important overseen artists. They all told me to go and see Maria Lassnig, who at that time wasn't well known outside Austria. And that is how the story began. I think that it is relevant to enable beginnings. But also, as Eric Hobsbawm said, to protest against forgetting. We live in an age where we have more and more information, but it doesn't necessarily mean that we have more memories. There are still artists, extraordinary artists, all over the world, who have been overlooked and haven't had the visibility they deserve.

That is still relevant to me. But there are also big changes. For example, at the Serpentine we introduced new departments in order to answer new artistic, cultural, social and political challenges. We think that the revolutionary changes in technology have an enormous transformative impact on art and on society. Museums need to have a tech department. Together with Ben Vickers, we built a whole technology department at the Serpentine, where we work with AI, VR, AR and where we develop video games. Today, we work with five digital curators. We have also created a new department for ecology. We were the first institution to employ a curator of ecology, *Lucia Pietroiusti* to address the climate emergency. We launch projects concerned with the environment and invite artists to do environmental campaigns. Then we have introduced a civic department where we go with art into the city.

It is important to keep in mind that doors prevent a lot of people from coming to see exhibitions. My parents once said, museums are not really for people. That is why I think art should not be hidden behind doors in museums, but we also urgently need to take art to the people. That means not only thinking about public art, but also about its civic notions. So, we created a civic project of Radio Ballads, with Sonia Boyce and many different artists that Amal Khalaf curated. It brings art into different communities in London, we worked on a big project with Barking Dagenham for example. We also commission architectural pavilions every year at the Serpentine. They are located in the park, and they have no doors. People can just walk in and encounter art and artistic ideas by chance. These are a couple of aspects where I feel we need to address relevance and maybe go from relevance to urgency.

GM: I remember when you came to gallery Krinzinger in Vienna. And what I noticed when talking to you was that you were really curious.

HUO: That's really interesting because I totally remember that we met on that first trip. You worked for Krinzinger and we were very young, I was 17 and you were probably 18 or something like that. And we were curious. It's not a coincidence that curare is so close to the word curious. I think curiosity is one of the keys. Endless curiosity is key to this profession.

GM: You were talking about relevance, and about communication with the public, about being open, even going into the city. What is the influence of identity politics? How does it influence a curator's work and communication with the public today?

HUO: I think the culture of identity politics is part of the theory and practice of curating. It is a way to engage people in thinking about different ways of being and to open their minds beyond the binary. The need for inclusion and diversity within all forms of work is absolutely urgent. But continuing with what Etel Adnan told me: the world needs togetherness and not separation, love not suspicion, a common future not isolation.

The consideration of identity politics in my work goes beyond its politics. It is about all those interesting people –artists, writers, thinkers—and my fascination with their work and ideas. I keep learning from people every day by listening.

It changes the way of thinking. I think listening is very important. That is another thing Adnan told me: that in our time we need to learn to listen again.

GM: You said, it is all about opening your mind. But can identity politics also close your mind? Could it create a kind of censorship attitude? But let's talk about this maybe later. I would like to continue with the question: How do you see the changing relations between curators, artists, collectors, galleries, museums and critics? What has changed here in the last years? Was there a shift of power?

HUO: How do we change?

GM: I thought for example of the role of collectors. They now open their own museums and engage curators. They have gained significant power in defining what art is and what the value and prices of art are.

HUO: That has happened over the years since the eighties. But what happened over the last five, ten years was the rise and—even more the emergence—of these private institutions. Initially they were more like collectors' museums. Since the eighties collectors have increasingly decided to open their own museums, to showcase, to offer a window for their collection. More recently, the idea emerged that those private museums function as laboratories, as places of experiment, as places of production. Many of these organizations are actually in Europe, not in the United States. The density, particularly in France and Italy, of these private foundations, makes these institutions somehow engines of change, of experiments, with residences and production possibilities. LUMA is such an example. I have been involved as an advisor with LUMA. It is a kind of ecological project. It has residencies and goes alongside production and a lot of experiments. Also, archives play an increasing role. In collaboration with LUMA, we have this archive project and LUMA Arles is also where my archive is located. It used to be in Berlin, now it is in Arles. And we look at a different aspect every year. I have many conversations with artists which have been recorded—about 4000 hours. Every year, we focus on another artist and make exhibitions of the archives. So, last year it was Etel Adnan, which is still ongoing, and later this year we look at Agnès Varda, with whom I worked very closely.

The year before it was Édouard Glissant, who was my mentor. And that is actually in relation to your previous questions about identity. The philosopher and thinker Glissant's notions of identity are amazing toolboxes.

Adnan says, we need to avoid the danger that identity becomes a prison. And I think Glissant's work is so relevant to all these thoughts, because he actually wanted to build his own institution, the All-World Institute, where all the world's cultures could be in exchange with each other. I think a real key to the identity question you raised earlier is the fact that we live in a world of globalization. When we met in the eighties, globalization was already en route and it has increased ever since. And that leads to a lot of pitfalls. There is the homogenizing force of globalization. It leads to an environmental disaster with a loss of species and mass extinction, but also to a loss of a lot of cultural phenomena. Languages disappear faster than ever before, for example. As does handwriting and calligraphy. That is why I devoted my Instagram to handwriting: it celebrates handwriting and calligraphy. So, it's not only species—not only our own species and many different species—that are in danger, but it's also cultural phenomena. The downside of globalization is homogenized globalization, which we have to resist. Glissant realized early on that there will be a counter-reaction to these homogenizing forces of globalization and that there will be new localisms and new nationalisms, which we can observe everywhere—in Europe and all continents. As Bernard Stiegler said, how can we be local without falling into the trap of becoming localist? Again, in these discussions Glissant is crucial. We made the first archive exhibition about him last year, also to make these interviews accessible.

But to come back to your question about private organizations. There are many in Europe right now. Just look at the transformation of Paris. Paris has all this energy right now and is extremely vivid. A key aspect of this are those private institutions and initiatives like Lafayette Anticipations, which do all these projects with young artists in a Rem Koolhaas building. There's the Fondation Cartier with its interdisciplinary program—shows on mathematics, shows on nature and trees, etcetera. They are now expanding with Jean Nouvel into a very big building. Another example is the Bourse du Commerce. Emma Lavigne, one of our dear colleagues and a brilliant curator, is now running the place with Caroline Bourgeois. And, of course, the Fondation Louis Vuitton with Suzanne Pagé as its director, with whom I worked when she was at the Musée d'Art Moderne for many, many years.

In Italy, you have a similar situation. There is this new foundation for contemporary art and Etruscan art—Fondazione Rovati. The Fondazione Prada, or the migrating Fondazione Trussardi. More and more foundations are opening. It is no longer just collectors' museums, but museums where curatorial experiments can happen.

GM: You see this development towards more private initiatives, more private collections as a positive one?

HUO: I see it very positively that there are laboratories and these new experimental organizations out there, which go beyond mere collections of objects. At the same time, of course, I'm concerned about the reduced funds for public institutions. I don't think that we can just hand over culture to the private sector. It is a very unfortunate tendency that governments don't prioritise culture more. Art is the highest form of hope as we live in turbulent times. Society needs art more than ever before.

Korea shows how important it can be for a government to back culture and to understand how relevant culture is. Before the financial crisis in 2008 began, the Korean government decided to fully court culture. And look at what is happening today –Korean cinema, Miky Lee's production, all these TV series and the visual art context, all of that exists because Korea understood that it is worthwhile to make major governmental investments in art. It is important that we make politicians understand how fundamentally important these institutions are for society, particularly post-COVID.

GM: Hans Ulrich, let me go back to your beginnings. Was there a personal hero, a curator whom you deeply admired?

HUO: Yes, there have always been. I mean, the hero is always a complex notion. I would say it is very rhizomatic. There isn't this one person from whom I would have learned everything. It was like a very complex kind of web of inspirations and influences. The biggest influence was the philosopher Édouard Glissant. He changed my thinking radically. That is also why I bring him into this identity question. Then I would address artists—Gerhard Richter from whom I learned so much. And as I mentioned Fischli/Weiss, Rosemarie Trockel, Alighiero Boetti, also artists like Christian Boltanski, Annette Messager, and more recently Arthur Jafa. We worked very closely with Arthur Jafa on his first museum show four or five years ago. And that was a transformative experience in every single way.

In terms of curators– professional curators or curating as a profession—I would say Lucy Lippard has been a great influence because in a way I've always done a lot of projects which have to do with dissemination, which have to do with portable exhibitions, exhibitions which can go to the people like Do It! or Take Me (I'm Yours). And these exhibitions were very deeply inspired by the great Lucy Lippard who, in the 60s, did an exhibition where all artists wrote instructions on postcards and then she did it in several cities, interpreting these instructions. That was a huge inspiration.

I had two mentors, from whom I really learned on the job how to make exhibitions and how also to bring the past, the present and the future together.

And that is Suzanne Pagé, who was at the Musée d'Art Moderne da la Ville de Paris for many, many years and who hired me in 1992. That was my first museum job. She always brought together sort of historic shows and contemporary shows and showed me that the future is invented with fragments from the past, that you cannot separate that. It's a very holistic process to run a museum. And she did this throughout the museum, where contemporary artists reacted to the collection. On a practical level, I learned so much from her.

And then, the second mentor was Kasper König whom I also met at the very beginning of my trajectory. And then he invited me to do a book about Der öffentliche Blick. I had never done a book before, so I learned how to do a book. And he knew about my very extensive research, which I had documented, and thousands of studio visits. And that is why the Wiener Festwochen invited him in 1993. At that time, I also saw you regularly, because I suddenly came to Vienna every second week.

GM: I remember it.

HUO: I went from a ten-square-meter kitchen to thousands of square meters of the Museumsquartier. At that time, it was still a chantier, a construction site. There was no mumok, there was no Leopoldmuseum. And we did this very big painting show there in Krischanitz's Kunsthallle, Der zerbrochene Spiegel. For me that was another milestone of experience, because within six months I learned how to do a large-scale exhibition, how to install it. And it was of course a celebration of Maria Lassnig as a pioneer.

GM: You've already answered some central questions I was going to ask you: Was there a show, which you consider to be a milestone for your current curatorial thoughts and practice?

HUO: That would have been shows from others that I have seen. Harald Szeemann's Hang zum Gesamtkunstwerk was the most important exhibition because I have always loved utopias, unrealized projects and dreams—and the idea of the Gesamtkunstwerk, which is of course a complex notion because it often leads to the late Wagner with the problematic notion of a total work of art overpowering the viewer.

GM: I remember this exhibition, which was also one of the most important exhibitions for my curatorial genesis—Wagner, D'Annunzio, Schnitters, Beuys, etcetera.

HUO: I think Szeemann's show gave us a whole other take on the Gesamtkunstwerk with Joseph Beuys and the whole environmental dimensions of Beuys, Goethe, Goetheanum, Rudolf Steiner. I saw this exhibition many, many times and I was very, very inspired by that show. It is interesting that these shows, which are also sometimes problematic, are not just shows one adores, but shows which really make you think. There was also Magiciens de la terre. I went to the opening of that show in 1989; I was 20. Of course, this was a very problematic show because it was still based on curators who somehow gathered the arts from all continents. But it was the first time in Europe we could for example see the avantgarde of China. I remember seeing Huang Yong Ping with his washing machine. I met Frédéric Bruly Bouabré at the opening of the show, the amazing visionary artist from Côte d'Ivoire who made this system of alphabet. Magiciens de la terre was one of the most important experiences in my life. You could see how incredibly Western centric big parts of European museums still are and too inert to cross that frame. At the same time, you could feel how problematic it is that one presents artists from all continents while the curators are still all European.

Soon after that in the '90s, a few years after, I got a phone call from the Secession, the space longest run by artists. Vienna has been really important in my trajectory as a curator because two of my early exhibitions took place in Vienna: Der zerbrochene Spiegel with Kasper König, which were my Lehr- und Wanderjahre, and Cities on the Move at the Secession. When the Secession asked me to curate the first anniversary show for them—I think Erwin Wurm was on the board at the time—I immediately thought there was this amazing scene emerging in Asia and we could do an Asian show. But I thought, I shouldn't copy Magiciens de la terre and just go as a Western curator to Asia and bring "my art" back. Then I rang Hou Hanru and asked him to co-curate the show with me. In the end, it was not just the Western gaze on Asia, it was a collaboration with the great Chinese curator Hou Hanru. We traveled together to many, many different cities in Asia and did this exhibition, which then went on a world tour. It evolved like a city. That is another aspect of exhibitions. If they tour, they become really famous like Cities on the Move. Other shows don't tour but are still very important. Sometimes people ask me which of my shows I'm most fond of.

GM: This would be my next question.

HUO: Of course Cities on the Move is a part of that. But I would also say Laboratorium. It was a really crucial exhibition that I did with Barbara Vanderlinden. It tried to go beyond this division between science on the one hand, and humanities and arts on the other. We invited practitioners from various fields to establish workplaces and workshops. I am always interested in laboratories and experiments. Zaha Hadid once told me there should be no end to experimentation. We also did an exhibition just on that theme. The laboratory studios were located in the city of Antwerp. So, we had the Fotografie Museum as the starting point—a kind of relay station—where people could pick up a bicycle, like in Münster, and then travel across the city to visit scientific and artistic labs. Panamarenko was still alive. His studio was a lab, and it started with a discussion, with questions. What is the meaning of 'lab'? What is the meaning of 'experiment'? When do experiments become public? When does the result of an experiment reach a public consensus? What happens inside the lab of a scientist? And inside the studio of an artist? These were all kinds of questions we asked ourselves. We danced with Xavier Le Roy. We had the Laboratoire Agit'Art from Dakar, the extraordinary artist collective inside an artistic lab. We also had Peter Galison and Isabelle Stengers, history of science labs, and Bruno Latour. He has just passed away. It was his curatorial debut. We had to convince him, as he initially said: "I am not a curator." I said: "Bruno, you have to try and be open." And then he did the tabletop experiments where he restaged experiments. He enjoyed it so much that he went on to curate three big shows with Peter Weibel in ZKM. It was a "theater of proof", a series of demonstrations where experiments were staged and restaged.

Bruno Latour gave the audience a better grasp of what to expect from scientific experiments, as he told me at our first meeting.

But maybe my absolute favorite is Do It! It isa long-term project and goes back to the beginning when you asked me what changed. We face very big changes now. Event culture is no longer sustainable. It is environmentally unsustainable. We need to think more about what Fernand Braudel called La Longue Durée. We need to think more about long-durational ways of working. And it is not a coincidence that over the last couple of years artists have become more and more interested in gardens. Precious Okoyomon is doing gardens rather than doing exhibitions, for example in Venice and in Aspen. Alexandra Daisy Ginsberg wanted to do an AI garden for pollinators at Serpentine instead of doing an artwork in the gallery, not for humans, but for pollinators. It is not only about gardens as a reality, but also as a metaphor. Artists are also starting farms. Yinka Shonibare started a residency on a farm. Organic projects which can evolve over time like living organisms are actually interesting.

Gianfranco Baruchello just passed away in his late nineties. He started his Agricola, his agricultural experiments in the seventies, making that link already. I think this idea of longer-durational formats is interesting and Do It! is such a project. It started exactly 30 years ago, but it never stopped. And there have been so far about 175 iterations. It is also fully sustainable because there is never any transport involved and the artists are locally adding instructions. We always do local research. It began out of a conversation with Christian Boltanski and Bertrand Lavier about instruction art and recipes. We discussed Fluxus, spoke about Alison Knowles, Yoko Ono, George Brecht, conceptual art of course, Sol LeWitt, Lawrence Weiner. The whole Fluxus movement was about instructions and conceptual art. And we basically started to write a sort of Western history of instruction art, from Duchamp to Moholy-Nagy and so on. We obviously realized that there are instruction art histories on all continents.

In Brazil, it played a big role with Tropicália. We wanted to do a vessel with this exhibition, a kind of device, a vehicle, which could learn wherever it goes. Having happened in 170 something places, the show has each time sucked up and learned from the local context and introduced these local artists into a more global context. For me, Do It! is really the direct application of Glissant's theory of mondialité. We must resist the homogenized forces of globalization, think about sustainable models, but at the same time we must not fall into localisms, into nationalisms, which reject the global dialogue. And Do It! is a truly global project, but it is also a truly local project. It addresses what is still at present and tries to be local without being localist.

There is a new book from the Shenzhen Architecture Biennale, where they invited 50 Chinese architects to do instructions of what you can do at home. Do It! also became completely meaningful during the lockdowns because people could do their instruction pieces at home. You can do the Wish Tree of Yoko Ono. Or everybody who has a broom, a Besen, in the cupboard can actually do their own Franz West piece, because West wrote an instruction. That's Do It! It never stopped and it will never stop. It will go beyond our lifetimes. It is an archive, it's a positive virus as Felix Gonzalez-Torres once told me, who was also involved in this project. If I have one project, it is this project just because of the fact that it never ended.

GM: This is very interesting. The shows Gesamtkunstwerk and Magiciens de la terre were also the most fascinating experiences with art for me in the eighties when I was young. And when you speak about gardening, I think of Derek Jarman, whom I met at that time in London, as an important example of what you were talking about. Much later, you organized an exhibition about Jarman at the Serpentine, which we also showed at Kunsthalle Wien.

HUO: With Isaac Julien.

GM: Yes. He did a great job.

HUO: We invited Isaac Julien to curate an exhibition of Derek Jarman. It was one of the first two or three shows at the Serpentine when I joined in 2006. I went with Julien to the garden and then he did this beautiful film and paintings. And I agree with you, the garden of Derek Jarman is a key example for that.

GM: Your way of thinking and working is often unconventional, surprisingly innovative and pluralistic. There seem to be very different ways in your curatorial work to go from the first idea to an exhibition. Are there also continuous elements in creating a show in your work, something which happens in all your different exhibitions?

HUO: What do they all have in common? I love your question. I think what they all have in common is that they share a deep empathy for and a deep dialogue with the artists. I have always been very concerned when I felt that art gets instrumentalized by curatorial agendas. For me, the idea that I develop is based on a process where I deduce or develop my exhibition projects out of a very close dialogue with the artists.

I would very often ask artists what the unrealized projects are, which projects they have not been able to do. This goes back to a very early conversation with Alighiero Boetti. He felt that artists get squeezed into formats and that basically people are not really listening to what they would like to do. I would say that what all these shows have in common is that they are developed with artists and address ideas which they feel are important. When, all of a sudden, artists are interested in gardens and farms and longer time horizons, I need to come up with exhibitions which address that. I can't just ignore it because otherwise we miss the needs, we miss where art goes. How does it go? Form follows function or function follows form?

In any case, it's never about art following curation—rather, it's curation that follows the lead of artists. I think that is what they have in common, from Do It! and Cities on the Move and Laboratorium to my most recent group show WORLDBUILDING. I am really excited about this show I have been working on for the Julia Stoschek Foundation in Düsseldorf, which also toured to the Centre Pompidou in Metz and then goes on a world tour. WORLDBUILDING is an exhibition we did on video games because I realized when making studio visits that more and more artists are interested in and even obsessed with doing their own video game. It is not only going into video games but also developing their own. It is so fascinating that 2.8 billion people last year played video games. I mean, that is a third of the world's population. It is bigger than the film and music industry together. Artists are fascinated by it because it is about world building. They can build their own worlds. And again, it is also a format where many things can come together. It is very collaborative. Music and sound can enter games and digital arts.

What my exhibitions also have in common is not only that they listen, but that they look—and look again—they listen out of curiosity; they are like curiosity machines. Like you said, it is fascinating because we have all these interactions we had in Vienna. We are of the same generation. We were inspired by the same shows. We met when we were very young, and the artists told you about my curiosity. I think all my exhibitions are kind of driven or fueled by my endless curiosity. Like with WORLDBUILDING, I wanted to find out what is going on with games. I am not part of the generation who grew up with video games, but I wanted to understand it and find out.

They have one more thing in common. It is a really interesting question. Nobody ever asked me that. What do these shows have in common? It is actually this idea of them being a kind of learning process. They are curiosity machines, and they are learning machines because, ultimately, I think it is quite arrogant if the curator claims to know. I always start with the fact that at the beginning I don't know. And I want to learn. That's why my exhibitions and my books are never finite. It's always Volume 1 and then we are going to hopefully learn more and do Volume 2. And, interestingly enough, that is how video games work. Even AAA games, when they are put on the market, they listen to the world and the developers evolve the games. So, I would say my exhibitions are evolutive. They are all evolutive—Do It! par excellence, but also Cities on the Move, WORLDBUILDING, and Uncertain States of America. These are all shows which grow over time, almost like a garden in that sense. They are a kind of living organism. And I think the idea of the living organism is important as artists are more and more interested in it, also in digital art. Ian Cheng talks about the artwork as a kind of living organism. I think this is an ontological change which deserves more attention.

GM: Hans Ulrich, now I come to the more practical side. Is curating also a struggle between vision and practical constraint?

HUO: Yes, of course. It is like an Olympian poem. I was friendly with Harry Mathews, who was elected as part of the Oulipo in 1973. Oulipo was a literary movement framed by constraints. And of course, there are always constraints. There are budgetary constraints, there are spatial constraints, there are temporal constraints. Curating is a practice which functions within constraints and needs to make these constraints productive. And I actually found very often that it is beneficial to approach these constraints. That is also why I think the curator has to be a generalist. There are so many dimensions to that profession, to that activity. It involves everything from working with the artists, the whole theoretical work around it to very practical aspects like fundraising, architecture, and how one transforms spaces. It all started in Vienna with Der zerbrochene Spiegel. Kasper König, curator of the show, always involved architects. I also think a lot about my work with architects. The spatial constraints are often such that we need to transform them. So again, we need to think to never be wasteful with resources. I think that is the main constraint in our time—that we are not wasteful with resources. I remember when we did Cities on the Move in London, Rem Koolhaas did the exhibition design. He rang Zaha Hadid. Hadid did a big show which was the preceding exhibition at the Hayward Gallery. He said: "We don't want to throw all this material away. Zaha, would you agree that I recycle all your vitrine stuff?" Koolhaas based the show completely on Hadid's architecture, and turned the vitrines upside down.

I would say one key constraint today is being environmentally conscious. At Serpentine we did an exhibition with the extraordinary artist Hervé Télémaque. He did this very political form of pop art. It was really his own way of finding. He also started his own movement and was recognized outside France only towards the end of his life. We did this retrospective, and I realized early on with our teams that it just didn't make sense to fly these paintings from the US, from all continents, from Martinique to London. So, we decided to do the retrospective, out of constraint, only from French collections. It would be one lorry, the lorry got us the paintings from Saint-Étienne and Paris. It was a constraint, but it produced a beautiful exhibition. I think environmental concern, for example building walls and throwing them away—that is no longer acceptable. We need to recycle these exhibition architectures or re-use them again.That is a big and important constraint.

GM: Today artists also work as curators. And curators work in a way very, very poetically and artistically. How do you see the relation between the artist as curator and the curator as artist?

HUO: I never thought that I was an artist because I work with artists. I produce reality with artists. I do not have my own art practice in that sense. But clearly, historically, there have been artists curators, artists working as curators. Duchamp was involved with the famous surrealist exhibition with the ropes. Leonora Carrington told me all about it when I interviewed her. I am from Zurich, so I am thinking of Dada, the Dada fair was an artist curated show in Berlin. Historically, also in Fluxus and the neo-avantgarde of the sixties, a lot of shows have been curated by artists. I have always been interested in this idea of artist curation. That is why I have quite often co-curated shows with artists. I find that very inspiring.

So, we did, for example, as a joint commission between the Manchester International Festival, Art Basel and Beyeler, Il Tempo del Postino, where we invited artists not previously known for their stage performances to do a 50-minute piece in front of an audience. It was a new format, a new rule of the game. And Philippe Parreno and I co-curated it as a kind of an artist opera or a new Utopia Station in an unusual collaboration with Molly Nesbit. Rirkrit Tiravanija built the stage for this show, Nesbit worked theoretically a lot on utopia, and I curated a lot of projects related to utopia. So, we joined all our forces, and it became a curatorial trialogue. I often co-curated exhibitions with artists.

GM: You work as a free curator, and you have been working, for a long time now, as a curator employed by a museum. Where do you see the differences? What about dependency versus freedom? A free curator is maybe more independent, but at the same time more dependent on funding and institutions to execute ideas. The curator in the museum has other restraints. You experienced both.

HUO: That is also a really interesting question. For me, Harald Szeemann was a real inspiration. Growing up in Switzerland, Szeemann was omnipresent. He was a public figure in Switzerland. And at a time when curating wasn't yet publicly so present as it is now, he really brought curation to the forefront. I remember we once had a talk in Appenzell. I had just begun to do my kitchen show, so I didn't have much to report on yet. And he had a whole life to report. After the talk we had dinner together. I asked him exactly that question. I said: "Harald, should I be an independent curator or should I be at the museum?" And he said: "You should do both." He was, of course, attached to the Kunsthaus in Zurich and at the same time a free freelance curator all over the world. When I was at the Musée d'Art Moderne, my job title was migratory curator. I not only did my exhibition project Migrateurs in the building, but I also migrated. The museum wanted me to bring in fresh and new ideas. And then I became co-director and now artistic director of the Serpentine. There was also, always from the beginning, the idea that I would continue to do shows, interdisciplinary projects in different fields, not only in the museum field, for example, the opera which happened at the Manchester International Festival. Things like that. I have always followed that credo of Harald Szeemann—both roles, instead of either/or.

The reason why I wanted to have an attachment to an organization is also that as a freelance curator one tends to do group shows and bigger curatorial projects rather than solo shows. After a certain while, this direct work with one artist becomes important. You have done that a lot at the Kunsthalle Wien. You know that it becomes important that one can work deeper with artists on solo shows and connect deeply in that relationship. And the deepest one can go with an artist is by doing a solo show. That is why in 2006, I went to the Serpentine, after having been the migratory curator at the Musée d'art Moderne, because I wanted to do solo shows. I did shows with Steve McQueen, Philippe Parreno and Dominique Gonzalez-Foerster, Arthur Jafa and more recently also Sondra Perry. And of course, also retrospectives of artists who need more attention, who should be remembered like Etel Adnan, or Faith Ringgold or Kamala Ibrahim Ishaq. You also did dozens and dozens of them in Vienna, like with Matthew Barney or Shirin

Neshat. I've done dozens and dozens of them in London and in Paris. I think that was really important to the artists and to me. And yet, at the same time, I think, it is important to do research about phenomena like gaming and continue to do these larger survey shows where we bring a pattern together as well. I have always been interested in patterns; there are patterns that connect. And this work keeps stimulating the institutional work and vice versa.

GM: It is a privileged position to be a curator as part of an institution, even to make the programs at an institution like you do, and at the same time to have the right also to create projects outside of the institution. It's not a common case. This is a position one has to create for oneself.

HUO: That is also why I never had a position in a museum which, in that sense, existed before me. Basically, Musée d'art Moderne and I created this position together. Then the same thing happened in London when I initially became director of international projects. It goes back to this idea—within an institution, you create new positions. That is what I try to do for younger generations. It's like in language—you have neologisms. You create new roles. And that makes it more stimulating.

I take pride in working for a museum

Álvaro Rodríguez Fominaya in conversation with Gerald A. Matt

GERALD A. MATT: What is a curator? Can you define your understanding and practice as a curator?

ÁLVARO RODRÍGUEZ FOMINAYA: A curator is the one that does the curating. This may sound like nonsense but given the number of "kinds" of curating, I can no longer find a definition that suits all. I'm not so comfortable with the so called "creative" curating any more, as it feels that often it just fits the curator's agenda. I'm not pursuing the idea of a curator as an artist. Though I can understand where it all comes from. Harald Szeemann was a master of this orientation; he was in the great tradition of Dada and Cabaret Voltaire. What do I have to say in that respect? But of course, a curator can help throw new light, new ideas and new interpretations on a work of art. A curator is someone with a torch throwing light on some object and saying "Hey, look at this". I like to take no compromises while curating. If for some reason I have made a compromise, I have instantly regretted it.

GM: When did you know that you wanted to be curator? How did it start?

ARF: There is no grand epic behind my decision to become a curator. I just wanted to pursue a field of knowledge that would allow me to work in a museum. Funnily enough my first job was with a modern masters art dealer in Mayfair (London) and not in a museum. But soon after, I was working at my hometown's contemporary art museum, CAAM Centro Atlántico de Arte Moderno in the Canary Islands; we did great projects there. Probably the first project I would like to recall was a four-venue solo show with Joseph Kosuth. He is one of the most generous artists that I have worked with. By then I had already been working in the art world for about a decade. It took me that long to commence to have some understanding of what curating is. And how intellectually tormenting and consuming the process can be. Sometimes, I now feel that I've said it all.

GM: How can curating be relevant to the challenges we face today and in what way does it differ from previous models?

ARF: There is always a place for interpretation and knowledge. Curating is obviously very much about this. But is curating a field that is becoming intellectually depleted? Maybe. The connoisseurship aspect of curating will always be current. We need curators with in-depth knowledge of an artist's work since that is very much needed to shape and edit an exhibition. But then again, there are so many artists that are great curators of their own work. When you operate as an in-house institutional curator, then there is so much red tape and politics to navigate that being an enabler, negotiator and facilitator becomes paramount. Sometimes, just to make a project happen is a victorious feat. This goes hand in hand with the risk-taking nature of this profession, there is no way to play it safe. It would be the death of curating.

GM: How do you see the changing relations between curators, artists, collectors, galleries, museums and critics? Was there a shift of power and influence?

ARF: Large global galleries have so much more power now than when I started working as a curator; over this 25 plus years there has been a shift. But that is no news. Now we can see museums like MoMA or Guggenheim lending to gallery shows in New York, this could never have happened before. Truth is there are some guidelines for these loans, but it still is a mind-blowing situation. Collectors are more actively aware of their leverage over the art ecosystem and the museum scene. Even museums like Reina Sofia that actively promote themselves as anti-market have embraced collectors and show their collections. Which is fine as long as there is transparency and a rationale to these curatorial decisions. Critics are less and less relevant, some people say there is no art criticism anymore, of course this is connected to the diminishing number and print runs of art magazines. In Spain there is currently no art magazine being published; they are all gone. The shocking fact is that Instagram is filling that void, partially for now. I bet you know many curators that select artists after seeing their work on Instagram, this is currently the curators' dirty little secret.

GM: Was there a personal hero, a curator whom you admired? And what were her/ his qualities and achievements?

ARF: Probably Kasper König. Münster Sculpture Project was always exquisite. I love the playfulness of Bonami too. Great Harald Szeemann is part of the Olympus as well. But sometimes a greatly curated exhibition doesn't necessarily have an obvious curatorial signature. So, all these great invisible curators are up there, most times you don't necessarily have to get yourself noticed.

GM: Was there a show which you consider to be a milestone for curatorial thoughts and practice?

ARF: There are exhibitions that I have greatly enjoyed as a spectator, but this doesn't necessarily translate into my curatorial projects. I learnt a lot from my colleagues at the Guggenheim, there were great exchanges with curators like Jeffrey Weiss, Valerie Hillings or Nancy Spector. From that period of my life the exhibitions of On Kawara, ZERO Group and Maurizio Cattelan remain in my memory in the most physical way. With great exhibitions one can achieve a higher level of consciousness, knowledge and pleasure.

GM: Can you describe a personal curatorial work and project you are really proud of, and also a project which didn't really work out?

ARF: For the first part that would probably be two recent projects: Pauline Oliveros retrospective and Etel Adnan. Both were projects with a very limited budget, but I consider them to be some of my most impactful work, and both were greatly affected by the pandemic. With the Oliveros exhibition the main challenge was to build a project about the polymath composer from the ground up. There had never been any exhibitions on her other than an homage with works commissioned from other artists; materials were dispersed in several archives while studies on her had exclusively focused on musicology or gender perspectives. I wanted to fill the voids and build a compelling story that was intertwined with the development of contemporary art. The exhibition was conceived as a great walk through an immersive installation where her voice was dominant. You could not only experience her music but delve in the archival materials, including text scores, photographs etc. Her widow IONE was instrumental to the success of the exhibition.

The approach to the Etel Adnan exhibition was very different—I was shaken by the sheer beauty and depth of her works at first. The idea of the show came from the desire to contemplate and experience them. She was involved in the selection of works but the pandemic prevented us from meeting. Sadly, she passed away a few days after the exhibition opened in Córdoba in the knowledge that she was comforted after seeing the images of the exhibition. The project included a broad range of works in the different media she cultivated, with a focus on the last two decades.

And a project that not so much didn't work out as was unfulfilled: In 2009, I found myself sharing a couple of beers with Rirkrit Tiravanija in an artist bar in Bangkok where I had curated an exhibition with Hong Kong artists in Gallery VER, his alternative space. I was working at Para/Site Art Space at the time. He shared the idea of this great unrealized project of driving from Thailand to Hong Kong, filming along the way. I was incredibly excited, but the project fizzled out when I realized I couldn't find the necessary funds to finance it once back in Hong Kong. I wouldn't have let it go now; it is one of my great regrets.

GM: Can you describe the path from the first idea to the exhibition based on one of your curatorial projects? What are the most important steps in developing and executing the project?

ARF: The process varies depending on the type of exhibition. Sometimes the starting point is an idea that is quite streamlined and focused, so then you just build on this initial concept. But many times, it's just the opposite, where a vague concept gets narrowed down along the way as you progress within the research. The title usually comes at a later stage. And sometimes the title is so much in flux that somehow "title freight" develops, even though it is one of the most fun parts. I find myself most at ease with historical research-based exhibitions, so I tend to use descriptive titles for these types of shows. The journey of discovery and amazement that comes along the way is the most rewarding part of any project. This is where your knowledge expands and informs you with a whole new vision on an artist, practice, collective or period. I have learnt a long time ago that a book is not an exhibition, and that it is easier to criticise a show than to make one. There is a whole journey of diplomacy and negotiation involved in any great exhibition. You have to build a show as if nothing is missing from the jigsaw, but in reality, only you know which works of art you wanted to have but couldn't get. Any great exhibition involves thinking about architecture a lot as well, the more familiar you are with the venue or exhibition space the better it is. There is a point where you become intimately connected with the space, and that is when you understand what can and cannot be done. There is no great architecture that is valid for all kinds of exhibitions. Every space works better with certain dimensions or media. Overlooking this key aspect can overwhelm and ruin an exhibition. You need also that sensitivity regarding exhibition design. Some curators excel at this, and others suck. No curator that I know of has defined this in scientific terms, most define it as a gift. To me a balance between creating relations and respecting the autonomy of the work of art is best, in that sense I prefer to research how and in what physical context the artist wanted his or her work to be shown. Another aspect of this is the unique experience from the rush of setting up an exhibition, and no matter how carefully it has been planned you are always thrown into the unknown. Many times, the relationships that you had planned between works in the gallery space don't work out, then you need to make split second decisions until you get it right. It is a physically exhausting process but a rewarding one, since most of your work in a museum is done in your office, I always feel grateful to be able to stay around the galleries so much for a period of time.

GM: Is curating always a struggle between vision and practical constraints? Can you give an example?

ARF: Financial constraints and availability of works are always a framework that defines what show you can do. But I don't think about it as a limiting situation, it's just the reality you have to work with, and it is also a matter of responsibility. I have always worked within an institutional setting, and I am fully sympathetic about this. There is always a way around it, but I would never accept compromising on the way works of art are exhibited, I would rather not include a specific work of art if I realise it cannot be shown as it should be.

GM: How do you define the relationship between artist and curator? Where are the conflict lines?

ARF: Depending on the level of intellectual trust, things can move into the field of the ridiculous pretty fast, and that's disastrous for any project. Even little details can scale up to life-or-death matters. On the other hand, through an exchange of ideas a meeting of minds can happen and that can enrich any project. Since an exhibition involves at least two years of close contact, it is instrumental to build this mutual trust, which often evolves into friendship. Sometimes budgeting becomes a conflict area if you are well into a project and new demands appear or you cannot keep things as promised for a variety of reasons. I would personally strive to make things happen in any case. At the end of the day, it is not different from any human relationship, and I feel that being upfront about what you can and cannot do always helps.

GM: Is curating artistic work itself or just a service to the public or an artist and their work?

ARF: I believe there is a creative aspect to it, but I don't mistake it with any artistic work, far from it, otherwise it would be competing with the artist's work. I don't believe in the curator as an artist. I respect it though, but I'm just not interested in this idea, and I don't practice it myself.

GM: There have recently been some examples of artists being called by institutions to curate also major shows and curators having their own artistic practice. In what way is the line and authorship of curators shifting/fading?

ARF: I believe this has been constant throughout history, not just a contemporary fade. Let us not forget the role Joshua Reynolds had in shaping the taste of his own time as president of the Royal Academy in the XVIII century. I find it quite obvious that artists have a great contribution to make to the curatorial field.

GM: How independent is an independent/freelance curator? How dependent is a curator employed by a museum?

ARF: Being employed by a museum is not contradictory to the principle of curatorial freedom. Both should coexist once you start developing a project, otherwise I would say the whole situation is messed up. When you work in an institution, how you decide on a project is defined by that context, and it should be. There is the history and mission of the museum, there is the board, the advisory committee, etc. These are safeguards of the museum's mission. It all makes sense when you think about it in this way.

GM: How different is their work and self-understanding?

ARF: Obviously when you bring someone from outside the institution, they don't need to think about any of this. If it gets to the point where a project is commissioned, then all these considerations have been taken into account before the approval. Then the freelance curator acts on a mandate. It is healthy to have a mix of in-house and freelance curators, sometimes specialist knowledge on certain fields is not available in-house.

GM: Are there two different art worlds, the art world of the museums and big collectors including star curators, auction houses and big fairs and the other art world based on smaller biennales, independent art spaces and curators as Robert Fleck once argued? Is there also a gap between curators serving one or the other world?

ARF: I wouldn't say it is so clear cut; it's probably an oversimplification and reductionist vision of the art world. I prefer to see more shades and colours to it.

GM: What is the impact of identity politics on the theory and practise of curating?

ARF: It has impacted on how we think about who we are exhibiting and about the opportunities granted or not. This reflection and conversation were not there thirty years ago. This lack of discussion created gaps in the history of art through actions of invisibility. Research together with new institutions in Latin America, Asia and Africa are making vital contributions.

GM: Did it change your way of thinking and working?

ARF: It has, this discussion has enabled an awareness that was not there three or two decades ago. It is helping redress the lack of visibility and opportunities for artists from certain groups that have been discriminated against. But at the same time identity politics should not be the only driver for curatorial decisions. Sometimes I feel that some curators are construct statements that are not about art and where the exhibition or the works of art are secondary and merely illustrate a curatorial thesis regardless of their quality.

GM: Has art to be moral? What are the values of art?

ARF: Art can be responsible or irresponsible. What if a work of art pushes you towards an immoral act. Are we to reject certain possibilities? We can't ignore the subjective perspective that a work of art represents. And as a curator, or better, someone involved in providing a public display for works of art, I'd say that rights are not limitless but must be exercised within certain boundaries.

GM: What is the role of institutions in your practice? Where does the boundary lie between curatorial and institutional responsibility?

ARF: I take pride in working for a museum. I am a great believer of the public good that museums bring to society. When you work in a museum, curating is only one of the many tasks that you perform. In that sense curatorial practice and institutional responsibility are blended into the core function of the museum with no separation.

GM: What will be the main challenges for a curator in the future? How will curatorial work change?

ARF: I'm never good at fortune telling, I would like to find the answers to this. I probably have more questions than answers myself, and I wish I could find someone that could answer them. How we engage with a younger generation is an obvious question for museums to stay relevant to their audiences. Museums are struggling with the use of the digital, being that they are bricks and mortar institutions. We have learnt a great deal about the digital realm from the pandemic but for obvious reasons smaller museums are being left behind. Another question is how to integrate AI in the visitor experience and even in the curatorial process. How to reassess our collections in the light of the changes brought by identity politics? All these are great opportunities lying ahead.

Everything depends on the personality

Anda Rottenberg in conversation with Gerald A. Matt

GERALD A. MATT: What is a curator? Can you define your understanding and practice as a curator?

ANDA ROTTENBERG: To make it short: A curator is a person who is an author of a visual narration, conceived and executed by him/herself by finding and placing chosen exhibits in space in a special order so that they create an added value.

GM: Fantastic! When did you know that you wanted to be a curator? Was there an initial experience?

AR: No. I started working at Zachęta already as a student. I was not allowed to make my own exhibitions, but I was a member of the team that executed the exhibitions, and I learned what an exhibition is and how to produce it. Then I moved to the scientific institute of art and suddenly was invited to make a group exhibition of Polish art in Cuba, Havana.

GM: I also did an exhibition in Havana years ago.

AR: It was in 1980.

GM: Mine was in 1997. I would have loved to see the differences between the exhibitions as well as their Cuban political, social and cultural contexts. That is all a long time ago. How can curating be relevant to the challenges we face today? And how did the role of the curator change in your opinion?

AR: Today it is much more complex. We have many more types of artistic expression, and exhibitions as such develop in its polyphony. On the other hand, it crosses the gallery walls and spreads out into a non-defined space interchanging with the current non-artistic reality, and it is open to multiple interpretations given also by the context of place. So, it is not definite anymore. We cannot really differentiate between what is an exhibition and what is not nowadays, partly due to the blending of art and non-art pieces.

GM: Was there a personal hero, a curator, whom you admired and what were his/her qualities?

AR: You know, I am old. In my youth, there was a strong division between the commissioner who made a list of exhibits, and the designer who decided about their display. My instinct told me to look for another solution. I wanted to govern the whole and did it in my first (already mentioned) show in 1980, when I exhibited a group of sculptures on a hillock of red Cuban soil. That was instinctive work. And much later, I displayed the sculptures by Alina Szapocznikow on elegant home tables as well as on hospital furniture. That was in 1998, after Harald Szeemann's exhibition *Austria im Rosennetz* where I discovered that you could show art objects and non-art objects next to each other. And that was a discovery that made me think differently about exhibitions.

GM: How do you see the changing relations between artists, curators, collectors, galleries, museums, and critics?

AR: The relationship between curators and artists is a matter of trust, responsibility and loyalty. One may elaborate on it and another not. The whole art system and its power relations are in permanent change but in the end good art survives, at least I hope so.

GM: And what do you think about the relationship: artist, curator, collector and museum?

AR: This is complicated. In relations with museums and collectors, the loan process is one of the increasing problems. Nowadays, getting a loan from a museum or collector is a nightmare, you never know the result of your request. And in relations with galleries, one should really be strong to resist their suggestions, their pressure to include their artists in your show. On the other hand, you must convince them not to interfere with the process of collaboration between you and the artist. I will skip the question about the critics because I never got a positive review.

GM: Do you think collectors are too powerful nowadays? They even create their own museums.

AR: They are. And they use this power. Museums explain to you why you don't get this or that loan. Collectors simply say: I don't want to. Why? Because.

GM: More and more artists curate shows. What do you think about this tendency?

AR: Everything depends on the personality. For example, I started to work with Kader Attia as an artist in 2004. I included him in the exhibition *Continental Breakfast*. And then he became a curator and made interesting shows as he has the vision. Another example is Luc Tuymans who makes exhibitions from time to time, quite complex, very interesting. He discovers something. So it happens, but it's not an everyday situation.

GM: Was there a show that you consider a milestone in your curatorial thoughts and practice?

AR: Yes, of course I already mentioned Harald and his work. By the way, I wrote a book consisting of my letters to Harald in heaven, trying to discuss curatorial practice with him. But it is not very well distributed, I am sorry to say.

GM: Maybe we can get it. Is it in Polish?

AR: No, it is in English. And it was produced in Switzerland.

GM: What is the title of the book?

AR: *From Poland with Love.* Scheidegger & Spiess.

GM: Can you describe a personal curatorial work that you are proud of and that you think is one of your important projects?

AR: I can mention some other curators, it is not that I learned from them, but it is about their achievements: Okwui Enwezor, for example.

GM: What about your own exhibitions? Your favorite show, your most important show?

AR: I've made so many. Obviously, there have been some really huge projects, like *Warsaw–Moscow/Moscow–Warsaw* or *Side by Side: Poland–Germany.*

A 1000 Years of History in Art at Gropius-Bau in Berlin. These exhibitions were hard work, and I consider them real achievements. But also, I made a very unusual show called *Grey in Colour*, at Zachęta in 2000. This was an exhibition aiming to reflect the hidden cultural life in Poland during the communist era in the 60-s and 70-s, in which I reconstructed many iconic places: student clubs, jazz cellars, libraries, cinemas, milk bars, fashion galleries, apartments and elegant stores, places of cultural, social and political importance. I really remade them, and they really functioned, you could listen to the music of the time, you could have coffee, cakes, snacks and wine in the way it was offered back then. I created a sort of repetitive reality, and I invited the heroes from that time, musicians, actors. They functioned as exhibits, sitting and talking with the public. This was a totally unusual show. I cannot define it, but it was very popular and an important exhibition for me.

GM: Was this like recreating a world?

AR: Not really, because it was a narrow margin of the communist period, more the outsiders, the subculture, the margins, but the important ones. It was about people blending with these small apartments, with the compact furniture, the music, all kinds of things.

GM: Curating is always a struggle between vision and practical constraints. Can you give an example where practical constraints deeply impacted you?

AR: I consider my first serious international show, which was called *Where is Abel, thy brother?* in 1995, when I convinced some very serious artists not to answer this biblical question but to repeat it. And they conceived new pieces, sort of commissions without payment and people like Boltanski, Lawrence Weiner, Gabriel Orozco, Jannis Kounellis, Jochen Gerz, Miroslaw Balka and Miriam Cahn worked *in situ* conceiving brilliant works. After that, the minister called me and said "Consider yourself dismissed", and soon after there was competition for my position in Zachęta. I had to win it the second time. That's a real constraint. I also did a show about independent art from Lithuania, Latvia and Estonia called *Personal time*. There was no public, no press. It was too early because it was 1996, too early. And of course, there are some permanent constraints related to budgets, space, and artists' expectations that you can't meet. Not to mention the level of the press. In 2014, I made the show *Progress and Hygiene* about the roots of fascism, rather complex, with serious widely international works, which was pretty popular with the public, but the press didn't understand my message at all.

GM: Let us go back to the relation between artist and the curator. Where do you see conflict lines?

AR: Conflict lines?

GM: You said, it is all about trust.

AR: The conflict line appears either when one of the parties, the artist or the curator, does not tell the truth, and beats about the bush, or when the curator doesn't work with the artist in an intimate way. The curator should be a little bit wiser than the artist but should never show it as the artist is a selfish person. So, you should go step by step when you talk about the future exhibition and should never impose anything. But also, you shouldn't let the artist have their way without discussion. In the case of a group exhibition of living artists, this is a totally different thing, then you are the boss. In my practice, I have usually developed the display and after that let the artists make corrections, change something. They would make an effort and try things out - which would finally stay as I had planned. But it's important to show your respect by letting them interfere.

GM: Right. Do you consider curating to be artistic work or a service to the artist?

AR: Yes, absolutely. Of course, not everybody is an artist in this profession, as we know. But you can compare it to being a theatre stage director or a movie director. It's the same process. You have a vision, then make a script, plan the display and build the narration using other people's talent to do your own work. And to do this, you also need imagination and talent.

GM: Can you say something about your education and training. Did you study art history?

AR: Yes, I studied art history and had my apprenticeship at Zachęta. Then I moved to scientific work, and finally, I came back. During the communist period, it was not easy because I was not in a privileged position reserved for communist party members. The case of Cuba in1980 was an exception. As a matter of fact, there was someone else to be nominated as the curator. But he got another proposal, and I simply replaced him.

GM: Did you become the director of Zachęta after the communist time?

AR: Of course. I became the director in 1993. There was a moment already in 1992 when they wanted to nominate me, but I insisted on a competition as a democratic procedure. They held it much later. And I won it.

GM: You experienced both: You were a curator in a museum and the director of a museum, but you also worked as an independent, freelance curator. How different is that? How different is life and work?

AR: No, I wasn't a museum curator, in the beginning I was a member of a technical team. Later on, I made exhibitions as a leader of different institutions and galleries (i.e. the Artists Union gallery 1991-1993 and the Egit Foundaton 1986-1990) or as a freelance curator after leaving Zachęta (2001). Being free and working outside an institution, as I am doing it now, is the most privileged situation. Of course, being the director and making exhibitions was also a privilege but there are always boards and politics—and you get the minister who tells you to "consider yourself dismissed". You are never safe from the so called "art scandals" they construct around you and certain projects as I experienced with the Uklański show with actors in nazi uniforms or with Cattelan's Pope John Paul II smashed by a meteorite. The Polish Pope attacked in a Polish museum—that was an opportunity for scandalizing art and popularizing prejudices against art. And me as a person "of Jewish origins". In the end I was forced to leave Zachęta. This is the price you pay as a director if you don't want to censor the show. In my practice, I feel much better as a freelancer because I elaborated a special contract, free from political pressure and censorship, free to create the exhibition I believe in. And insist on it before starting the work. Then I feel the master of the situation and I have the luxury of working according to my own rules.

GM: Right. But in your position is it easy to survive also as a freelance curator?

AR: No, I have never lived from exhibitions. Sometimes I get a high honorarium, but it doesn't happen often. You should always have other, possibly permanent sources. I now have my weekly radio broadcast and the position of culture editor in Vogue. Also, my texts, conferences and books help me to keep the financial balance.

GM: You live in Poland, a country where politics is becoming more and more authoritarian and illiberal. Hence, my question: How dependent is curating on the state of democracy in a society or in a country? What is the situation for curators in Poland today? I'm thinking back to our debate on censorship some years ago before you were attacked for doing the exhibitions with Uklański and Maurizio Cattelan. But things haven't changed for the better, have they?

AR: The exhibitions you have mentioned were made by other curators, but I was responsible for them as the director of Zacheta. Now, it has become worse. First of all, most directors of state art institutions were exchanged and replaced by people favored by the minister of culture and the PIS party. In many cases they are not professionals, but dilettante opportunists and command receivers, as in the case of Zachęta or Muzeum Sztuki in Łódź, for example. The curators don't want to stay and work there anymore but there are not many places to go, and younger people may end up jobless. And on the other hand, there is a sort of boycott, for example, I don't visit many places like the Ujazdowski Castle, the art museum in Łódź or Zachęta Narodowa Galeria Sztuki anymore, I simply don't show up there. Many other people do the same.

GM: Are curating and the state of democracy very closely related to each other.

AR: Definitely. Absolutely. We have no democracy in Poland at all right now. The constitutional regulations are not being respected. This government doesn't follow them. I have the luxury of being a freelancer, I work for private enterprises (like the radio, Vogue, publishing houses, etc.) also outside of Poland. But the curators who have left museums are in a really very difficult situation. They don't have a field of activity. Of course, there are municipal galleries or museums, but not that big and not that many, except for Krakow or Warsaw city institutions.

GM: Maybe also the Museum of Modern Art which is now under construction in front of the Culture Palace in the heart of Warsaw.

AR: Yes, because it has recently become a city museum. But it is the only big new museum in Poland which is more or less independent, except for MOCAK in Krakow.

GM: So the state museums don't need censorship anymore because their directors do what the government expects and wants anyway?

AR: Precisely.

GM: Let us go back to the international field. What, in your opinion, is the impact of identity politics and "wokeism" on the practice of curating?

AR: Basically, they are dependent on one another.

GM: You don't feel it is a new kind of censorship?

AR: In state institutions in Poland the directors are censors. This is inner censorship, connected to the government, which is against artistic freedom, of course. As it has always been under authoritarian power. But in municipal galleries—and there are many very good ones—the attitude is often radical, "wokeism" could sometimes be a problem, but it isn't comparable to the new censorship that exists in the governmental institutions.

GM: But when curating in Western countries, are you aware of identity politics? For example, if you make an exhibition, there should be the same number of women artists as men. Do you also think about the community, about sentiments of minorities?

AR: I have already done these kinds of exhibitions before. For example, I did a feminist show including 20 women artists called *White Mazurka* in Berlin in 2002. I am flexible, and of course I take it into consideration because this is a process of opening our minds. But I would not consider creating an exhibition following all these aspects of politically correct participation. Because this would tie my hands. In 2012, I did an exhibition in my native city in Galicia about four nations that vanished from it after WWII. I called it *VOID*. And there were Germans, Jews, Roma and Lemko people, the Ruthenians relocated by force in 1947. So, I am sensitive to these questions, but I don't want anybody to impose them on me. Regulations and limitations, censorship in any case, I didn't want it before, and I don't want it now.

GM: A polemic question: Must art be moral?

AR: It depends. Morality doesn't have a clear definition. In general art is moral. But art means also freedom of expression. If you have to put something first, in the end it is freedom. If someone considers art immoral, this is their problem, not the art's problem. Artists are always ahead of us because of their sensitivity.

GM: Must the artist be a moral person?

AR: I believe every artist has their own morality which can be different from the superficial social morality or the Christian morality, the Protestant morality, the Buddhist morality. I believe that an artist follows their own evaluation scale. If this conflicts with the commonsense morality, I will always stand on the side of the artist.

GM: There is an article that Robert Fleck wrote saying there are two different art worlds: the art world of big galleries, big collectors, big museums, auction houses, big fairs, and star curators—which you are in fact part of, one could say. And then there is the other art world of independent spaces, independent curators, smaller biennials etcetera—you are also part of this world. Do you see this dualism or borderline?

AR: Big museums, the top museums in the world with their immersive collections and infrastructure have the tendency to make blockbuster shows because they look or have to look for the money coming back and the public visiting their programs. They would rather not risk making exhibitions which are not that popular. Also, private collectors, let's say, Pinault, look for reputation and attention. They may be more open but also follow the existing evaluation scale. Pinault doesn't discover new artists. He shows those who are great and interesting, and those are good exhibitions. In general, only the secondary biennials, provincial biennials are fresh. They bring unknown artists, unknown artistic situations, and open our minds. Yes, there is this dualism, but it is not excluding, it is osmotic.

GM: Are small, perishable alternative biennials and exhibitions more interesting for you than the big ones?

AR: No, of course, to be honest, I go to the big ones, but I also happen to attend the smaller ones. Let me tell you why. Because I am old, and I am tired, and I don't look for new generations as I have done for the last 50 years. So, I have the luxury of just enjoying mature art and artists. But new biennials, like the Latvian or Bukarest biennial, yes, they are interesting.

GM: What is the role of institutions? Where does the boundary lie between curatorial and institutional responsibility? You have been a curator and director, even in your own house, you were responsible for the institution and the exhibitions at the same time.

AR: As a director, I was responsible for everything, i.e. also for the institution and the public. When I am a curator, I primarily take personal responsibility for the show and the artists. When I was in both roles, my advice always was: "Say, it wasn't me, it was Mrs. Rottenberg."

GM: You were two people.

AR: Well, I mean that is a situation of two different positions and understanding these positions. I am probably the only institution's director who took full responsibility for the curators and also my staff.

GM: As a director, one has to look more at the budget and the public.

AR: That is the statute of the museum, to keep to the budget. But there should also be a way in big institutions to do other projects, you can always find space for flexibility and experiments. That's what makes a good director.

GM: What will be the main challenges for curators in the future? What do you think?

AR: There is more and more merchandizing work. And more and more artists look—besides at themselves—at the market and how to sell. The market is a dictator. The auction houses are earning much more money than the galleries and they sell whatever happens. I am afraid that the old evaluation scale built on expertise and experience in trying to recognize the value of the art is now melting. Now people say someone is good because they sell at a very high price. And I say that I don't know why anybody would pay that price because I wouldn't even like to have it, either in the museum or at home.

GM: Will this make it more difficult for curators to work?

AR: Yes, there is a lot of pressure. Curators are less and less independent nowadays, especially if you are invited by a private institution to curate a show. I remember one example in Austria. I wouldn't say which collection, but they proposed that I do a show out of their collection, and I conceived an exhibition in a sort of radical way. I gave it the title *If you only love me,* and I proposed that Elfriede Jelinek write for the catalogue. After two months, I received an answer that they would rather make an exhibition with highlights from the collection. Period. No further explanation. But it was clear to me that my choice of radical artists and Jelinek were not accepted even in Austria. So, this was not formal censorship, but it is an example which shows that there are kinds of exhibition you may not do even if you are invited. So, I quit.

GM: You started your career as a curator in communist times. If you had a choice to start it today, what would you prefer?

AR: I only made one exhibition in 1980. And in the mid-80s, I opened my own private foundation, and I made illegal exhibitions outside censorship. They were not big, but in so-called alternative spaces. A time I would never like to have missed. And now, I'd probably do the same.

GM: Thank you very much, Anda.

AR: Thank you.

We don't need another hero

Francis Ruyter
in conversation with Gerald A. Matt

GERALD A. MATT: What is a curator? Can you define your understanding, and practice as a curator?

FRANCIS RUYTER: I am an artist.

GM: How can curating be relevant to the challenges we face today and in what way does it differ from previous models (if you think it does)?

FR: Relevance is maintained through an independent and conscientious practice of being in the world.

GM: How do you see the changing relations between curators, artists, collectors, galleries, museums and critics? Has there been a shift of power and influence?

FR: Artists are increasingly appropriated and excluded from something people like to label 'artistic production', and yet are often the only force that moves the discourse to another direction. As in other fields, these efforts will be increasingly supplemented by machines and automation, which is exactly why what artists do is relevant, even under these conditions, to the present and future of human life.

GM: Was Harald Szeemann replaced by François Pinault?

FR: This question is way too far from my personal experience for me to answer. I imagine that kind of information would be in a public record somewhere.

GM: Are the young artists taking over the role of curators?

FR: They are assembling an army that will take over the world.

GM: Was there a personal hero, a curator whom you admired?

FR: We don't need another hero.

GM: Can you describe a personal curatorial work and project you are really proud of, and also a project which didn't quite work out?

FR: They might be one and the same thing. I invited a group of artists who were meeting weekly in Berlin to discuss feminist topics to come to Vienna and take over my space as a Temporary Autonomous Zone. I am extremely proud that the format we developed for the project in Vienna laid a great foundation for FF to continue for quite a few more years, manifesting in different cities and forms despite radically different approaches to feminism represented by the individual participants. It was a project far beyond my experience or comfort zone. In terms of not working out, I thought it would help me find the hybrid model of an art space that I was looking for, but I ended up paying for the whole thing myself with no chance of support after being turned down for public funding. Instead, it was the catalyst for enormous personal change. And I do suspect that it might have nudged Vienna a bit in a better direction.

GM: Can you describe the path from the first idea to the exhibition based on one of your curatorial projects? What are the most important steps in developing and executing the project?

FR: Each project is different, and the methodology is highly dependent on the surrounding conditions.

GM: Is curating always a struggle between vision and practical constraints?

FR: No.

GM: How do you define the relation between artist and curator?

FR: Colleagues.

GM: Where are the conflict lines?

FR: Self-interest.

GM: Is curating artistic work or a service to the artist and his work?

FR: No.

GM: There have recently been some examples of artists being called by institutions to curate also major shows and curators having their own artistic practice. In what way is the line and authorship of curators shifting/fading?

FR: Those who see this as a struggle for power or authorship might consider getting out of the room, taking some fresh air, and making space for new voices.

GM: Are there two different art worlds, the art world of the museums and big collectors including star curators, auction houses and big fairs and the other art world based on smaller biennales, independent art spaces and curators as Robert Fleck once argued? Is there also a gap between curators serving one or the other world?

FR: There is one planet Earth that we all live on and, unfortunately, take an increasing part in destroying.

GM: What is the role of institutions in your practice? Where does the boundary lie between curatorial and institutional responsibility?

FR: It is not a boundary but a skin—a membrane which allows for transfer in both directions.

GM: What will be the main challenges for curators in the future? How will curatorial work change?

FR: Survival. The same challenges we will all face as the climate changes.

Art embodies openness. Morals always scared me in the sense that is a world of constraints, barriers and rules.

Jérôme Sans
in conversation with Gerald A. Matt

GERALD A. MATT: What is a curator? Can you define your understanding and practice as a curator?

JÉRÔME SANS: Having an attitude, a direction and a vision. Specific choices and sticking to them are essential to a curator. It is a life choice. In the 1980s and 1990s, I was one of the first independent curators in Europe, experimenting with new forms of exhibitions outside institutions, in places of reality (airports, apartments, stores, neighbourhoods, on the road, rural landscapes…). There were almost no opportunities to be invited to do projects within institutions at the time. Then in the 2000s, I decided, together with Nicolas Bourriaud, to build our own institution—thinking of what an institution of the new era could be. Today, I develop a more transversal approach between the permanent and temporary, between the inside and outside, between individuals and communities.

My entire curatorial practice has consisted in placing artists at the heart of the debate, at the heart of society—giving space and voice back to those who reinvent the world.

Artists put our current history in perspective, they make us aware of the perpetual rebirth and the permanent reinvention of the way we inhabit the world and build our relationships. For a curator, each project and each exhibition is a challenge. You must constantly renew yourself. It is important not to be influenced by the fashions and aesthetics that follow one another at a frantic pace, today more than ever. Being a curator is about bringing one's own vision to the chessboard-like quandary of what an exhibition is and how to make exhibition models evolve permanently into myriads of new experiences. And on my side, a long-term engagement with the artists, always supporting and accompanying them, is something essential. It is the human relationship we build together and make it last a lifetime. That is why I consider all my exhibitions from the beginning to be a continuing platform, a kind of *cadavre exquis*, a continuum of exhibitions that keeps reinventing itself in different forms, shapes and contexts, but in the end, it is one.

GM: How can curating be relevant to the challenges we face today and in what way does it differ from previous models, if you think it does?

JS: Nowadays, I feel that one of the major stakes—beyond constantly rethinking the limits of art and exhibition formats—is to throw the spotlight on those who have often been hidden from view and who deserve to be exposed on the front stage: artists of all generations, nationalities, genders and backgrounds; and to embrace the extraordinary vitality of creation… Decentralizing the Western-centric gaze to reveal other artistic scenes, other dynamics of creation has always fascinated me. In parallel to the ecological stakes, the current economic situation invites us to deploy other strategies to make *in situ* exhibitions and to work with local circular economies and communities to produce the works on the spot. It is a revival of curatorial practices, initiated in the 1970's, with a certain economy of means which metamorphosed exhibition-making into a really vibrant creative workshop, directly with the curator and the artists. They are coming back into force today, in particular when it comes to setting up exhibitions on new artistic scenes. It was a real revolution a few decades ago, then, with the professionalization of curatorial practices in museums, it was largely lost from sight, but it is on my horizon when I imagine exhibitions.

GM: How do you see the changing relations between curators, artists, collectors, galleries, museums and critics? Has there been a shift of power and influence?

JS: The art world has undergone a radical shift in the paradigm of its structure. Previously, what mattered most was the artistic invention conceived jointly with institutions and curators, and followed by the orchestration of galleries. The collector was the transmission belt that made the economy of this ecosystem work. Since the years 2000-2010, the private world has gradually taken the place of the public world, completely changing the cosmogony of the art world, like the faces of a Rubik's cube. Suddenly, the collectors, who sometimes produced works, and the companies who financially supported the production of institutional exhibitions, started to open their own places.

From partners, they became actors. Today, the world of private institutions, foundations and collectors prevails over the public institutions and curators. In this new ecosystem, galleries also play a considerable role since they are market operators. This is why some exhibitions today are entirely produced by a gallery or a brand, which was absolutely unimaginable 20 years ago.

However, there is no judgment of value to be made. The world is constantly changing. The public world was not an ideal world. A fully private world is not ideal either, but the conjunction of the two creates a balanced world that seems to me to be more just than either one. The public one was, first of all, political, since the city (polis), the State or the region managed culture almost on their own. Today, it is healthy that culture is taken charge of by companies that are aware of the importance of their social responsibility. While some people see behind these implications a presence that could be negative, I see above all a richness that has made it possible to multiply the productions and the opportunities for artists to exist. It is this diversity that allows a spectrum of more or less interesting programs to exist.

GM: Harald Szeemann replaced by François Pinault.

JS: Harald Szeemann was passionate about utopias. Like many of the curators who worked with him, he was an inspiring figure in the world of culture. His generosity, simplicity and modesty were exceptional. I was lucky enough to be able to talk to him regularly. I don't think that one has replaced the other. Through his foundation and his sites, in Paris and in Venice, it is clear that François Pinault has become one of the great actors of contemporary creation, but he does not replace Harald Szeemann.

François Pinault provides an extraordinary and unique setting for the artists he welcomes within his walls. Harald Szeemann opened up mental paths.

I have a lot of admiration for this whole generation of committed and engaging curators who fought for the culture of an era and a certain knowledge. I am thinking in particular of Pontus Hulthén or Kasper König. From this "other world" of the post-war period, they invented the history of curating, tracing the genealogy of multiple paths of what an exhibition can be today. Before them, an exhibition was a scientific and theoretical writing project. They opened the freedom of writing to other sociological and philosophical fields. From their proposals, making an exhibition was no longer simply showing an artist, but taking a position through different fields of thought.

GM: Was there a personal hero, a curator whom you admired?

JS: I was lucky enough to meet Harald Szeemann, whom I saw as a sort of ideal uncle. He had a real lightness, a real poetic approach, always interested in listening to new voices and meeting new artists, refusing any form of dogma. The other head of this tutelary duo, or of my double curatorial paternity, is Pontus Hultén. On the one hand, Harald Szeemann, the libertarian hero, and on the other, Pontus Hultén, the inventor of new institutional models. He invented the Modern Art Museum in Stockholm, an absolutely radical revolution of intelligence, interdisciplinarity and generosity, and one of the most avant-garde institutions, together with the Pompidou Centre, which opened in 1977.

With him, the museum was no longer a sanctuary but a house open to all, allowing access to knowledge, to culture, to artists, with the possibility of going from a performance to a film, from a film to a concert and from a concert to an exhibition, a multiple programming, in dialogue, in perspective and in friction with itself. At the time, the entrance to the Pompidou Centre was precisely called the forum. Not the one at Les Halles, but in its Latin sense, that is, a place where thought can be shared with the population and where public affairs are dealt with. I was lucky enough to be present at the opening and to walk around this place every day afterwards. Until then, it was a permanent wonder to see culture in all its forms in such a state of proximity. This way of doing things has not only nourished my practice but also my way of expressing myself, making exhibitions, accompanying artists over time and inventing the different models of institution that I have been lucky enough to be able to develop throughout the world. All of them are rooted not in the typology of the sanctuary places of the 1950s but in the one that, born in the late 1970s, developed in a more libertarian, joyful and transversal way. For me, it was a question of thinking of culture not as the bastion of a few people who would hold all the knowledge, on the contrary. Culture is not a bunker; it is a house with wide open windows. It is a space where the outside is not a dangerous world, but a world that nourishes and ventilates the inside.

GM: And what were their qualities and achievements? Was there a show which you consider to be a milestone for curatorial thoughts and praxis?

JS: Harald Szeemann's exhibition, *When Attitudes Become Forms,* is inevitably a point of rupture and historical evolution. He succeeded in showing how non-traditional practices, which are part of a whole new vocabulary, can be considered as works of art. It is a whole part of our history which opens with him, and which forms the premise of all that one could see in art since. The catalogue of this exhibition, for example, is a folder and not a book. You can open one card in two, replace it with others or change the order. The approach to this serious object sums up a certain simplicity combined with the richness of the plurality of meanings and methods proposed. Another exhibition that I consider to be a milestone in my thinking and approach is *Les Immatériaux*, an absolutely mind-blowing exhibition that took place at the Pompidou Centre in 1985. As its name indicates, it sought to leave materiality to go towards something else. It marked the sudden arrival of another part of contemporary creation, another way of writing the exhibition, which is in a way the beginning of what we talk about a lot today: the immersive and the experiential. These proposals were of the order of the infra-thin, of the spectacular with very little, accompanied by a formidable theoretical field.

GM: Can you describe a personal curatorial work and project you are really proud of and, also, a project which didn't really work out?

JS: Since the first one, in 1982, I consider the whole of my curatorial practice a big exhibition. Not having access to the institutions of the time, I started naturally in the real world with projects at airports and other incongruous everyday places, on a docked boat, between two cities. Today I'm back to projects in the public space. I was lucky enough to be able to invent my own models. First, with Nicolas Bourriaud at the Palais de Tokyo, it was a question of conceiving a model coherent with the world in which we live. Later, I had the chance to develop the first private foundation in China and now in Mexico. Each project is a continuation of another, without repetition. Some, without necessarily being better, simply go further than others. When you are experimenting, there are, nevertheless, sometimes things that don't work. In this sense, the *Infra Sound* exhibition that took place in Hamburg, Germany in 1995 was a disaster. It was on the beginnings of sound in public places (supermarkets, shopping malls, train stations, subways, etc.). The idea was to invest in public places and to show how sound information broadcasted everywhere was beginning to invade urban space. This exhibition wanted to put forward a new type of urban pollution, insidious and generalized. I had invited a number of international artists to produce pieces designed specifically for certain sites in the city. On the day of the opening, only one out of four pieces was working, while I was opening the show myself, taking a hundred people from one place to another in the city. The failures are as important as the successes. Pride is not really a word in my vocabulary, but if I had to have only one, it would be to be alive today and to be able to continue to build my own path. Every day I tell myself that it is great that it continues even though everything can stop at any moment. I am happy with what I have done but I am aware that everything is ephemeral. This is also what justifies my independence. I chose to live the danger of my reality, a reality that is precarious, difficult and complex. I am happy to be able to continue like this.

GM: Can you describe—based on one of your curatorial projects—the path from the first idea to the exhibition? What are the most important steps in developing and executing a project? Is Curating always a struggle between vision and practical constraint? Could you give an example?

JS: There is no project without constraints. A project without constraints is unreal and utterly naïve. It is the famous "draw me a sheep" by Saint Exupéry, which can be answered by drawing whatever we like however we please. Each project has its very own structural, economic and political constraints, whether it is the creation of a magazine, an exhibition, an institution or a project in an urban space. On the contrary, the constraints make the project. To give an example, for the Palais de Tokyo, the architects Lacaton and Vassal didn't have the budget to remodel the entire building. They embraced the constraints and used the budget to ensure safety conditions, and this 'brutalism' contributes to its renowned and unique aspect today. That is how we were able to re-open this place fast, in less than 2 years. The constraints are necessary. It is always best to know them from the start.

GM: How do you define the relation between artist and curator? Where are the conflict lines? Is curating artistic work or a service to the artist and their work?

JS: To make an exhibition is to be in a dialogue with an artist and invent together a project that they may never have done without you. To showcase an artwork in a traditional way doesn't interest me. However, I'm interested in inventing a project that pushes their vocabulary, their practise, their system. To curate is to live this collective adventure. It is writing a score together that pushes us to our boundaries. What would we say of a musician that replayed exactly the score of another? It is rather about interpreting it in one's own way—a curator brings their touch by helping the artist take a new step in their work.

GM: There have recently been some examples of artists being invited by institutions to curate major shows and of curators producing their own art. In what way is the line between authorship and curating shifting/fading?

JS: I have never made a distinction or put barriers between these practices. Numerous artists—I notably think about Félix Gonzalez Torres, a great international artist that was part of Group Material in the 1980's, a conceptual art group based in New York—part of his work was to conceive interventions and exhibitions, that were fully part of the members' artistic practises. When Elmgreen & Dragset became curators of the Istanbul Biennial, Kader Attia of the one in Berlin, or when BMPT present their own projects, it is to me the same thing. Their work, their artistic vision, extends to exhibition curation. There are also artists, like Francesco Bonami and Hou Hanru, who became curators. There is no hierarchy or uncrossable border. It isn't a novelty, and I don't think that there is, today, a particular development of this phenomenon. I find the approach of one artist to another fascinating. They can bring a vision, a reading grid utterly different from what we could have seen before them. I don't see why exhibitions should be exclusively reserved for historians or self-proclaimed curators.

GM: What is art and its values?

JS: As my dear friend Chen Zhen once said better than I ever could: "Art as such is not all that important. What matters is giving meaning and thought to what one does and relating it to life itself."

GM: How independent is an independent/freelance curator? How dependent is a curator employed by a museum? How different is their work and self- understanding?

JS: These are two worlds that have nothing to do with each other. In an institution, curators work on a timescale, an established budget, and a pre-existing location. They work in general on projects with a perspective of 3 to 5 years ahead. It is an impossible scheme for a person that lives from their practise alone. Working 5 years in advance before realising a project is an enigma that doesn't match the pace of the contemporary world of work. Inevitably, someone that is not attached to an institution must provide more work to survive, produce and exist. All those who went down the road of independence understand its extreme difficulty, the precariousness it implies, and even its long-term impossibility. Being an independent curator also means having a position, affirming a vision. In the early 1980's, being independent meant not being in an institution and inventing one's own way, one's own curatorial writing. Today it often means looking for a position, and rarely a theorical or affirmative one. It is impossible to live with one project a year, to work on an artist for three full years, to write, to meet and travel the world thinking the same thing. None of us have this luxury.

GM: Are there two different art worlds—the art world of museums and big collectors, including star curators, auction houses and big fairs, and the other art world based on smaller biennales, independent art spaces, and independent curators, as Robert Fleck once argued? Is there also a gap between curators serving one or the other world ?

JS: I would add to what Robert says that there aren't two but many art worlds. A multitude of galaxies compose this universe. That is what makes it complex to someone who is a stranger to it at the beginning. Most don't understand a thing because it isn't a clear world, classified and organised, but an ecosystem composed of numerous subgroups that sometimes intersect and overlap in a highly complex way, which is also what makes it so rich.

GM: What is the impact of identity politics on the theory and praxis of curating? Did it change your way of thinking and working?

JS: I don't feel like I've changed. This identity dimension, more generally diversity, was already here at the dawn of my projects. In 1989, I worked with the General Idea group, filling a stairwell with AIDS posters replaying Robert Indiana's *LOVE*. At the time, AIDS had stricken Europe and the whole world. To carry this societal message with a group of artists among whom two of the members were disappearing, hit by this dreadful scourge, was absolute evidence. Neither a question or a subject, the disease was here, and we could not neglect it. In the same way, we speak today of artists from different territories, but I have always been into the mix, the diversity among others—whether they be African, Latino, Asian, American, European or from anywhere else. I have never thought in terms of quota but on the contrary: a fluid population of personalities from different parts of the world, different obedience, cultures and identities. I have never been close to a dogma and a sole position. I have always loved being drawn into doubt by different positions. What made me evolve was the sum of artists, creators and thinkers that I had the chance to meet over 30 years—not a fashion or a trend that makes me bend to one side or the other.

GM: What is censorship in society and what is it in the art world (if there is a difference) today?

JS: Censorship is everywhere and evermore present. Let's not be naïve, it is as much in the United States, China as in France. If we open a magazine from the sixties or seventies and one from today—as with exhibition programming, then and now—it is day and night. Regarding what was showcased in photography, it seems to me that we are moving backward rather than forward, and in a catastrophic manner. Censorship is gaining ground and is insidious. Like smoke, it enters beneath every door. The world becomes more and more conservative: in the media, on television, in speeches, and in institutions, we hardly dare to show anything. We can no longer showcase certain photographers that we used to on a massive scale 20 years ago. The constraints are ideological.

Art embodies openness. Morals have always scared me in the sense that it is a world of constraints, barriers and rules. The world I was born into was full of morals, an old world that I felt was wasting away. Morals induce a judgment and criticism based on differences. Morality is the beginning of the end, the start of all and every misunderstanding, all wars and all the world's atrocities.

GM: What will be the main challenges for a curator in the future? How will curatorial work change?

JS: If there is one, the biggest challenge today is to be able to express oneself freely. In the years to come, the real difficulty will be to think outside the box of the right-minded, the non-abrasive, the decorative or the academic. To achieve that, the only thing to do is resist. In order not to succumb to temptation, we must know where we must be and where we naturally position ourselves. Personally, I have always loved to be in an uncomfortable position and in constant questioning. To me, the important thing is not to take the easy way out and be mediocre, to live without compromise.

I still believe in the concept of Avantgarde

Felicitas Thun-Hohenstein
in conversation with Gerald A. Matt

GERALD A. MATT: What was your reaction when the minister of culture called to tell you that he had chosen you as the Venice biennial's commissioner for the Austrian pavilion? Complete surprise? Or perhaps some satisfaction as well?

FELICITAS THUN-HOHENSTEIN: Joy, yes—and energy. The line appeared at once: gather voices, open rooms, carry decisions. Venice is teamwork. Not a pedestal, a rehearsal—the space of the possible.

GM: There is nothing better.

FTH: The best is when something remains: relationships that hold, attention that doesn't fray—and enough momentum for the next round.

GM: It is very courageous to take on one name. So far, I have always had the feeling that curators find it difficult to ultimately decide on one or another single artist. They compromise and show multiple artists instead. Were there also people who were irritated, who perhaps criticized you?

FTH: I think there is always criticism. The response has been consistently positive—at least from what I have heard. I like courage; I need clarity. A solo is not a snub—it's a lens. Friction is a rehearsal for change. The question that stays: artistically, does it hold? If yes, it stands and - it does.

GM: Why not a man?

FTH: A better counter-question is: why so rarely a woman? Selection follows artistic necessity—and it can correct old imbalances without becoming a gesture.

GM: I have to follow up on that. We know that there are biological differences between men and women, but do you see a difference between male and female art?

FTH: Art has no gender; visibility often does. So we work on the conditions—criteria that keep the work, not the label, at the center.

GM: So, the reproach is irrelevant.

FTH: As reproach, irrelevant; as symptom, instructive. The aim is parity—without grandstanding, with consistency. However, at this biennial we consider a structural imbalance. It is simply about time a woman had a solo presentation in Venice. In the entire history of Austrian contributions, there has never been an individual presentation by a woman artist. We looked at the statistics. Since 1975, thirty-eight male and eleven female artists have been represented. Fifteen of the male artists had individual presentations. So, I think it is about time that we addressed this anachronism. In my experience, solo presentations are generally more sustainable, also in terms of artistic work. They get more attention after the biennial unless the curatorial concept is exactly to the point.

GM: As for Austria, the minister of culture appoints the commissioner directly. There are countries where a jury decides. Do you think this is a good selection system?

FTH: This selection system has been questioned for a long time. I also think there were always plans to change it. I would be in favor of an open call, as in many other countries, a competition where curators can submit concepts which then go through a review. From my point of view, the decision should be transparent.

GM: We have seen a proliferation of biennials in recent years. From Gwangju to Riga. Even Vienna has a biennial. Venice stands out. It is the oldest biennial. It is in fact a world exhibition as well as an international competition. My first question is: Do we have too many biennials? Can there ever be too many? And my second question is: Is the Venice Biennale unique and special precisely because it is still based on the idea of national pavilions? Or, perhaps, the concept should be abandoned altogether in the face of the rising nationalism?

FTH: Numbers don't decide—ethos and care do. Biennials matter when they produce research, encounter, and continuity. Abolish them? No. Inhabit them critically and make the history speak. The Venice Biennale is the mother of all biennials. It was founded in 1895. I think it is quite interesting that it was initially an exhibition concept based on the world exhibitions in Paris and London with one large pavilion. In 1907, the Belgians made themselves independent because the other big countries like France, Germany, USA took up too much space in the first big pavilion. The Belgians would no longer put up with being relegated to the last corner.

GM: Then everyone else followed suit.

FTH: Yes. The pavilion model grew over time—through diplomacy, urban planning, and art politics. What interests me now is how artists annotate that history from within: turning a national frame into a site of relation rather than a border.

GM: Outdated? Or is that exactly what makes it unique?

FTH: Both can be true. The form is old; the conversation inside can be urgently contemporary. That tension is not a flaw—it's the fuel. Work with it, not around it.

GM: In the meantime, are there too many biennials worldwide?

FTH: Too many begins when they become interchangeable. Distinction comes from local proximity, time for research, fair production, and live mediation—not from scale alone.

GM: There is never enough art on display?

FTH: Display isn't enough. We need legibility—frames that support looking without smoothing everything out.

GM: Robert Fleck talked about this divide in a lecture when he took up his professorship in Düsseldorf. On the one hand, there is the biennial art, which is non-commercial, more process-based, and perhaps more political. And on the other, there is museum art and the art of major collectors and major galleries. Of course, the boundaries are quite permeable. Do you think this separation benefits art, or is it simply the way it is?

FTH: I think that there are and should be alliances. As Robert Fleck said in his lecture about the so-called B-artists, there are also B-curators on the road on all continents.
The fields are porous. Moving between them is productive if the ethics and integrity of the work remain intact: economically informed, aesthetically responsible.

GM: Independent curators.

FTH: Exactly.

GM: Artists and curators who travel and receive grants, etc.

FTH: Yes, that is good too. Because every time you travel and work somewhere else, you learn an enormous amount. My greatest professional experience was doing the Cairo Biennial many years ago, which once again completely re-shaped my Western view of art.

GM: Coming back to the biennials: I noticed—also at other major art events—that when you come to the openings, they are very lively, the videos are working, art globetrotters from all over the world trickle in. But then, they leave the place again like grasshoppers, so to speak. And when you go back later, the videos are no longer running. There is no one there. No one seems to be interested anymore. Don't you sometimes worry that this has become a kind of self-satisfaction machinery for the art world and the real world is actually completely excluded, even though the art itself and the art discourse constantly deal with its problems?

FTH: Openings are confetti; the work is day to day. Treat exhibitions as living systems: keep things running, reactivate, host conversations. Less toasting, more tending.

Basically, it is important to take the communication of artistic language and art in general more seriously. That is the topic of the research project, *Six Formats*, where we are investigating different formats of mediation and display. I don't want to share your somewhat negative view, because most of these biennials, whether in Gwangju or in St. Petersburg, perhaps less so in St. Petersburg, also arose in part from an urban development impetus, just as the Venice Biennale did originally. And I do think that the regions are also on display as a result.

GM: Of course, there's often a tourist and urban planning aspect.

FTH: In Venice, it was like that too.

GM: Yes, also in the case of the world exhibition. But you were talking about mediation. Isn't one of the problems of mediation that the art institutions and the curators—not the artists—speak a language that makes sense in the context of their self-image, their legitimation and their profiling but no longer reaches the audience and people? For example, the word installation: I once had a debate at the MAK, and we mentioned the word installation. An older lady pointed out that in the past installations were done by a plumber. Why use such an absurd term in art? Or the word practice. People usually associate it with a doctor's office. Art has occupied this word, but most people don't understand it. And there are ghastly words like context, which partly just obscure the fact that there is no content. It's the emperor's new clothes via language instead of trying to say things clearly. Don't you see this problem? After all, you are active in both areas, theory and practice.

FTH: Language can be precise and still welcoming. I like a small triad: plain sentences, precise terms, and, now and then, a poetic image. Translate without dilution.

GM: Hiding behind post-structural discourses.

FTH: Theory is a tool, not a shield. No experience, no theory; no theory, no experience—they need each other. The point is connection, not cover. You have concepts such as the avant-garde or context. These are all concepts that also relate to social situations or artistic practice at their respective times. But it is indeed very important to formulate the area of mediation in different languages and think of the visitors, who are numerous. One should not forget that 600,000 people visit Venice every year.

GM: There is a huge number of visitors who have no direct connection to art, who are just curious.

FTH: Curiosity is a gift. Our task is to shape approaches—clear paths, time, small cues—so strong works can do what they do. Curiosity isn't a deficit; it's the beginning.

GM: I would be interested to know how you became a curator and a professor at the Academy of Fine Arts. Can you tell us what kind of background you come from? Did art play a role in your upbringing? Did your parents support your idea of studying art?

FTH: My mother used to take me to Venice every year. And my first intensive encounter with art was at the Guggenheim Museum in Venice, Giacometti's *Walking Man* was in the garden at the time. For me, art is a method of orientation—a place to test questions, listen closely, and make room for others to do the same. I'm a theorist, not an artist; the work is dialogic—co-thinking with practitioners and publics. *Con-spirare* here is modest: a shared breath, a common vocabulary.

GM: Was there another career aspiration before you knew that you wanted to be involved in art?

FTH: Yes—dance.

GM: That fits wonderfully with your focus on performance, dance, space, and people. But you still went through the classical art history program. There really wasn't any contemporary art there.

FTH: It trained my eye for how history is made—classification, narrative, omission. Since then I've been interested in how images circulate socially—between bodies, media, and institutions—and how exhibitions can rewrite those routes.

GM: With big names.

FTH: Yes, of course. But I became more interested in thinkers like Arnold Hauser very early on, because I was drawn to the socio-critical component. On the one hand it preserves autonomy, but on the other, it shows that art always exists in relation to social contexts and above all to forms of communication.

GM: You must have been interested in *The Social History of Art and Literature* by Arnold Hauser, for example. That is an important book.

FTH: Exactly. Aby Warburg was also a very important figure for me. I then actually did my doctoral studies externally at the Albertina. Konrad Oberhuber was the director at the time. That also had a very strong influence on me, because sitting and working in those study halls was particularly beautiful. Unfortunately, they no longer exist today.

GM: If we look at the whole art system—at this interplay of galleries, museums, collectors, the state and universities—it is based on the fact that art is ultimately a concept of agreement in which different forces participate and thus, of course, also of interpretive sovereignty, a struggle for interpretation, a struggle over what is art, what is good art, what is expensive art. What has changed since you have been active in this area? Have the forces shifted there?

FTH: On the question of what is art, or the development of the art scene in general?

GM: The individual scenes. There are people who say, now wholesalers are buying auction houses. Some galleries have larger exhibition spaces than museums. I would be interested to hear your perspective on curatorial power. It is perhaps declining today, but it used to be so considerable that one had the feeling that curators determined the exhibitions by selecting the artists like stamps to fit their concepts. How do you see this? What has changed decisively in the last 20 or 30 years?

FTH: We're living through genuine plurality—of forms, voices, and cultural approaches. Contemporary art hasn't just widened the field; it has, remarkably, reached market parity with modernism and the old masters. But the deeper shift is conceptual: from selection to relation, from the object to the score, from authority to co-authorship. Institutions are learning to hold time—rehearsal, restaging, iteration—so works can live rather than merely premiere. We are in the thick of a very interesting transition.

GM: Contemporary art has even partly taken over.

FTH: Yes. This interest is not just thrilling; it's an opportunity to keep plurality high. When we present work from across geographies—how people think, what they ask, what they face, and how they shape it—the conditions for a more open society improve.

GM: We talked about the problems of mediation followed by the question of how much impact art can have. Sometimes one naturally has the feeling that art is something, as Bourdieu might put it, a thing for the happy few, the few who are privileged by education or other means. And they don't like to share the added value of art with—in quotation marks—the masses. They consciously speak a language that others do not understand and visit those deserted places like tourists who prefer not to talk about them so that no one else goes there. At the same time, however, the artists actively address political and social issues. But there, too, the feeling is that they are only preaching to the converted who then pat themselves on the back saying: "Yes, that is my opinion too, anyway". In other words, they don't reach the others at all. What can be done? Is that a good thing or should something be done, especially by curators like you?

FTH: That is also my approach to the biennial. When I got the invitation to curate the biennial, it became clear to me pretty quickly that I wanted to reach the widest possible public. So, I decided to extend this temporality, this time corset of the biennial. And that is why we are already starting the so-called Biennale Lectures in the fall, which are open to the public, and will also have a platform on the website with live stream transmissions and an archive. Here in Vienna, we will also try to address the biennial themes such as the national pavilion, feminist themes, feminist artistic practice, the question of mediation, the question of temporality, of formats, of concepts of time and the concept of time in the exhibition. All of this will be addressed at various events. The artwork will be shown again in Vienna in the same time frame of six months in the Upper Belvedere to give as many people as possible the opportunity to actually see the work. Duration helps. Build programs that outlast the event: city and education partnerships, open archives, returns and reactivations. Publicness grows with time, not with volume.

GM: You mentioned the term avant-garde before. Art has always believed, and its environment has always believed, that art is the cultural moment that advances, that recognizes more, that is a sensorium for social change. I ask you deliberately: Isn't art overrated in that sense? Because if you look at what is really changing the world, it is technological innovations, it is the introduction of the Internet. That has changed the world much more than the artistic avant-garde. To put it in Marxist terms, the conditions of production ultimately determine the superstructure, not the other way around. Is this concept of the avant-garde actually dead? Is it a pure cliché? Or do you still believe in it or in the function of art as being advanced and progressive?

FTH: I still believe in the concept of the avant-garde because, above all, it is always interrelated. It is always changing in relation to the respective society, the respective culture, the respective time, it rubs up against it and puts itself in relation to it. Technology rearranges infrastructures; art rearranges attention. They work on different tempos. We need bridges between both—otherwise we change the world and fail to notice how.

GM: But they're an important commentary.

FTH: Commentary—and often a compass. Sometimes even a decent Plan B.

GM: I can't help but address a debate or a socially powerful moment that has increasingly dominated the discussion in recent years: political correctness. And I ask quite provocatively, is it a necessary regulation—also for art—or the beginning of censorship? And a very specific question: Would you present the work of an artist like Otto Mühl, who was convicted under criminal law? We could also name Carl André. He was acquitted for lack of evidence but there was a trial because his wife, Ana Mendieta, fell out of a window and they never found out exactly why. Would criminal conduct be a reason for you not to show an artist?

FTH: Language as care, yes; moral monopoly, no. With contested biographies: clarify the facts, frame responsibly, include affected perspectives. Showing is never neutral—context is part of the work.

GM: But it shouldn't hinder language.

FTH: No, it should not hinder or censor it.

GM: Otto Mühl at the Biennale, you a curator?

FTH: No, that wouldn't work.

GM: You have known Vienna's cultural life for quite some time and are a close observer, but you also travel around a lot internationally and can certainly judge the international presence of Austrian art. In my opinion, Austrian art has lost its international presence in recent years. Would you agree? If so, do you see a reason for that?

FTH: I think it's a structural problem. The production is strong; the bridge in the middle is fragile. We need durable mid-scale institutions, multi-year budgets, and co-production funds—continuity over façade.

If you look at Germany, for example, you'll find many art associations. Practically in every larger city there is an art association where young artists can have their first exhibitions. In Vienna, we have the Neuer Kunstverein Wien, for example. These are very committed projects of course but have far too little money and can hardly consolidate through it. It would be very important to finally get a strong commitment from politics for the visual arts.

GM: That brings us to cultural politics. Has anything changed in the last 20 or 30 years? And has the shift to a right-wing government had any consequences? Or does this actually change nothing since we have a continuity of funding anyway? And if we think further: What needs to change?

FTH: Culture needs reliable frameworks: clear responsibility, predictable funding, fair pay, and protected spaces for disagreement. Then it can also speak clearly when it must.

I think the visual arts should get more attention in Austria, politically. It is the theater and music still that matters most. The greater the attention, the greater the financial support. Of course, a lot has changed in terms of funding. Art universities have changed and developed a lot. I think that the art scene is very dynamic. It just needs a stronger commitment from cultural politics, and a ministry of arts would be the first step in this direction. That is something we have been calling for, for a long time. It would open more institutional possibilities.

GM: Isn't that thinking too institutionally? The U.S. does not have a ministry of arts either, but they have a very strong presence of artists worldwide. That is also true for some other countries. Isn't this a bit of an Austrian way of thinking—that the whole thing needs to be bureaucratized in order to work better?

FTH: Austria needs a clear political home for the arts—call it a ministry or not, but give it responsibility and budget. Models aren't copy-paste; accountability is.

GM: Should you be able to write off art acquisitions?

FTH: It's a pragmatic lever—if tied to public benefit: lending obligations, transparency, and access.

GM: Isn't that favoring the rich in our country?

FTH: It can—if designed poorly. With caps, disclosure, and public-access requirements, it can widen access and reduce precarity across the field.

GM: How do you explain the fact that the first time an ÖVP/FPÖ coalition formed a government, there was strong artistic resistance, which hasn't happened this time? What has changed?

FTH: That's a development I also observe with concern. I think we are called upon to look very carefully and attentively at what is happening here and to counter certain developments with clearer words. And art is called upon here, too. Because if we look at who revolted or spoke up clearly in 1968 Austria—it was art. The task remains: speak clearly, build coalitions, and keep rooms open where disagreement can breathe.

GM: That's right, the artists.

FTH: For example, with the university action in the New Institute Building in Vienna—*Art and Revolution*.

GM: It was otherwise relatively quiet, but the artists were the revolutionaries. When you talk about your curatorial self-image, are there any role models? Curators who were relevant to you, or whom you admired?

FTH: Lucy Lippard as an icon of American feminist exhibition making. Harald Szeemann: all his exhibitions were great! For me, they were like chambers of wonder, of knowledge production. He had a very exploratory, also a very passionate approach. Of course, Cathrin Pichler, who came from the same generation and made wonderful festival exhibitions in Vienna, like the *Wunderblock*. I learn from stances: feminist clarity, generous research, archival care and habits of attention matter.

GM: An essential task of a curator is to make decisions about what's important, what's less important, what's good, and what's not so good. When is art "good" for you? That is such a simple question, yet not so easy to answer.

FTH: It is not an easy question at all. And I would never utter whether art is good or bad. I don't presume to do that. There are many different approaches to creativity and many different art scenes. For me, the most interesting thing is when seemingly incompatible things come together. When it shifts perception without shouting—when it lets you think and feel, and still echoes once you've stepped outside.

GM: We've touched on some of your key themes—body, space, dance and performance. You've worked with these academically, but also in exhibitions. What draws you to this topic? And to what extent are these boundary crossings even possible? I am asking this quite consciously because, for example, a colleague, Chris Dercon, took over the Volksbühne in Berlin and tried to transfer theatrical and performative elements from visual arts into theater—and ultimately failed. What appeals to you about it? Where does it work and where are the limits?

FTH: I'd say my approach clearly comes out of the visual arts and is intermediary. I am interested in the shifting relationality of the artist, the audience and the artwork, both aesthetically and conceptually, but across all media. Crossings work when they're context-true. Not every transfer holds. The test is simple: does the form let the room breathe differently?

GM: Could you give an example?

FTH: For example, Renate Bertlmann—now in preparation for the Austrian Pavilion (2019). Over four decades she has built a complex practice: live actions and camera-based studio performances; insistently performative yet in sustained dialogue with so-called traditional media—drawing, photography, objects, painting. In her work gesture and material think together—performance braided with image and object over time. We treat the pavilion as a score, not a container—following Guattari's idea of an existential experiment: a live test of relations in which audiences co-author and the room's tempo shifts.

GM: Right. They are essential to her way of thinking, actions and work. In short, you are also associated with feminist art. To what extent has art, and those art works, influenced your life? To what extent would you describe yourself as a feminist?

FTH: In the early 2000s, meeting Carolee Schneemann in Vienna reset my compass. From there—and through my work at the academy—a stubborn, generous network of women artists took shape. I learned that visibility is labor: who is named, archived, listened to. My understanding of feminism is therefore practical, not declarative: an ethics of attention—seeing, speaking, opening doors—and it keeps moving."

GM: So you're a different woman now than you were 30, or 25 years ago, in terms of that position.

FTH: In some ways, yes—same questions, different tempo. I'm less interested in purity and more in practice: shared authorship, care, parity, infrastructure. I listen harder, make more room, and argue more precisely. If anything, I dance the work differently now—quicker to open the floor, slower to close it.- Above all, I have to say, the attitude is now being strengthened by the political situation, which is very backward-looking, especially as far as questions about feminism or women in society are concerned. I would say I am all the more alert, which will grow stronger.

GM: You are involved in contemporary art. Are you also interested in the past? Can we imagine you doing a Caravaggio or Mantegna exhibition one day, and going into art history?

FTH: Of course. The past is present. Feminist and postcolonial re-readings reopen what we think we know—history becomes a current rehearsal, not a monument.

Taking a new look at what seems to have already been discussed. Of course, it is very exciting to analyze Caravaggio from a feminist point of view.

GM: Did you sometimes doubt art? You do lead, like all of us, a very, I don't want to say pleasant, but inspired life in the environment of art. Maybe a privileged life. Have you sometimes felt like you were missing the real problems of the world and actually wanted to do something completely different? Has there ever been a doubt?

FTH: Doubt visits me regularly. I give it a chair and questions. It keeps the practice flexible—and kind. But I've never had a doubt because visual art is the most important companion to my thinking which permanently longs for the increase of knowledge and the expansion of one's own boundaries. Within my field I am trying as hard as I can to push forward small changes, even of perceptions and perhaps standardizations. I think you must be accurate in what you do and in what you have perhaps slowly worked out. I wouldn't do anything else. I might still become a dancer.

GM: For you, art and life are one.

FTH: They interpenetrate. Art condenses life—and, on good days, gives it a better grammar.

GM: Can you tell me the last time you felt real happiness in relation to art? An artist, a work of art that made you feel happy.

FTH: A great book, I would say, gives me that happiness. There are a few women authors who are very radical thinkers, like Christine Lavant, Ingeborg Bachmann, Susan Sontag etc. Whenever I can turn a page in one of their books and see myself reflected in it, I have great moments of happiness. And I can think of a great exhibition: I was in Berlin and saw *Neolithic Childhood* at the Haus der Kulturen der Welt curated by Tom Holert. A careful montage around Carl Einstein—clear, slow, wide. A quiet happiness: orientation through composition.

GM: Felicitas, thank you very much for the interview.

This interview is an edited version of the conversation between Felicitas Thun-Hohenstein und Gerald A. Matt from 24th September 2018 as part of the talk series Matt spricht mit... for the Viennese TV broadcaster W24.

It's not only about artists, it's about people

Olesya Turkina in conversation with Gerald A. Matt & Synne Genzmer

GERALD A. MATT & SYNNE GENZMER: What is a curator? Can you define your understanding and practice as a curator?

OLESYA TURKINA: A curator is a person who takes care, who cures and who combines different functions, aesthetically, sociologically, politically, etcetera. For me, the word 'curator' came together with Perestroika. Because in the Soviet era, a 'curator' meant a person from the KGB, who followed artists or musicians or writers. It was a specially appointed person, who had to observe an artist and, let's say, report on what the person spoke about, etcetera. So, with the Perestroika the word 'curator' was introduced in Russia. Many people, especially artists from the older generation, didn't understand us, the younger generation. In the beginning of Perestroika, I was very young, and when I went, for example, to an artist's studio—let's say, an official artist's studio—and declared proudly I was a curator, they looked at me with great surprise thinking: "I'm sorry, you are too young to be a KGB, and why are you speaking about it so blatantly?" In the beginning of Perestroika, it was a transliteration and then, finally, it became, let's say, a normal word adopted by the Russian language. To me, the practice of a curator is the same as the practice of Karl Marx: to combine theoretical, political and everyday life in the form of unity. Because there is no curator without taking care, without curing, without being involved in the complexity of the problem and the present situation.

GM & SG: We face many new challenges today. How can curatorial practice face these challenges? How can it be relevant to these challenges? Or do you think that the challenges have simply changed?

OT: I would like to come back to a personal experience. Let's say, I am a survivor of two revolutions—one revolution and one counter-revolution. At the beginning of Perestroika, it was a great challenge. The very word and profession 'curator' appeared. Curators were being actively involved in the current situation—in this case, local art. Russian avant-garde artists supported the state and were forced to create work to change the situation. And so, what to do right now? You see, I have students. I teach at the Faculty of Liberal Arts and Science. And speaking with my students, I have to answer questions they ask me every day. What can we do? What is our task today? What can be done? And so, what can be done? I recollect Felix Guatteri's and other philosophers' ideas that in our contemporary situation, the major—let's say—creative forces that can rise are among curators and artists. There are no organized proletarians, because we have no working class any more than we have creative class. The workers have been divided into different strata by corporations, salaries, and privileges. So, who are the people with nothing to lose? Only artists, writers, and curators. Our task today is to be the avant-garde of the new changes, analyze and criticize what is going on, and try to be actively involved in the situation. In a way, we play the role of the working class in Karl Marx' time.

GM & SG: Do you feel that you still have all the possibilities to criticize, analyze, and express?

OT: They have become more and more narrow. Every day, I feel that there is less and less free space left. That's it. That is what I can say. It is really a very heavy situation. And I feel this every day.

GM & SG: The following questions are about the role of curators and their relation to other professionals in the art field. How do you see the changing relations between curators, artists, collectors, galleries, museums and critics? Has there been a shift of power and influence? Is there another new type of curator: Francois Pinault instead of Harald Szeemann? Or, are young artists taking over the role of curators? What are your observations?

OT: You see, we live in another sphere now. Before, I would have discussed the influences. Now, it is completely different. Nobody has the power. Museum directors have been replaced one after another over the last months. It is hard for me to speak because I live here, I cannot yet analyze what is going on. I guess we need time to just observe. When you ask if Harald Szeemann was replaced by Francois Pinault, I say "Never ever!" I would like to explain it with a kind of metaphor. It happened to me during the 48th Venice Biennial when I was curating the Russian pavilion. Harald Szeemann, was walking around and looking to see what was going on. And then he was dancing like mad at the final party. I could hardly imagine that

I could dance with Francois Pinault. I don't mean to offend him, but that is the difference. About artists taking over the role of the curators, I hope they will get the chance. Because we need a new point of view. Young artists make a revolution by heart, by situations. They must change the situation. It depends of course on the conditions they live in, but here they are privileged. When young artists become curators, they just jump up and look at what is going on. Of course, they are not so much connected with collective institutions and all this, let's say, political ideological power. They are fearless. They have a new point of view. You must be fearless. I know it, again, from my personal experience, because I teach at the curatorial studies section, and in 2014, I became the director of Curatorial Studies Program in St. Petersburg at the Faculty of Liberal Arts and Science. When I thought of the program, I asked them, what point of view do you have on this? They said we would love to see what is going on, through studies, through a theoretical view. And I understand both. Sometimes it is hard. Artists become curators. We know such cases. But I also have examples among my students where curators have become excellent artists.

GM & SG: Would you say that artists as curators are more privileged in the sense that they have more freedom in a way?

OT: That is true, yes. They have no more fears. Because their position does not depend on the institutional field, on the curator. Once they become established, they have those limits. Curators and galleries could say: "What are you doing? Just continue to do what you were doing. I am still thinking of those strange and crazy works that you were producing." Young artists are art institutional par excellence. That is why I love them so much and deeply hope they will enter more and more into the context of the curatorial field.

GM & SG: When you think about how you became a curator yourself or how you entered the curatorial field, was there a personal hero, a curator whom you admired? And what were her/his qualities and achievements? Or was there a show which you consider a milestone for your own curatorial thoughts and practice?

OT: That's very simple. My personal hero is Pontus Hultén. He curated the *Paris-Moscow, Moscow-Paris* exhibition. I was very young. I went to Moscow to see the show. But the most important moment for me was in 1990, when St Petersburg was still Leningrad. Pontus Hultén brought his students and his friends—Hans Haacke, Daniel Buren, Sarkis—to Leningrad to the

Institute des Arts Plastique and the Russian Museum for the first time. It was still the Soviet Union. And for me... I know Pontus Hultén curated enormous exhibitions—I teach them to my students. The exhibition he created at the Russian museum was, maybe, not the most exciting example. But for me, it was exciting because I realized that this was the real process. Pontus Hultén worked together with the young artists. They divided the exhibition into two floors. The first floor was just for Russian artists. The other one, the basement, was dedicated to young artists. One of the artists was Chen Zhen who came in 1990 and told the most amazing stories. I was appointed as Pontus Hultén's assistant. I was working at the museum and adored him. I was working from early morning until night, because after the work was over and the museum was closed, Pontus Hultén took all the young artists out to drink and eat together at his own expense. For Pontus Hultén, art life was not separated from the rest of life. He respected the artists in every aspect. From this moment on, I also started a very simple, but very important thing. As a curator, you cannot grant yourself better conditions than the artist. I don't like it when the curator stays in a five-star hotel and the artists stay wherever. I can't do that. The curator is not a capitalist. Which brings me back to the Marxist notion. The artist, of course, is a proletarian worker. But they work together. The curator is a worker as well. There is no capitalization. Sometimes, the curator invites the artists to a very fancy dinner, but it does not happen very often. You see, Pontus Hultén was working on the exhibition wherever necessary, putting the works up, speaking with the artists, feeding them, giving them vodka, whatever. Pontus Hultén was so involved. And he was also fearless, like the young artists. He was not so young in the 1990s. When he did the exhibition and showed Russian artists in Paris, it was not the best time. The Afghan war was going on. It was just when a boycott was announced against the Soviet Union. It was something incredible. Everything he did. For me, he was a person who showed you *jouissance*—joy and fearlessness. Those are the two things a person could achieve. Do what you like to do and don't be afraid. If you are afraid, just try to keep going.

GM & SG: That is even general advice for life.

OT: Yes, that is true. Again, I still remember this funny story when this exhibition at the Russian Museum was supposed to open. Sarki prepared an installation using wooden boxes that the museum packed pictures in. But the workers decided that it was something left over and started to clear them away. And Pontus Hultén run after them shouting: "What are you doing? Stop, stop! That's a work of art!" They didn't understand and

I explained it to them. They didn't want to believe it. "This? It looks like boxes from our storage." Pontus Hultén was so engaged he could do it—he could show this kind of art in Leningrad.

GM & SG: Thank you for sharing your memories. Can you also describe a curatorial work or project of your own that you are really proud of? Or another one that you think did not really work out? What about success and failure of curatorial work?

OT: Success? There are different types of success as you know. Capitalist success, economic success, money, power... For me, I felt very successful when I got to make my exhibition at the Pulkovo Observatory in 2007. The observatory is from the beginning of the 19th century and is very famous. They catalogued stars there. It was a really, really important place. During the Second World War it was completely destroyed, bombed, and then it was reconstructed. It worked well until conditions became really bad. And the astronomists went to an observatory in South America and other countries where the conditions for observation were better. And so, it became quieter and quieter. It was like that in the whole city. And so, I had an idea to create an exhibition there. I went to the director of the observatory, and he said "Okay, if the artists are not working with astrology." If there is something astronomists hate, it is astrology. I assured him that there would be no astrology. So, he agreed. I invited different artists; even international artists were included, like the German-Russian artist Joulia Strauss and Moritz Mattern. The artists chose their spaces, inside the reflector telescope, for example. One artist chose the first radio telescope, an open field for site-specific work. Then there was the observatory museum, and one even picked the spot for a scientific meter. So, it was something very special. And then, a very famous astronomer, who had the flu at the time, looked out. He thought he had a delusion, because he'd never seen so many people at the observatory. He checked his temperature. But no, people really had come. There were amazing works, like, for example, the work of two artists from St. Petersburg. They installed a very small wooden chair, a kitchen chair and a device to listen to sound. You expected to hear the sound of the stars or some minimalist or post-minimalist music, but instead you could hear the artist's voice saying something like "Vanya, I'm back home". It was amazing. I loved that show very much. I would love, maybe, not to repeat it—and times have changed—but I hope to do it again in some way or the other.

GM & SG: Furthermore about your own curatorial practice: Can you describe one of your projects, the path from the first idea to the exhibition? What were the most important steps in developing and executing the project? Maybe you have a special personal method.

OT: Oh, yes. It is very simple. For me, the most important thing is to fall asleep. I take my favorite book. As a kid I liked sci-fi very much: H.G Wells and Jules Verne, the early sci-fi before real space travel. So usually my method, my first step is to take my favorite sci-fi novel and fall asleep. And when I fall asleep, I get an idea. I don't think about spaces, money, sponsorship or artists any more. I just feel as if I'm floating in a space station, weightless. Anyway, to get an idea it is very important to feel this weightlessness, this floating around. Otherwise, you have too much gravitation. We stand with our two legs on the earth, and that is not good if you must invent something.

GM & SG: Is curating always a struggle between vision and practical constraint?

OT: Yes, of course. First you have a vision, then, allegorically, you make this vision come true. You try to realize it, but then it becomes hard. You think you have this vision and if you write it down, at least you can control it. And then something happens in the middle of the process. You have a new idea, a new flash, let's say. And then you become more and more interested in developing that idea.

GM & SG: What about the relation between artist and curator in this regard? You have mentioned that curators become artists, and we talked about artists becoming curators. Is curating also a sort of artistic practice? Is curating a service to the artist? Where are the conflicts?

OT: The conflict is in-between. The most important thing for the curator is not to become very artistic, not to interfere with the artist, not to tell him or her what to do. From the point of view of the exhibition it is easy, and you think that you need exactly this work here and the other there, because of this size or this subject. You can't be too artistic, but of course you can become artistic between the lines, let's say. The curator is a reader. You know very well the real author is a reader. So, in this sense, the curator is also a reader. But he/she has to read between the lines and not tell the writer what to write. Like asking, for example, to just change a line, because you don't like it, because it doesn't fit in with the exhibition. No. Try to find the space in between.

GM & SG: You have worked in many various curatorial roles, as a freelance curator with institutions, as a teacher, and a researcher. How do you see the difference between these roles in relation to the institutions, in terms of independence, in terms of aligning with the vision or mission of the institution, for example?

OT: It depends. I was very lucky, and I am happy that my institution changed while I was working there. When I started there, it was still the Soviet Union, and the Russian Museum was very conservative—despite the fact that it had the best collection of Russian avantgarde art. With Perestroika, my generation started to collect contemporary art. Of course, we started to collect contemporary Russian art, and then, there was the great gift by Irene and Peter Ludwig given to the Russian museum. From that moment on it became totally international. We started programming with the help of different countries and making exhibitions, and it started with the exhibition by Pontus Hultén in 1990 when it was still the Soviet Union. It was the first time Marcel Duchamp, Daniel Buren, Chen Zhen, and others were presented in Russia. It was amazing. My institution was changing, and I grew together with it, I changed as well. I did my best to collect, curate, etcetera. Now we have other changes. It is hard to speak about them. And speaking about other institutions, of course, there are different ones. I liked the Stedelijk Museum in Amsterdam very much, where I have co-curated the exhibition called *Kabinet*, after the journal which we started to produce in 1990 in St. Petersburg. We created it by making copies on Zerox machines before it became fully published with 200 copies, and it still continues. The Stedelijk Museum was great in supporting us. We asked to create an exhibition at Malevitch's place which was supposed to travel to Warsaw and Berlin to explain his theory of additional elements. They made it possible; it was no problem. Another thing that I was really amazed about at that time was the trade unions. In Russia trade unions meant nothing. It was just an empty word. When I saw trade unions prohibit workers from using certain substances to clean works of art, or from being overworked, I was really amazed by how labor was protected. I was amazed. But again, I was so lucky back then. I would stay in the museum until midnight reading books that I could find in the museum library, think about exhibitions and then speak with people. I didn't feel like I was working for a big institution, even though it was a big institution. Somehow, it was an example of democracy for me. And I thought that it should be like this. People loved what they did. They cared about art. It's an amazing museum, you can just dream of working there.

GM & SG: You are describing the museum, or the institution, as a democratic space and a field of possibilities.

OT: Well, in Russia the old institutions changed. They became new and open to contemporary art and international activity. At the same time, Western institutions became very supportive and open to Russia when the Iron Curtain was forced to go down. It was a time of discovery for both sides. I don't know how to work in another way, if it is more formal. I never had a feeling of strict formality. For me, it was human to human, even with people like Pontus Hultén or others. There was something very human at the base, and I didn't feel awkward or shy towards a person because he or she represented all this institutional power. It didn't mean anything to me. From the beginning of Perestroika our hierarchy changed, it was broken, there was no more hierarchy. It was an open space, an open field.

GM & SG: What is your opinion about the impact of recent debates and discussions around identity politics or ethical questions?

OT: It is a new and extremely important field. Again, I feel this through art. You can really be involved with and touched by art. Because both questions are crucial for human beings. It is of course important that you can read and discuss things, but you should look at the work. I was so lucky that I could visit the last 15th Sharjah Biennial. It was absolutely great because of how it dealt with the identity question. The idea was based on the question of identity—thinking about from the past to the present. One of my favorite artists, Cao Fei, made a piece about the history of theater representing the journey back into the past and into the future. It was installed in a former hospital. It was fantastically made. Of course, art is about trauma, about curing trauma, about remembering and recollecting, and about repeating trauma. And we are going through a traumatic experience. Look at the world. We are being wounded, let's say, every hour. It is terrible. It is a terrible world. When we can reflect on it, it's art. I mean not only visual art. For me, it is primarily visual art, but there is, of course, music and literature. On this occasion, people are talking about prophecies because of writers like Vladimir Sorokin. Now, people are saying that he kind of envisioned what is going on. In a way, he did. It doesn't mean that he actually foresaw it, but he is very sensitive to these waves.

GM & SG: One last question. What about the future of curating? Where do you see challenges for the future, or where does curating go? Or where could it go?

OT: Well, I guess it goes back again to taking care. It is not only about artists but about people. I mean, all we need is love, not hate. And love means co-existence. People are kind of self-isolated because of all these devices they have in their hands. They become very alienated. They do not like to share anything. They are afraid, or ashamed, or whatever. So, the future is about love. We live in hard times. What can we do? We can criticize them. If we cannot do exhibitions, we can teach our students. I can transmit my plans and my visions to the next generation. Let's say, if I can't do anything anymore, they can do it. I hope so.

It's essential to keep coming back to the conviction that art is free

Kasia Matt-Uszyńska
in conversation with Gerald A. Matt

GERALD A. MATT: What is a curator? Can you define your understanding and praxis as a curator?

KASIA MATT-USZYŃSKA: A curator is not just someone who manages or organizes an art collection or art exhibitions. The curator never works alone - always with artists and/or artists' works. Since there are different ways of looking at or perceiving art, an exhibition concept is always a combination of the artist's thought and the curator's subject view. By selecting the works for an exhibition, juxtaposing them with other works, establishing intellectual and visual connections between them, contextualizing them with other works or even with art history, a curator attempts to convey these thoughts to the public.

GM: When did you realize that you wanted to become a curator?

KU: I come from a sleepy suburb of Warsaw and used to spend a lot of time in the capital going to exhibitions, theatres and jazz clubs. The first art books I read were about the Impressionists, then Cézanne and the Salon des Indépendants, the autumn salon, which made a big impression on me at the time. I was only 17 but I was impressed by the idea of the *Salon* and the role of Ambroise Vollard, an art patron, dealer and curator at the same time who enabled many unknown artists to exhibit in the Salons. I drew a lot during this time. I enjoyed it and was fascinated by how your perception of time changed when drawing. But I also realized that I probably lacked the obsessive, this exclusive and unconditional desire to make art, and that I didn't want to make art but rather wanted to work for art and wanted to concentrate on its theoretical and practical side. And so, I decided to study art history.

GM: You curate shows and are the director of the Neuer Kunstverein Wien. Can you tell us something about how you got into this position, about the steps of your career?

KU: Having graduated in art history, I embarked on a thrilling adventure, working for renowned museums like the Leopold Museum and galleries in both Vienna and New York. But deep down, I felt this burning desire to break free from the conventional art world and do something unique and innovative. And that's when fate intervened in the form of a generous private entrepreneur and collector who offered me a space. Together with some dear friends, I founded the Neuer Kunstverein Wien. We started small with a modest exhibition space but have since expanded to encompass two interconnected exhibition halls spanning almost 2000 square meters. These halls have become a haven for contemporary art, offering an extraordinary platform for artists to showcase their work.

GM: How can curating be relevant to the challenges we face today and in what way does it differ from previous models (if you think it does)?

KU: As a curator, despite all the political and social pressure, it is possible to concentrate on the actual task of serving the art world and the artists and presenting their ideas in a political, social and art-historical context. I work almost exclusively with the contemporary art world, which tends to reflect and artistically process social changes and issues. I have also shown projects at the Neuer Kunstverein that deal with controversial issues related to ecology, economy and identity politics. Nevertheless, it is particularly important today to protect the freedom of art from political and actionist appropriation. I think it is essential for a curator to keep coming back to the phrase: art is free.

GM: Was there a personal hero, a curator whom you admired?

KU: Yes, Alfred Barr Jr. I've read a lot about his work as a curator and museum director, which deeply resonated with me. During his tenure as director of MoMA, he not only acquired works by living artists for the collection and visited their studios but also managed the museum's funding. Barr's approach to exhibition design was also ahead of its time. As an educator, he was deeply committed to making modern art accessible to a wide audience. He envisioned the museum as a kind of laboratory, where he used innovative pedagogical techniques to create wall displays and installations. He used tools like leading questions, juxtapositions and humour to engage the audience. Although his art-historical approach seems traditional by today's standards, his idea of what constituted modern art was actually very broad. For Barr, modern art encompassed not only painting and sculpture, but also applied art, design, architecture, film, photography and theatre. What speaks to me most is his commitment to the idea of the museum as a laboratory, aiming to educate and engage viewers. His dedication to reaching a broad public remains, in my view, one of the most vital tasks of a curator today.

GM: There is a number of examples recently of artists being called by institutions to curate major shows and curators having their own artistic practice. In what way is the line and authorship of curators shifting/fading?

KU: I love getting to know the artists views and ideas - also on the works of their colleagues or other artists. Artists have their own sensorium for art and see Kunstverein very much from an artistic perspective and are therefore less susceptible to the political appropriation of art. Artists, whom I always invite either to work closely together on the design of an exhibition or as curators of exhibitions, always bring new perspectives and ideas to the projects. I am very grateful for these collaborations and see no problem at all with curators or curatorial handwriting or even independence. It's always incredibly enriching, like the recent experience with Jakob Lena Knebl, an artist who not only curated a large exhibition at the Neuer Kunstverein Wien, but also gave the whole thing a personal touch by integrating parts of her exhibition design and architectural elements which she also uses in her own exhibitions, into the exhibition. By including the artworks of her students and graduates and, as the exhibition title *Transmodular* suggested, not only moving beyond the outdated boundaries between art and fashion but also exploring the relationship between art and media, she created an artistic biotope reflective of her personal vision while simultaneously addressing essential social issues from her own distinct perspective.

GM: Can you describe a personal curatorial work and project you are really proud of?

KU: I think it was the exhibition of works by Glenn Brown, a major exhibition I curated for the Kunsthistorisches Museum, and the first Austrian exhibition of works by Glenn Brown - one of the most inspiring artists I have ever met. The exhibition took place in parallel with, or indeed in the context of the *Arcimboldo Exhibion*. Working with such an erudite and thoughtful artist as Glenn Brown was not only incredibly enjoyable, but it was also incredibly exciting to explore the art-historical context of his works with him and to show their roots. With his exhibition at the Kunsthistorisches Museum, Glenn Brown's works point back to the artistic universe from which he draws his inspiration. Brown's painting is deeply rooted in art history, its iconography, myths and clichés. He repeatedly refers to the intellectual and pictorial worlds of classical painting, quotes them, satirizes them and reinvents works by old and modern masters as well as unknown artists from past eras by charging and transforming them with conceptual ideas from modern and contemporary art, literature, film and music—just think of the titles of his works. It was very important to us to show this in the context of Mannerism.

At the centre of Glenn Brown's exhibition are his portraits - the portrait, as in Arcimboldo's work, is both an image of himself and others, a kaleidoscopic, shimmering, mysterious mirror of the world.

However, Brown is not only interested in art-historical iconography, the similarity and transformability of motifs, the simultaneity of the non-simultaneous, but also in the phenomenon and act of painting itself, the nature and laws of colour, its atmospheric and material effects, its possibilities and limitations. "I paint colour" he says, declaring art to be a form of witty "entertainment", or studies for connoisseurs and the curious who allow themselves to be fascinated and intoxicated by his enigmatic riddles.

With his love and passion for the grotesque, the anamorphic, the paradoxical, for distortions and exaggerations, for the artificial and the enigmatic, he finds himself in congenial, friendly proximity to the work of Arcimboldo, for example.

With the museum he recently opened in London, which houses his collection of works by artists from earlier centuries, he demonstrates a personal continuity in the history of art and thus performs an incredibly important task in the mediation of contemporary art.

GM: Was there a show which you consider to be a milestone for curatorial thoughts and praxis?

KU: I hadn't been born yet when Harald Szeeman made Documenta, I could only read about it but I was lucky that the first Biennale that I saw was curated by him. That was a brilliant example for me of how to think and organise large exhibitions. It was incredibly inspiring for me, a starting point. His biennial united intellect and spirit, was curious and open, and showed that outstanding art is to be found not only in the West; it opened the view onto the world. It was not cramped, top-heavy or even pedagogical, it was full of poetry and humour.

GM: Is Curating always a struggle between vision and practical restraint? Can you give an example?

KU: I think this is a conflict that every curator has to resolve in each project - with themselves, with the artists, with the institution they are working for or that is financing their project. It is crucial that in the end the financial and practical limitations do not become visible or damage the vision. There must be no compromises when it comes to the content, quality and vision of an artistic project. The focus must be on the art and the realisation of the artistic ideas. If this is jeopardised, it is better to cancel a project. On the other hand, as I now run an artistic institution myself, which I personally created to provide a means of funding, a catalyst for my artistic projects and dreams, I have experienced and learned in my daily practical institutional work how important it is to reconcile content with organisational and financial concerns. What too many resources you use on one artistic project, you take away from another project, from other artists, as there is only a limited (annual) budget. In my dual role as curator and director of the Kunstverein, I have learned a great deal in this respect - namely, not to see vision and organisation as opposites, but as an enriching dialectic.

GM: How do you define the relation between artist and curator?

KU: The curator and the artists are part of one world in which art is the centre of their lives. Good relationships between artists and curators are characterised by respect, interest, expertise, teamwork and a shared vision of art and its communication.

GM: Where are the conflict lines?

KU: If there are any, there might be between two egos and ideas, between a vision and budget, between the curator and institution, between free and shifting ideas and timelines, between integrity of the artwork and the formation and translation of ideas to the public, and many others.

GM: Is curating artistic work or service to the artist and their work?

KU: Both, and only both make quality curating.

GM: You are a curator, who created her own institution, which is a rare and also highly strenuous endeavour. What was your idea, your impetus?

KU: I've always been interested in bringing works of art, ideas and concepts closer to the viewer. After working for entities such as the Leopold Museum or the Kunsthalle Wien, and as a freelance curator for various institutions, I realised that my projects and visions as an employed curator were even more dependent on other institutional or personal considerations and preferences than as a freelance curator. Founding my own platform or institution was my way of conquering the space for my curatorial freedom.

At the beginning, the Kunstverein was only a space of about 60 sqm. Sometimes it was only possible to show a single work in this small space, but it was important that I could work freely and, above all, closely with the artists without being restricted by institutional constraints or even audience expectations. It was also important to me what the visitor could take away and remember about the exhibition and its message. In the meantime, I have been able to develop a different dimension of exhibition organisation and presentation with the Neuer Kunstverein. We have large, wonderful temporary exhibition halls, which a sponsor made available to us in a former car dealership. I now work with a great team, an assistant curator, a technician and staff.

The Kunstverein has two exhibition spaces of 800 sqm each and can realise great projects, although I concede that these wonderful opportunities are of course always associated with a struggle for resources.

Nevertheless, I see our programme, which took place in very different spaces - from an office to a flat from the 1920s in a landmarked Bauhaus building, to a machine workshop, and currently, to the large halls in former garages and Porsche showrooms - as being in a great continuity. All of the projects were characterised by an examination of the architecture, its surroundings and history. Polish artist Robert Kuśmirowski, for example, thematised the Second World War and the destruction of the castle in Warsaw by reconstructing it in a flat in Vienna's first high-rise building in Herrengasse. Kuśmirowski reflects his complex relationship with the history of his native Poland. *Träumgutstrasse* circles around Czapski Palace that was destroyed in a bombing in 1939. The Krasiński Library, situated in the south wing of the palace, was the centre of political and cultural events in Warsaw between 1862 and 1913. He rebuilt a part of this sculpture in the state after the fire in 1939 in the 60m2 flat of a tower block in Vienna. With its impeccable execution down to the smallest detail, including every minutely copied document and the burnt smell that filled the room, the installation transported us into a dream world of the traumatic events of World War II.

Or, an artist who recently made a reference to the history of the Porsche showroom by building a sculpture modelled on exhaust fumes and tried to capture the atmosphere of a moment.

My projects have always been about crossing the boundaries of art genres between art, fashion, architecture, film, dance, performance and other forms of artistic expression, so we showed exhibitions such as Carsten Fock/William Forsythe, The Digital Effect, Kai Walkowiak, Mary Reid Kelly or Natalie Djurberg and Hans Berg or Barbara Hammer or Aleksandra Wasilewska.

I see art as a continuity.

GM: You now lead an institution. What do you think is being neglected?

KU: As a curator in charge of a larger structure such as an art association or even a museum, you also have to learn to be able to make sacrifices. You can't do everything at the same time and the tasks of managing a museum, from project planning, programming, securing funding and personnel policy to marketing the projects, are extremely challenging. What remains and gives me great pleasure is the constant search for dedicated and interesting artists and curators with whom interesting projects can be realised. Yes, and of course, given the current size of our art association, I still have the opportunity to curate projects that are very close to my heart myself, which I would be very reluctant to give up. What I often miss in Vienna, however, is the exchange with other art spaces, galleries and museums.

GM: Can you tell us more about the history of the Neuer Kunstverein and you are now Director of?

KU: The Neuer Kunstverein Wien was originally supposed to be called COLA (Contemporary Laboratory for Art), but since our neighbours at the time were called Coco (the fact that it sounded so similar to Coca-Cola was something only I found funny), I named the space the very serious-sounding Neuer Kunstverein Wien. This was also a kind of contrast to the small 60-sqm space. At that time, there were more and more independent spaces with bars, which became places to meet, party, and exchange ideas, but I wanted to show a single artist, perhaps just one artwork, an installation, so that people could focus on just one work, thus engaging with the art or a particular position. I remember that one of the visitors to our newly opened space was a collector of this artist who had seen a newspaper article about our exhibition with James Beckett and visited the show, and we talked about the work for two or three hours.

I also invited well-known artists such as Nathalie Djuberg, Robert Kuśmirowski and Shirin Neshat to the small spaces like the one we had in the Hochhaus.

We moved from room to room, which we got sponsored, and there was also a short period in between where we were homeless for a few weeks in 2019, and we did a project curated by Felicitas Thun-Hohenstein 4by12, with several live stream performances. Also, Jakob Lena Knebl did a performance with Markus Pires Mata in a hotel room of the Intercontinental.

GM: You define the Neuer Kunstverein as a "free space". How do you live this idea?

KU: It has always been important for me to grant artists as much freedom as possible and to free them from commercial and institutional constraints. I believe in offering them opportunities and freedoms that they may not have in the rigid structures of museums and larger institutions. At the NKW, artists have the opportunity to produce their works on-site and to experiment. For example, artists work on their installations for months in the NKW's spaces. A notable example is Charlotte Gash, who created car sculpture installations in response to the previous use of our exhibition hall. In our recent exhibition *Hello, Dear Ruth, Questions—Déjà Vu? Unknown Subscription!*, which celebrated the 20th anniversary of a magazine developed by an artist collective, we gave the artists complete freedom in designing the exhibition space. The exhibition space became a walk-in layout, a large editorial backdrop and a temporary laboratory for this project.

GM: You also organized the exhibition *Here and Now, Vienna Sculpture 2022*, an exhibition which was followed by part II in 2023 and part III in 2024, a series of shows presenting the sculptural scene living and working in Vienna, a kind of tribute to the Vienna art world?

KU: First of all, it was a cooperation with an initiative called Verein Skulptur and it was clear to me from the beginning that the garages of a car dealership were perfect for presenting sculptures and object art. These spaces have the ideal dimensions, size, and height to exhibit works that might not fit in galleries, museums, or public spaces. The halls are located in a space between inside and outside, characterized by their rawness and transparency. Naturally, an exhibition of this magnitude and importance required special effort, and the successful implementation of such a project depended on the enthusiasm and commitment of the artists involved. With the *Here and Now* exhibition, my co-curator and I wanted to provide a platform and a venue for Viennese artists working with sculpture or object art. My primary goal with this project was to bring visibility to artworks, sculptures, and objects that are often unseen - stored away, hidden in warehouses, or accessible only to a privileged few in studios - and have yet to find their place in museums or public spaces. The exhibition presents different generations of artists and their sculptural concepts, which are specifically tailored to the spaces of the former St. Marx car dealership. This new contextualization and juxtaposition lend the artworks new perspectives and interpretations. The second part of the sculpture project showcases the thematic and media diversity as well as the exceptional quality of the Viennese sculpture scene. Ambitious projects like this survey of Viennese sculpture also require cooperation with partners and additional funding.

GM: Back to your programmatic vision to incorporate different disciplines and combining different media from sculpture to video to performances like you presented in shows as "The Burrow" (2019) by Agnieszka Polska or "Thingness" (2017) by Yingmei Duan, or group exhibitions such as "The Devil to Pay in the Backlands" (2022) and "Autohaus St. Marx" (2021). How is the response of the artists and the public?

KU: When I arrived in Austria, I noticed that the art scenes here—from visual arts to dance, film and theatre—don't communicate much with each other. They tended to separate themselves, unlike in Poland, where the scenes overlapped more. In Warsaw, unlike here, I often saw actors, musicians at exhibition openings. Poles seemed more involved with theatre, music, jazz and film in their everyday lives, and the different disciplines merged more naturally. I missed that in Austria. That's why I find the cross-border character and the mutual influence of the different disciplines extremely compelling, both to myself and the Kunstverein. The direct experience of art is very important to me. By combining various media, we enable visitors to enter different artistic worlds. I think that this programmatic approach is rewarded by the artists and their enthusiasm working with us and the positive response from our visitors now also coming from different art worlds. It is different now, the art scene has changed also in Austria, you see more and more artists working in a range of fields like music, art or performance. Crossing borders comes naturally.

GM: The exhibition *The Devil to Pay in the Backlands* (2022) investigated the contemporary art scene and created a critical discourse about today's political, social and cultural phenomena and crisis. How important is art as a critical reflection on contemporary society?

KU: I deeply believe that contemporary art is inherently political, albeit in a broader sense. It challenges our habitual ways of thinking and experiencing and encourages us to develop a critical awareness and to see and think in new ways. Just as socio-political issues are incorporated into art, I strive to integrate art into socio-political life. That's why I want to engage even more intensively with current issues as we did with the show *The Disagreement. A Theatre of Statements* dealing with post-colonial structures, class struggle, climate change, identity politics and heterogeneous belief systems in Brasil.

GM: What about the young art scene?

KU: I also want to involve more young artists as well as young visitors alongside the art scene. It's not easy to compete with the abundance of images and "art" on the Internet. People, especially young people, need to understand that what they encounter on social media is not necessarily art and the social media doesn't necessarily broaden our perspectives nor is objective and should always be critically questioned. Artists like Philipp Timischl or Simon Lehner deal with these issues in their work; they are a young generation that knows and can combine both worlds. I am fascinated by the new ideas and approaches of the young generation of artists who are just finishing their studies, and I think they are an important part of the program of Neuer Kunstverein Wien.

GM: What is the impact of identity politics on theory and praxis of curating? Did it change your way of thinking and working?

KU: Art and life have always intertwined. If identity politics means respect for and communication and cooperation with the other, I think it is rudimentary for curatorial work, but if it means new borders and exclusion, it's poison to the arts and curators. There is a strong interest by artists in highlighting these issues, and they are now combining them with other content and other complex themes. This is one of the relevant contemporary themes, and our program is based on new themes and new ideas.

GM: Must art be moral?

KU: May I quote Oscar Wilde: "There is no such thing as a moral or an immoral book.

Books are well written or badly written. That is all." I believe that art does not necessarily make the world a better place, but it also poses questions of social and political relevance and, most importantly, enriches our lives and makes our lives worthwhile.

GM: What would you tell young people when they ask you what is important to become an excellent curator?

KU: Oh, in short, just believe in your dreams and ideas.

Art is moral per se because it's purpose is to question the facts and processes of life

Dean Zahtila & Damir Stojnić
in conversation with Gerald A. Matt

GERALD A. MATT: What is a curator? Can you define your understanding and practice as a curator?

DEAN ZAHTILA & DAMIR STOJNIĆ: Although we curate exhibitions for our own art collective, LAE, and its sound & vision fraction, Metal Guru, as well as five to six exhibitions of other artists a year in the Lamparna Socio-Cultural Centre in Labin, you must know that we are not engaged in curatorial work in the professional sense. The position of curator *per se* is not very interesting to us. The artistic direction and management of the Industrial Art Biennial, which LAE has been organizing since 2014, is one of the strategies we use to realize our fundamental project, Underground City XXI, whose constitution would be based on art and culture as the basic premise of a more humane society. We believe that the 'above-ground' systems, built on strictly economic-political interests, have shown their deficiency and unsustainability because they focus exclusively on profit-driven interests, and therefore more and more obviously suppress universal human values by creating a discursive analogy between the human being and the commodity, trying and succeeding to make such a vision of man more and more globally acceptable. Of course, curating is a good way to highlight certain issues in society and fit them into a wider context, but also to make certain ideas more visible. We believe that today it's not enough to diagnose problems; it's also necessary to act therapeutically. Through our biennial, we as curators try to bring together not only artists, but also scientists and philosophers who think in a similar way to us. That's why our curatorial practice, for the reasons we mentioned, is very specific. It's related to the local, Underground City context, although, of course, the realization of this project would be an extremely important global event.

GM: How can curating be relevant to the challenges we face today, and in what way does it differ from previous models?

DZ & DS: At this moment in civilization, the only relevant action is one that brings some solutions. We believe that it's more necessary than ever for people, locally and globally, to gather around ideas whose realization would be directly related to solving the most pressing problems we face at the civilizational level: the neoliberal market of capitalism that needs to be abolished, climate change that needs to be taken extremely seriously and addressed with many good solutions that already exist but are not popular on the market—which is why we advocate the abolition of a market generated solely for profit. Furthermore, we are faced with the increasing dehumanization of human beings, with increased control, as is most blatantly implemented in China. Artificial Intelligence is increasingly making a person a useless member of human society, lately even within the cultural and artistic sector, which is a dangerous situation that opens countless, extremely sensitive questions. AI is slowly but surely evolving to the level of a demiurge. What do you think might happen when we entrust AI with genetics and the creation of humans, for example? If we are talking about relevance, then let the curators not only ask questions and hold intellectual debates, let them, through their curatorial projects, not only provide insight into existing or probable local or global issues but also offer possible answers.

GM: How do you see the changing relations between curators, artists, collectors, galleries, museums, and critics? Has there been a shift of power and influence?

DZ & DS: Of course. Rich collectors, as well as elite private museums and galleries, with the help of curators on their payroll, have taken over and have the power to do whatever they want in the field of visual art. More precisely, those who present art have become more important than those who produce it: the artists. Billionaires run this art world ghetto, and it's no secret. With the help of art, they grant themselves greater importance than money alone could provide. There is no great subtlety to this. That's the state of affairs.

GM: Was Harald Szeemann replaced by François Pinault?

DZ & DS: In an intellectual sense, it would be extremely frivolous to consider such a question at all. Szeemann was an artist of curating but, in financial and marketing terms, Pinault certainly won over him. The only problem is that Pinault is not able to problematize an exhibition as Szeemann could. He does not have that strength or artistic gene, so with the help of his wealth, he compensates with grandiosity and spectacle. Szeemann was driven exclusively by passion whereas Pinault also by interest—that is, profit.

GM: Are young artists taking over the role of the curators?

DZ & DS: Yes, because there are more and more young artists who have less and less need for curators and want to curate exhibitions themselves. As curators, we encourage artists to curate their own exhibition projects.

GM: Was there a personal hero, a curator whom you admired?

DZ & DS: As curators, we didn't overly admire anyone, but as artists we especially appreciate Harald Szeemann, who helped by giving us some concrete and not just general *pro-forma* advice, and who immediately recognized our idea of an underground city as a never-ending work of art in progress. He dubbed the art we practice as artists "event art". I (Dean Zahtila) was the one who persuaded him to do it and consulted him regarding the exhibition *Blood & Honey—The future's in the Balkans* in the Essl Museum. Unfortunately, his premature death interrupted our cooperation on some other projects, such as the planned *La Mama* exhibition in Brazil. Among the Croatian curators, we especially appreciate Branko Franceschi, who together with us designed and curated the pilot project of the Industrial Art Biennial in 2014. So, as we have already stated, our curatorial work is only a continuation of our artistic work and stems exclusively from it.

GM: And what were his qualities and achievements? Was there a show which you consider to be a milestone for curatorial thoughts and practice?

DZ & DS: Everything has already been said about the exhibitions he curated, some of which are the most important and influential exhibitions of the 20th century, but I think that his greatest quality and achievement was that he discovered and presented to the world many of the greatest artists of the 20th and 21st centuries: Christo, Rama, Ai Weiwei, etc.

GM: Can you describe a personal curatorial work and project you are really proud of, as well as a project which didn't really work out?

DZ & DS: So far, we have not had any failed projects, only projects with which we have been more or less satisfied. After all, what are the other criteria for the success of an exhibition? If we and the artists are satisfied with the exhibition, neither the reception of the audience nor any other professional opinion concerns us. Although we do not curate but organize and direct it, we are very proud of every Industrial Art Biennial held so far (2014/2016/2018/2020, the next edition will take place from May 13–June 30, 2023), which continues the historical avant-garde's idea of the identification of art and life. For the two of us the Industrial Art Biennial is a kind of experimental laboratory where we study processes that could be useful in designing a better and more humane social order, which we intend to implement within our futuristic project Underground City XXI.

GM: Can you describe, based on one of your curatorial projects, the path from the first idea to the exhibition? What were the most important steps in developing and executing the project?

DZ & DS: Regarding the idea or concept creation, we never have a problem with that. It is enough to read the news in the morning, and you immediately get an idea for several projects. The biggest problem is financing the production of art works and setting up an exhibition, which has unfortunately become the most important issue.

GM: Is curating always a struggle between vision and practical restraint?

DZ & DS: Of course!

GM: Can you give an example?

DZ & DS: Again, it's about financing. Sometimes we simply don't have enough funds, nor do we have the logistic support or spatial-technical conditions to show some more production-intensive work, and that can be frustrating.

GM: How do you define the relation between artist and curator?

DZ & DS: A small manual could be written about it. We have never had major problems with artists. Maybe because we are artists ourselves, which makes us appreciate that position and simplifies mutual relations.

GM: Where are the conflict lines?

DZ & DS: In our experience, most often along the lines of the ego. But as we have already said, we have never had major conflicts with artists' egos—only with certain curators we invited to curate our biennial, within the framework that we gave them. As in everything else, honesty and respect are essential, and if they exist then agreements are possible.

GM: Is curating artistic work or service to the artist and their work?

DZ & DS: A good exhibition requires both.

GM: There have recently been some examples of artists being called by institutions to curate also major shows and curators having their own artistic practice. In what way is the line and authorship of curators shifting/fading?

DZ & DS: If we can be sure of one thing, it's that all positions will be reconsidered over time—that is a fact of life. It's the same with the outdated paradigms of artists and curators. We believe that it is ontologically healthy for that line to be ambivalent. After all, we work that way ourselves.

GM: How independent is an independent/freelance curator?

DZ & DS: Independence is just a platitude. Many independent curators have to think about how to get the funds not only for their projects, but also for themselves personally. How independent can they be if they must look for funds from various sources? Only those curators who have enough of their own money to finance their projects are independent. Apart from the previously mentioned Pinault, we (unfortunately) do not know anyone like that.

GM: How dependent is a curator employed by a museum?

DZ & DS: Curators employed permanently by museums, especially public ones, have greater freedom—and thus also the potential to realize truly independent projects—than freelancers. Thanks to their regular income, they have a certain security which, at least on a more modest scale, allows them to do what really interests them without having to think whether whoever finances the exhibition will like it.

GM: How different is their work and self-understanding?

DZ & DS: We are not familiar with any specific issues they face within the museum.

GM: Are there two different art worlds, the art world of the museums and big collectors including star curators, auction houses and big fairs and the other art world based on smaller biennales, independent art spaces and curators as Robert Fleck once argued? Is there also a gap between curators serving one or the other world?

DZ & DS: Of course. The extent of the "abyss" between them is dictated solely by the amount of money. But from a qualitative point of view, this gap is much smaller, and it often happens that financially modest biennials present much better conceived and executed exhibitions.

GM: What is the impact of identity politics on theory and practice of curating?

DZ & DS: Unfortunately, it's quite large, especially considering the absurdity of such policies. If we respect the principle that art should be identical to life, as well as vice versa, and life in its processes does not care about political correctness, then it's clear what the state of affairs is. Identity politics are inartistic by themselves. Art transcends identity, questions it, and doesn't flatter it. Isn't the very question about the identity of art and artists the axis of contemporary artistic practice? Therefore, complying with such policies can only result in an anemic decline of artistic freedom.

GM: Did it change your way of thinking and working?

DZ & DS: Apparently yes.

GM: What is censorship in society, and what is it in the art world today—if there is a difference at all?

DZ & DS: Was Wagner a bad composer because he was anti-Semitic? Recently, there was a discussion about the removal of a huge sculpture of North American Indians, by Croatian sculptor Ivan Meštrović, in Chicago. Allegedly, it offended the feelings of Native Americans by their stereotypical portrayal. We believe that they should be much more offended by the American policy and laws, the reservations they are ghettoized in which are hotbeds of crime, drugs, alcohol, murders and suicides. Are they not offended by the amount of land that was violently taken from them and the miserable living conditions that have been imposed to them since then? The concept of identity hypersensitivity lends itself to masking fundamental problems with superficial interventions.

GM: Must art be moral? What about art and its values?

DZ & DS: Please define morality in art. Art is moral *per se*, because its purpose is to question the facts and processes of life, both past, present and future, rather than to share lessons about them. The greatest value of art is its radicalism in relation to all possible existing paradigms. That is what all artists should be true to.

GM: What is the role of institutions in your practice? Where does the border between curatorial and institutional responsibility lie?

DZ & DS: We do not deal with any other institutions except our own, LAE. It's our institutional responsibility to choose appropriate curators for the projects/exhibitions that the institution wants to realize in accordance with its programming concept, and it is up to the curators to choose the appropriate artists and guide them in their creative process from the idea phase to the production and presentation of a new work.

GM: What will be the main challenges facing curators in the future? How will curatorial work change?

DZ & DS: The main role of curators must be research, discovery and mapping of new emerging artists and new art forms not in established museums and galleries but in marginalized cultural provinces far from the public eye, which are currently of no interest to anyone, and only after that, conceiving and implementing exhibitions. The future of curatorial work should be about ways of turnings exhibitions themselves into works of art. The biggest challenge is, of course, who will pay for it.

Curators

BRANKA BENČIĆ is a Croatian curator and art historian. She curated the Croatian Pavillion at the 57th Venice Biennale and co-curated the Pavillion at the 16th Venice Architecture Biennale. Benčić is co-founder of Apoteka—space of contemporary art in Vodnjan. She is the director of the Museum of Modern and Contemporary Art in Rijeka, Croatia. She curated the third Industrial Art Biennale (IAB) in Labin, Raša, Pula and Rijeka (Croatia) together with Christian Oxenius and Gerald A. Matt.

PAOLO BIANCHI is a Suisse curator, art critic, cultural journalist and creativity researcher. He lectures as "Dozent" at the Züricher Hochschule der Künste ZHdK. Bianchi is also author and guesteditor of the Magasin Kunstforum International.

BERNARDO JOSÉ DE SOUZA is a Brazilian curator and art critic. He worked as artistic director of Fundação Iberê Camargo, in Porto Alegre, Brazil, from where he departed to work as an independent curator based in Madrid and Rio de Janeiro. Previously he worked as the Director of the Department of Cinema, Video, and Photography at the Secretary of Culture of Porto Alegre, Brazil.

CHRISTOPH DOSWALD is a Suisse curator, art critic and university teacher. Doswald was member of the board of Shedhalle Zürich. He was president of the board of Arbeitsgruppe Kunst im Öffentlichen Raum (AG KiöR) of the city of Zürich and responsible for its art in public space programs. He curated ART AND THE CITY and recently the forth Industrial Art Biennale (IAB) in Labin, Raša, Pula and Rijeka (Croatia) together with Paolo Bianchi.

OKWUI ENWEZOR was a Nigerian curator, art critic, writer, poet, educator and museum director. Enwezor served as artistic director of several major exhibitions including Documenta 11 and the Venice Biennale 2015, becoming the first non-European and Africa born curator to lead both. He was director of the "Haus der Kunst", München and founding director of Anka:Journal of contemporary African Art. Previously Enwezor had the role of adjunct curator of the International Center of Photography in New York City and at the Art Institute of Chicago. He also served as artistic director of the 2nd Johannesburg Biennale, the 7th Gwangju Biennale in

South Korea, and the Triennale d'Art Contemporain of Paris at the Palais de Tokyo.

Enwezor was Dean of Academic Affairs and Senior Vice President at San Francisco Art Institute. He held several other important academic appointments. Enwezor died in 2019.

HEDWIG FIJEN is founding director of Manifesta 1 in Rotterdam and executive director of the Manifesta Foundation in Amsterdam since it's beginning. The biennial has developed into one of the three most important major art events in Europe. She regularly gives lectures and publishes texts on the context of Manifesta as a biennial. Before Manifesta, she had worked as a curator at the Netherlands Office for Fine Arts, and has worked in Eastern Europe, the Soviet Union, Cuba and many other countries.

JONATHAN FINE is an American curator and art historian. He is Generaldirector of the Kunsthistorisches Museum Vienna and served previously as director of the Weltmuseum Wien and as a curator for and director of the Ethnologisches Museum der Staatlichen Museen in Berlin. In the United States Fine worked as a lawyer specialised on human rights and international trade.

YUKO HASEGAWA is a Japanese curator, museum director and university teacher. She is director of the 21st Century Museum in Kanazawa and the Artistic Director of the Museum of Contemporary Art, Tokyo. She is Professor in Curatorial Studies at the Graduate School of Global Arts, Tokyo University of the Arts and curated numerous exhibitions and Biennals (7th International Moscow Biennale of Contemporary Art and the Sharjah Biennial 11. Hasegawa is a member of the Advisory Committee of the Istanbul Biennial.

MAX HOLLEIN is an Austrian art historian, curator and the director of the Metropolitan Museum of Arts in New York, previously he served as director of the Fine Arts Museums of San Francisco, which he joined from his position as the director of the Schirn Kunsthalle and Städelmuseum Frankfurt. Hollein started his career as project manager at the Solomon R. Guggenheim Museum. He worked closely with Guggenheim director Thomas Krens on the development of the exhibition halls Deutsche Guggenheim Berlin and Guggenheim Las Vegas as well as exhibition tours.

VERENA KONRAD is an Austrian art historian and curator. She is director of the Vorarlberg architecture Institute. Previously she was responsible for the

"Premierentage Innsbruck" and worked as a curator of Kunsthalle Vienna. She lectured at the University of Art and Design Linz and at Innsbruck University. Konrad was commissionar and curator of the Austrian participation to the Venice Biennal.

KOYO KOUOH was a Swiss Cameroon curator and culture producer. She was appointed the Chief Curator and Executive Director of the Zeitz Museum of Contemporary Art Africa (MOCAA) in Cape Town, South Africa and the appointed director of the Venice Biennale 2026. Previously she founded and directed the RAW Material Company in Dakar. As a specialist in photography, video and public installations, she has curated exhibitions and published numerous articles on contemporary art with a focus on the African continent. She was a member of the jury for the Golden Lion at the 50th Venice Biennale and acted as an advisor to the artistic directors of documenta 12 and documenta 13. She was also a member of the selection committee for documenta 14. Kouoh died in 2025.

GERALD A. MATT is an Austrian curator, writer and the director of the Vienna Art Institute and former longterm director of Kunsthalle Vienna. He hosts a variety of TV talks with personalities from the cultural, social and political field. He was instrumental in establishing the Kunsthalle Vienna as an international reputated institution for contemporary art and the Museumsquartier Vienna as an important museum complex. He was also a promoter of the temporary Kunsthalle Berlin. He is associate professor at the University of Applied Arts Vienna and taught at the CIAM in Cologne. He also lectured art theory at the Institute of Art History at the University of Innsbruck. At the same time he worked as a senior consultant at Graf & Partner, a museum and art advising company. Matt published several books on art and museum management.

KASIA MATT-USZYŃSKA is a Polish-Austrian art historian, curator and founder and director of Neuer Kunstverein Wien, NKW. She studied art history at Vienna University and worked as a curator for several institutions like the Kunsthistorische Museum, the Kunsthalle Vienna and the Leopold Museum. She founded the Neue Kunstverein Wien and expanded it from a small appartment space to an institution of contemporary especially space related and trans media art in two major exhibition halls. In the meantime Kasia Matt-Uszyńska served as artistic director of the Kahan Art Center. The Neue Kunstverein Wien organized, in cooperation with the Verein Skulptur, a major three-year overview of contemporary sculpture in Vienna.

ABASEH MIRVALI is the Artistic Director of the art fair Viennacontemporary. Her prior roles include Executive Director of Fundación/Colección Jumex Arte Contemporáneo (Mexico City), the Museum of Contemporary Art Santa Barbara, and the Biennial of the Americas. She has also held key curatorial and advisory roles with major art fairs including ArteBA, Buenos Aires, Artissima-Torino, miart-Milan, and Art Basel.

SIMON NJAMI is an independent lecturer, curator, and art critic. He was the Curator of the 12th Edition of the Dak'ArtBiennale and a visual-arts consultant for Cultures France, the French Ministry of Foreign Affairs. Njami has curated numerous exhibitions of African art and photography. Njamiis also co-founder and editor-in-chief of the Paris based cultural magazine Revue Noire. Njami was member of the first search committee to decide on the curatorial leadership of Documenta 16.

HANS ULRICH OBRIST is a Suisse art historian, curator, critic, writer. He is the co-director and artistic director of the Serpentine Gallery London. Obrist is the author of the ongoing "The Interview Project" based on an enormous number of interviews with artists, architects, filmmakers, scientists, philosophers and musicians. He is also co-editor of the Cahiers d'Art review. He lives and works in London. Furthermore, Obrist is a jury member of the Iron Curtain art project, which museum in progress has been implementing at the Vienna State Opera. Obrist founded the mobile museum Robert Walser and was a member of the board of trustees of the Allianz Cultural Foundation. He is the author of various works of art literature. Obrist was ranked First in the list of the 100 most influential people in the art industry by the trade magazine ArtReview in 2009.

ÁLVARO RODRÍGUEZ FOMINAYA is the director of the Museo de Arte Contemporáneo de Castilla y León (MUSAC) in Spain. Previously, he was the director of El Centro de Creación in Cordova, Spain. Fominaya served as the curator in charge of collections and exhibitions at the Guggenheim Museum Bilbao. Before he served as executive director and curator of Para/Site Art Space, Hong Kong and served in successive positions at Centro Atlántico de Arte Moderno (CAAM), Spain, as curator, chief curator, and acting director.

ANDA ROTTENBERG is a Polish Art historian, art curator and art critic, writer and TV host and former director of the Zacheta National Gallery of Art in Warsaw. She launched Egit, one of the first foundations for art in Poland and served as Director of the Department of Art at the Ministry of

Culture and Art. She was curator and commissioner of the Polish Pavilion in the Venice Biennial and was instrumental in establishing the Museum of Modern Art in Warsaw.

FRANCIS RUYTER is an American artist and freelance curator. Ruyter often paints using photographs as a source material, in a style that has been compared to Pop Art. He produced a billboard work, as part of MoMA Projects 77. His work is included in the permanent collections of the Museum of Modern Art, New York, the SFMoma, the Pérez Art Museum Miami and the Denver Art Museum. Ruyter also operated a gallery in Vienna for some years.

JÉRÔME SANS is a curator, cultural agitator, and director of institutions, known for his pioneering approach to new models of cultural institutions and exhibitions. Sans was the co-founder and co-director of the Palais de Tokyo in Paris. He served as director of the BALTIC Centre for Contemporary Art in Newcastle (UK) and was director of the Ullens Center for Contemporary Art in Beijing. Sans was creative director and editor-in-chief of the French cultural magazine L'Officiel Art and has curated numerous exhibitions around the world, including the Taipei Biennial and the Lyon Biennial.

DAMIR STOJNIĆ is an artist and the artistic director of the International Industrial Biennale Labin. He lives and works in Rijeka, Croatia.

FELICITAS THUN-HOHENSTEIN is an Austrian art historian and professor at the Institute for Art and Cultural Studies at the Academy of Fine Arts Vienna. Thun-Hohenstein has curated numerous international exhibitions. At the 58th Venice Biennale in 2019, Thun-Hohenstein curated the installation "Discardo erga sum" for the Austrian Pavilion with Renate Bertlmann. She is also the author and editor of numerous publications, the initiator and director of the Cathrin Pichler Archive for Science, Art, and Curatorial Practice, and a member of the board of trustees of the Museum Moderner Kunst Stiftung Ludwig Wien.

OLESYA TURKINA is a Russian art critic and curator based in St. Petersburg. She is a Senior Research Fellow at the State Russian Museum, Associate Professor on the Faculty of Liberal Arts and Sciences, St. Petersburg State University, where she also worked as a founding director of Curatorial Studies MA programme. She has curated numerous exhibitions in Russia and abroad, including Beyond Zero at Calvert 22 Foundation and MIR:

Made in The XXth Century, Russian Pavilion, 48th Venice Biennale and has contributed to numerous publications.

DEAN ZAHTILA is a Croatian artist and Director of the International Industrial Biennale Labin. He is the founder and member of the association Labin Art Express (L.A.E.), an independent underground cultural and art association, based in the ex-coal mine in Labin, Region of Istria, Croatia. L.A.E.operated the first independent radio station in Croatia, closed by governmental decision and the international multimedia Cultural Centre “Lamparna” in one of abandoned ex-coal mine buildings.

Interviewers

JOHANNA DI BLASI is an Austrian art historian and cultural journalist. She has written for publications including Die Zeit, NZZ, Merkur, and Lettre.

JONATHAN FISCHER is an artist, social worker, DJ, journalist and Africa expert and writes for the Süddeutsche Zeitung, among others.

SYNNE GENZMER is a German art historian and curator. She has worked for the Kunsthalle Wien and the Akademie der Bildenden Künste, among others.

JÖRG HÄNTZSCHEL is an editor in the arts section of the Süddeutsche Zeitung. He was a journalist at taz and has written for the Neue Zürcher Zeitung, Die Zeit, Bauwelt and Monopol, among others.

CATHRIN LOCH is an arts editor in the arts section of the Süddeutsche Zeitung.

GERALD A. MATT is an Austrian curator, writer and the director of the Vienna Art Institute and former longterm director of Kunsthalle Vienna.

KASIA MATT-USZYŃSKA is a Polish-Austrian art historian, curator and founder and director of Neuer Kunstverein Wien.

ALEXANDER MÜHLAUER heads the business section of the Süddeutsche Zeitung. Previously, he worked as a correspondent in London and Brussels.

REINHARD SPIELER is a German art historian and director of the Sprengel Museum in Hannover. Previously, he was director of the Wilhelm Hack Museum in Ludwigshafen am Rhein.

JÜRGEN WEISHÄUPL is an Austrian cultural manager and cultural producer.